ART ART ART ART
OPS OPS OPS OPS
ART ART ART ART
OPS OPS OPS OPS
ART ART ART ART
OPS OPS OPS OPS
ART ART ART ART
OPS OPS OPS OPS

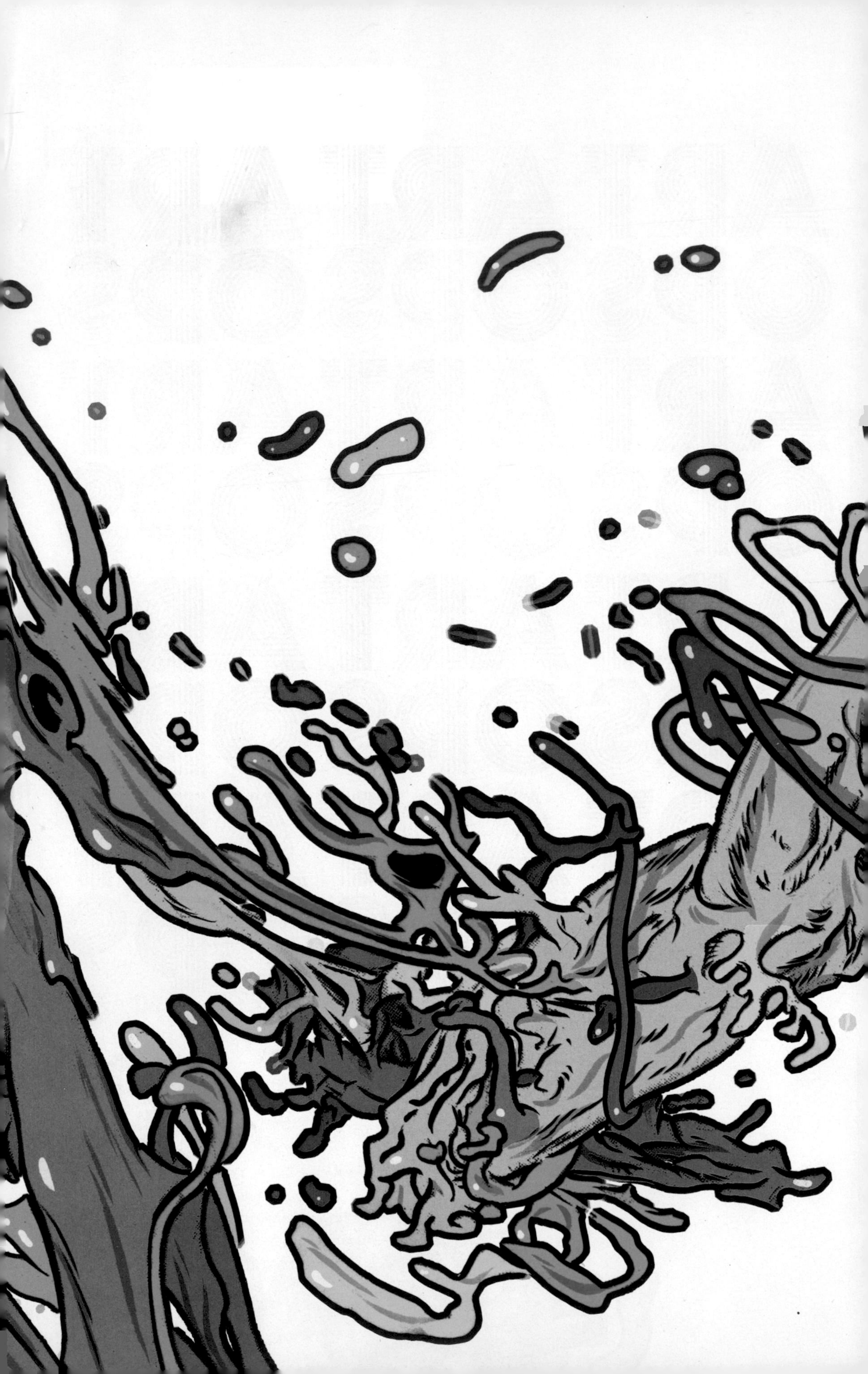

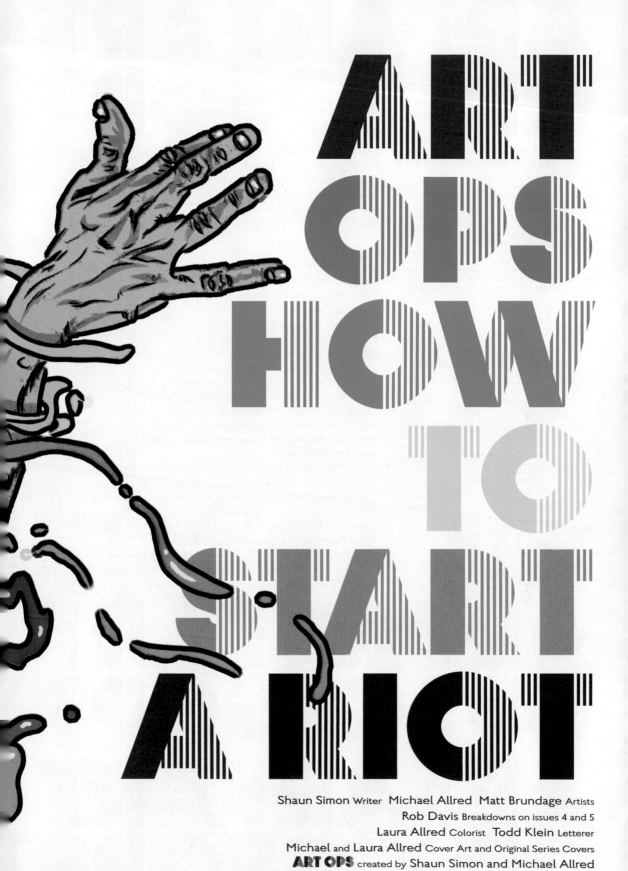

ART OPS HOW TO START A RIOT

Shaun Simon Writer   Michael Allred Matt Brundage Artists
Rob Davis Breakdowns on issues 4 and 5
Laura Allred Colorist Todd Klein Letterer
Michael and Laura Allred Cover Art and Original Series Covers
ART OPS created by Shaun Simon and Michael Allred

Logo design by Steve Cook

ART OPS: HOW TO START A RIOT

Published by DC Comics. Compilation and all new material Copyright © 2016 Shaun Simon and Michael Allred. All Rights Reserved.

Originally published in single magazine form as ART OPS 1-5. Copyright © 2015, 2016 Shaun Simon and Michael Allred. All Rights Reserved. All characters, their distinctive likenesses and related elements featured in this publication are trademarks of Shaun Simon and Michael Allred. VERTIGO is a trademark of DC Comics. The stories, characters and incidents featured in this publication are entirely fictional. DC Comics does not read or accept unsolicited submissions of ideas, stories or artwork.

DC Comics
2900 West Alameda Avenue
Burbank, CA 91505
Printed in the USA. First Printing.
ISBN: 978-1-4012-5687-6

Library of Congress Cataloging-in-Publication Data

Names: Simon, Shaun, author. | Allred, Mike (Mike Dalton) illustrator. | Brundage, Matt, illustrator. | Allred, Laura, illustrator.
Title: Art Ops : how to start a riot / Shaun Simon, writer ; Michael Allred, Matt Brundage, Laura Allred, artists.
Description: Burbank, CA : DC Comics, [2016] | "Originally published in single magazine form as ART OPS 1-5."
Identifiers: LCCN 2016006067 | ISBN 9781401256876
Subjects: LCSH: Comic books, strips, etc.
Classification: LCC PN6728.A75 S56 2016 | DDC 741.5/973—dc23
LC record available at http://lccn.loc.gov/2016006067

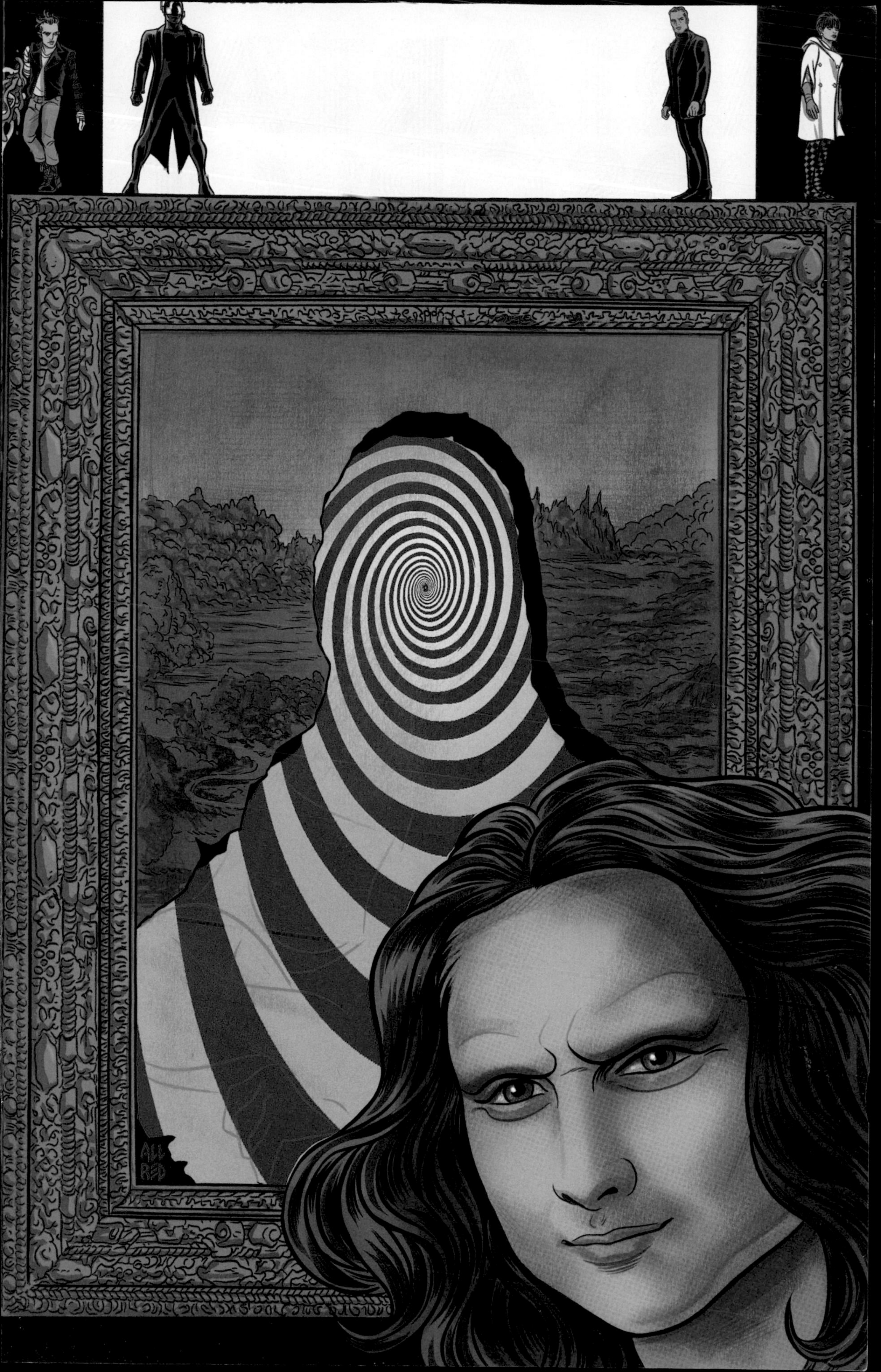
ALL
RED

ART ART ART
OPS OPS OPS
ART ART ART
OPS OPS OPS
ART ART ART
OPS OPS OPS
ART ART ART
OPS OPS OPS
ART ART ART
OPS OPS OPS
ART ART ART
OPS OPS OPS

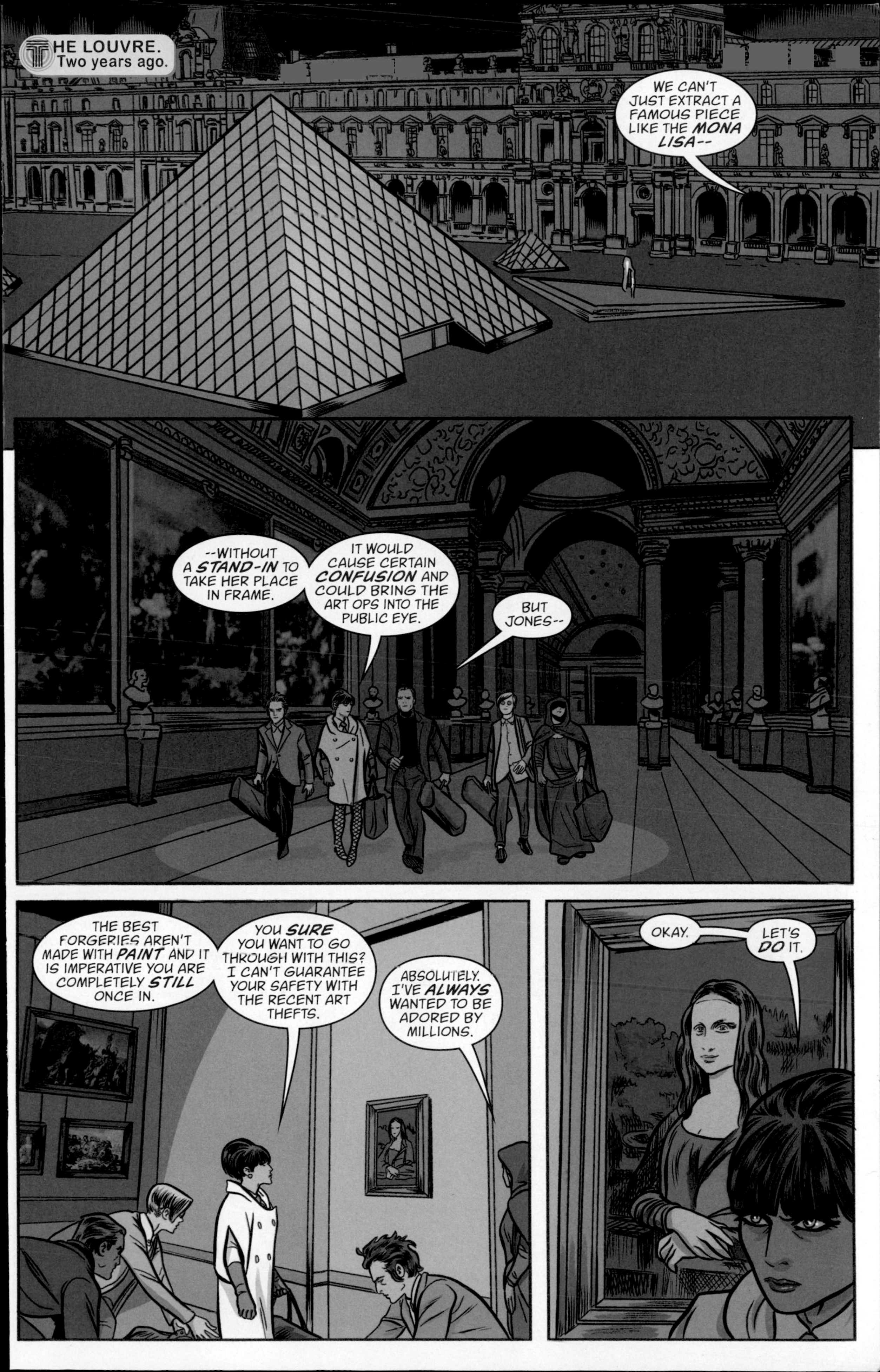
THE LOUVRE.
Two years ago.
WE CAN'T JUST EXTRACT A FAMOUS PIECE LIKE THE MONA LISA--
--WITHOUT A STAND-IN TO TAKE HER PLACE IN FRAME.
IT WOULD CAUSE CERTAIN CONFUSION AND COULD BRING THE ART OPS INTO THE PUBLIC EYE.
BUT JONES--
THE BEST FORGERIES AREN'T MADE WITH PAINT AND IT IS IMPERATIVE YOU ARE COMPLETELY STILL ONCE IN.
YOU SURE YOU WANT TO GO THROUGH WITH THIS? I CAN'T GUARANTEE YOUR SAFETY WITH THE RECENT ART THEFTS.
ABSOLUTELY. I'VE ALWAYS WANTED TO BE ADORED BY MILLIONS.
OKAY.
LET'S DO IT.

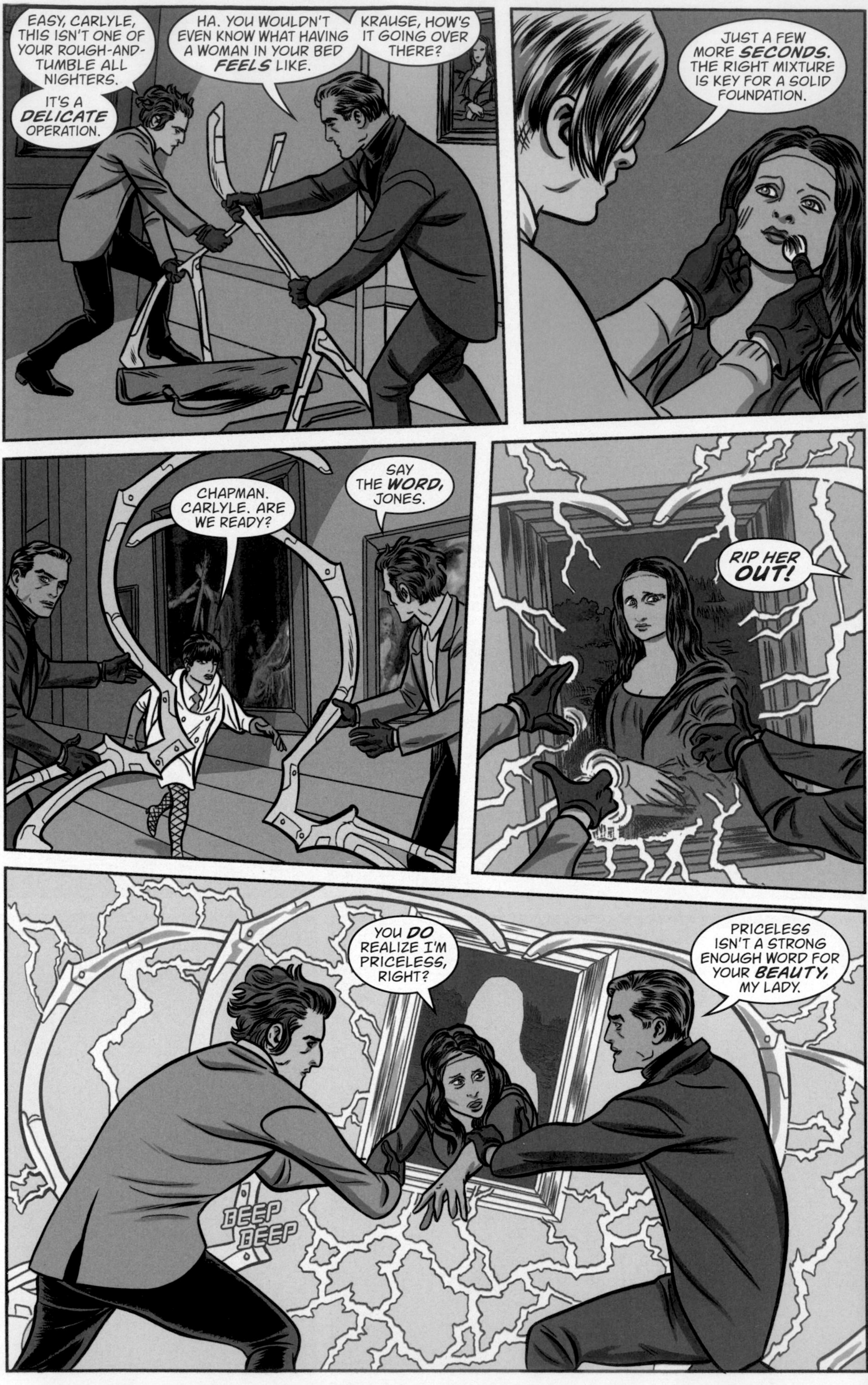
EASY, CARLYLE, THIS ISN'T ONE OF YOUR ROUGH-AND-TUMBLE ALL NIGHTERS.
IT'S A DELICATE OPERATION.
HA. YOU WOULDN'T EVEN KNOW WHAT HAVING A WOMAN IN YOUR BED FEELS LIKE.
KRAUSE, HOW'S IT GOING OVER THERE?
JUST A FEW MORE SECONDS. THE RIGHT MIXTURE IS KEY FOR A SOLID FOUNDATION.
CHAPMAN. CARLYLE. ARE WE READY?
SAY THE WORD, JONES.
RIP HER OUT!
YOU DO REALIZE I'M PRICELESS, RIGHT?
PRICELESS ISN'T A STRONG ENOUGH WORD FOR YOUR BEAUTY, MY LADY.
BEEP BEEP

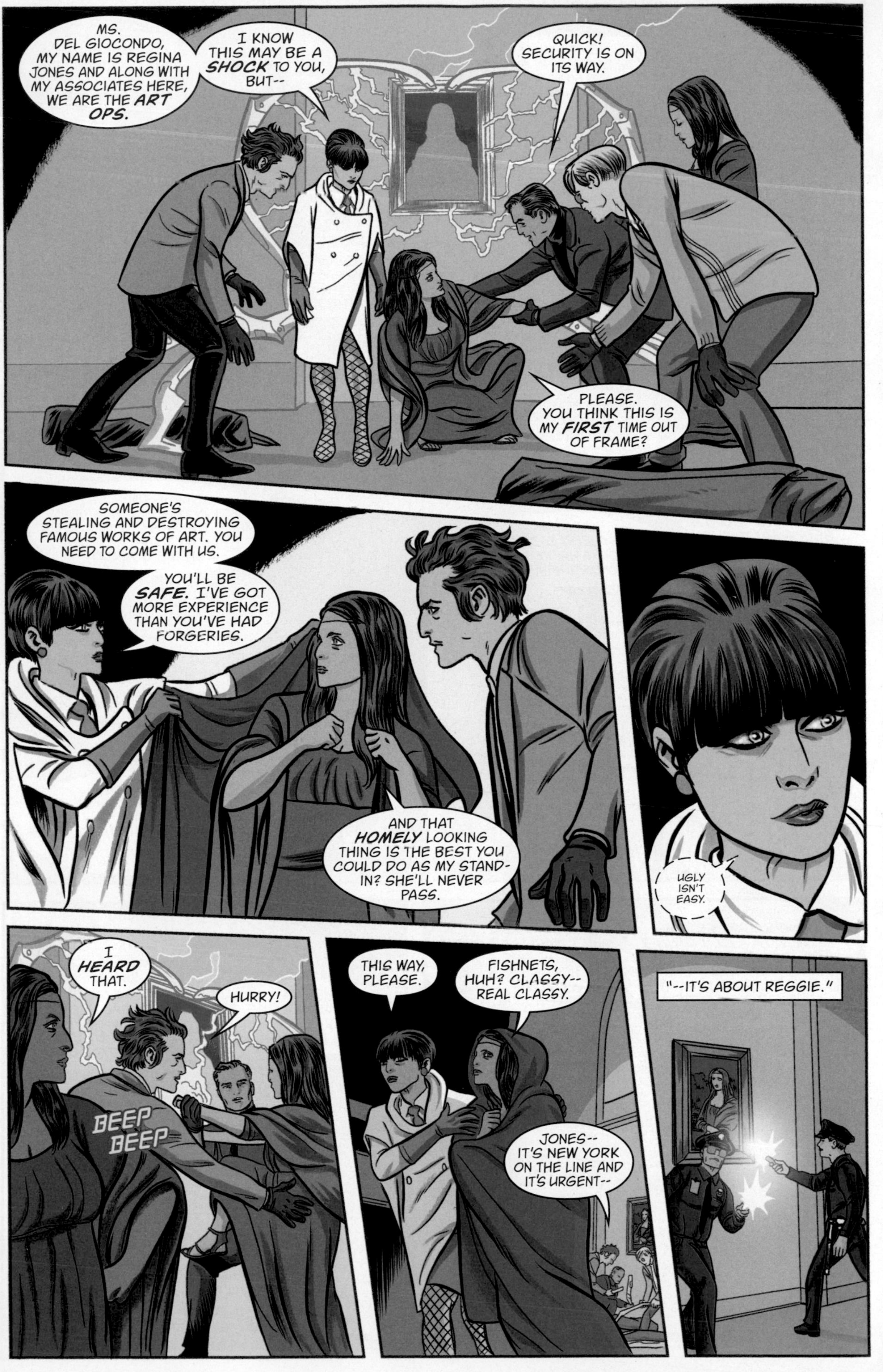
MS. DEL GIOCONDO, MY NAME IS REGINA JONES AND ALONG WITH MY ASSOCIATES HERE, WE ARE THE ART OPS.
I KNOW THIS MAY BE A SHOCK TO YOU, BUT--
QUICK! SECURITY IS ON ITS WAY.
PLEASE. YOU THINK THIS IS MY FIRST TIME OUT OF FRAME?
SOMEONE'S STEALING AND DESTROYING FAMOUS WORKS OF ART. YOU NEED TO COME WITH US.
YOU'LL BE SAFE. I'VE GOT MORE EXPERIENCE THAN YOU'VE HAD FORGERIES.
AND THAT HOMELY LOOKING THING IS THE BEST YOU COULD DO AS MY STAND-IN? SHE'LL NEVER PASS.
UGLY ISN'T EASY.
I HEARD THAT.
HURRY!
BEEP BEEP
THIS WAY, PLEASE.
FISHNETS, HUH? CLASSY-- REAL CLASSY.
JONES-- IT'S NEW YORK ON THE LINE AND IT'S URGENT--
"--IT'S ABOUT REGGIE."

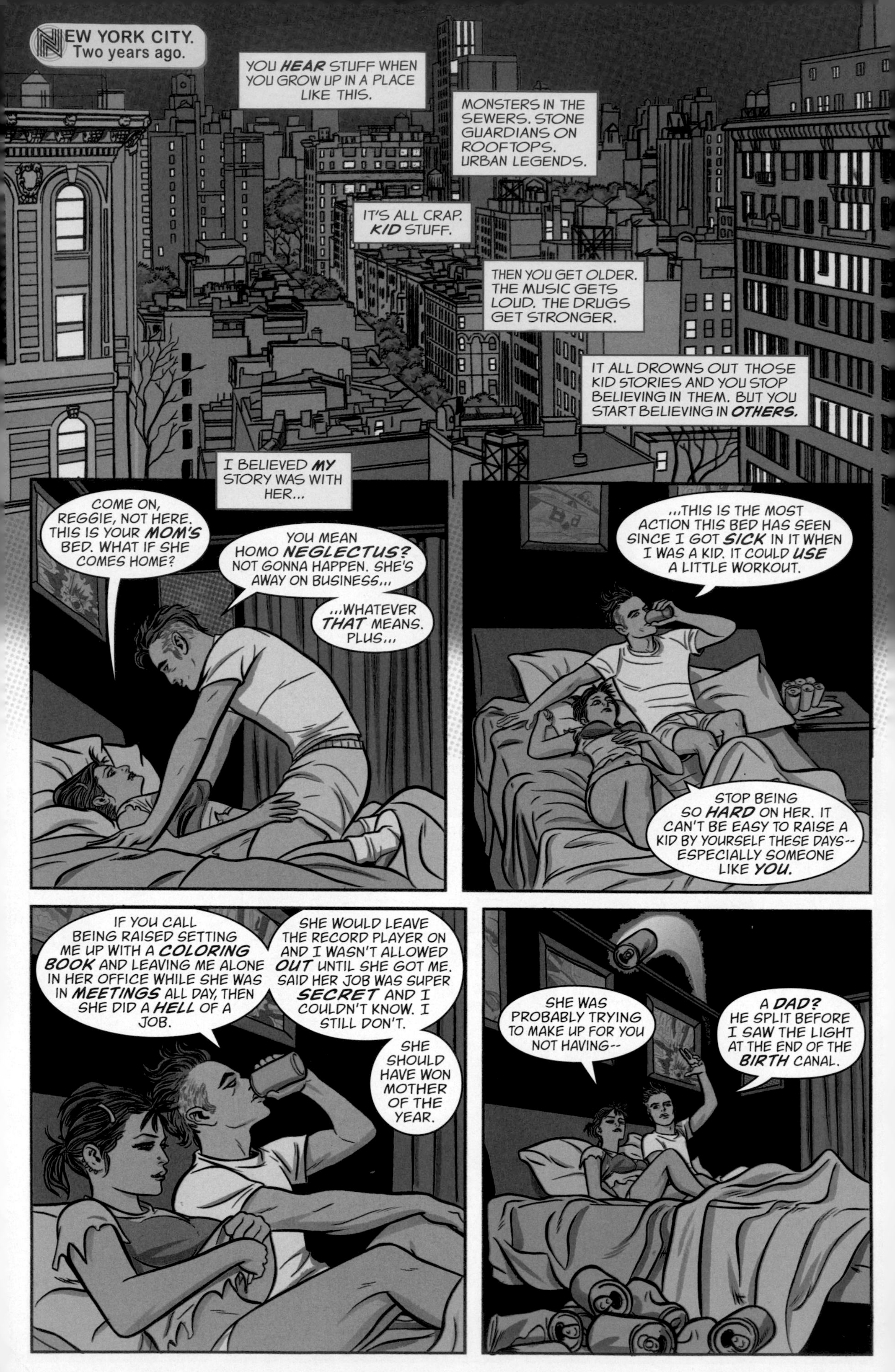
NEW YORK CITY. Two years ago.
YOU HEAR STUFF WHEN YOU GROW UP IN A PLACE LIKE THIS.
MONSTERS IN THE SEWERS. STONE GUARDIANS ON ROOFTOPS. URBAN LEGENDS.
IT'S ALL CRAP. KID STUFF.
THEN YOU GET OLDER. THE MUSIC GETS LOUD. THE DRUGS GET STRONGER.
IT ALL DROWNS OUT THOSE KID STORIES AND YOU STOP BELIEVING IN THEM. BUT YOU START BELIEVING IN OTHERS.
I BELIEVED MY STORY WAS WITH HER...
COME ON, REGGIE, NOT HERE. THIS IS YOUR MOM'S BED. WHAT IF SHE COMES HOME?
YOU MEAN HOMO NEGLECTUS? NOT GONNA HAPPEN. SHE'S AWAY ON BUSINESS...
...WHATEVER THAT MEANS. PLUS...
...THIS IS THE MOST ACTION THIS BED HAS SEEN SINCE I GOT SICK IN IT WHEN I WAS A KID. IT COULD USE A LITTLE WORKOUT.
STOP BEING SO HARD ON HER. IT CAN'T BE EASY TO RAISE A KID BY YOURSELF THESE DAYS-- ESPECIALLY SOMEONE LIKE YOU.
IF YOU CALL BEING RAISED SETTING ME UP WITH A COLORING BOOK AND LEAVING ME ALONE IN HER OFFICE WHILE SHE WAS IN MEETINGS ALL DAY, THEN SHE DID A HELL OF A JOB.
SHE WOULD LEAVE THE RECORD PLAYER ON AND I WASN'T ALLOWED OUT UNTIL SHE GOT ME. SAID HER JOB WAS SUPER SECRET AND I COULDN'T KNOW. I STILL DON'T.
SHE SHOULD HAVE WON MOTHER OF THE YEAR.
SHE WAS PROBABLY TRYING TO MAKE UP FOR YOU NOT HAVING--
A DAD? HE SPLIT BEFORE I SAW THE LIGHT AT THE END OF THE BIRTH CANAL.

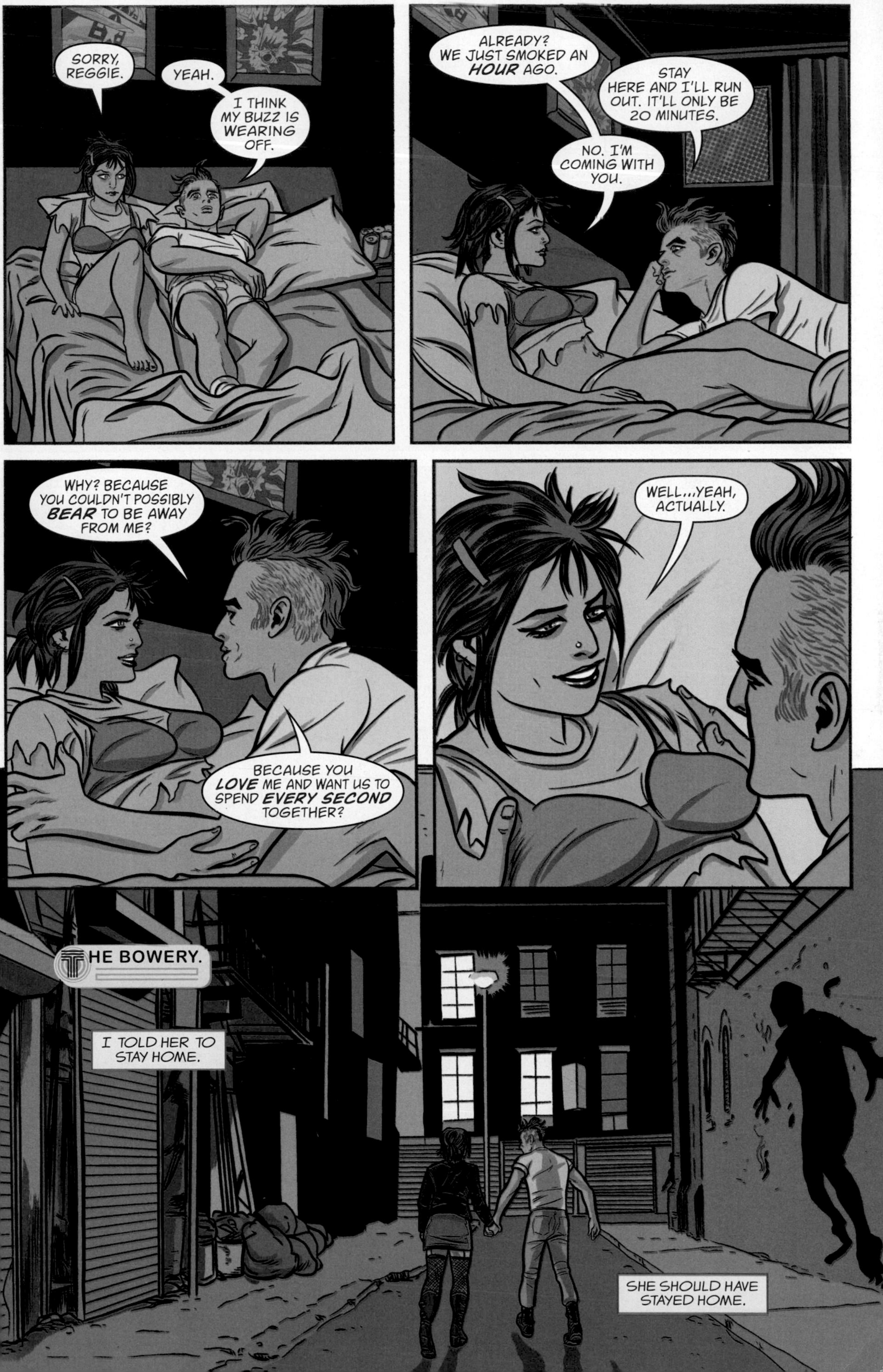
SORRY, REGGIE.
YEAH.
I THINK MY BUZZ IS WEARING OFF.
ALREADY? WE JUST SMOKED AN HOUR AGO.
STAY HERE AND I'LL RUN OUT. IT'LL ONLY BE 20 MINUTES.
NO. I'M COMING WITH YOU.
WHY? BECAUSE YOU COULDN'T POSSIBLY BEAR TO BE AWAY FROM ME?
BECAUSE YOU LOVE ME AND WANT US TO SPEND EVERY SECOND TOGETHER?
WELL...YEAH, ACTUALLY.
THE BOWERY.
I TOLD HER TO STAY HOME.
SHE SHOULD HAVE STAYED HOME.

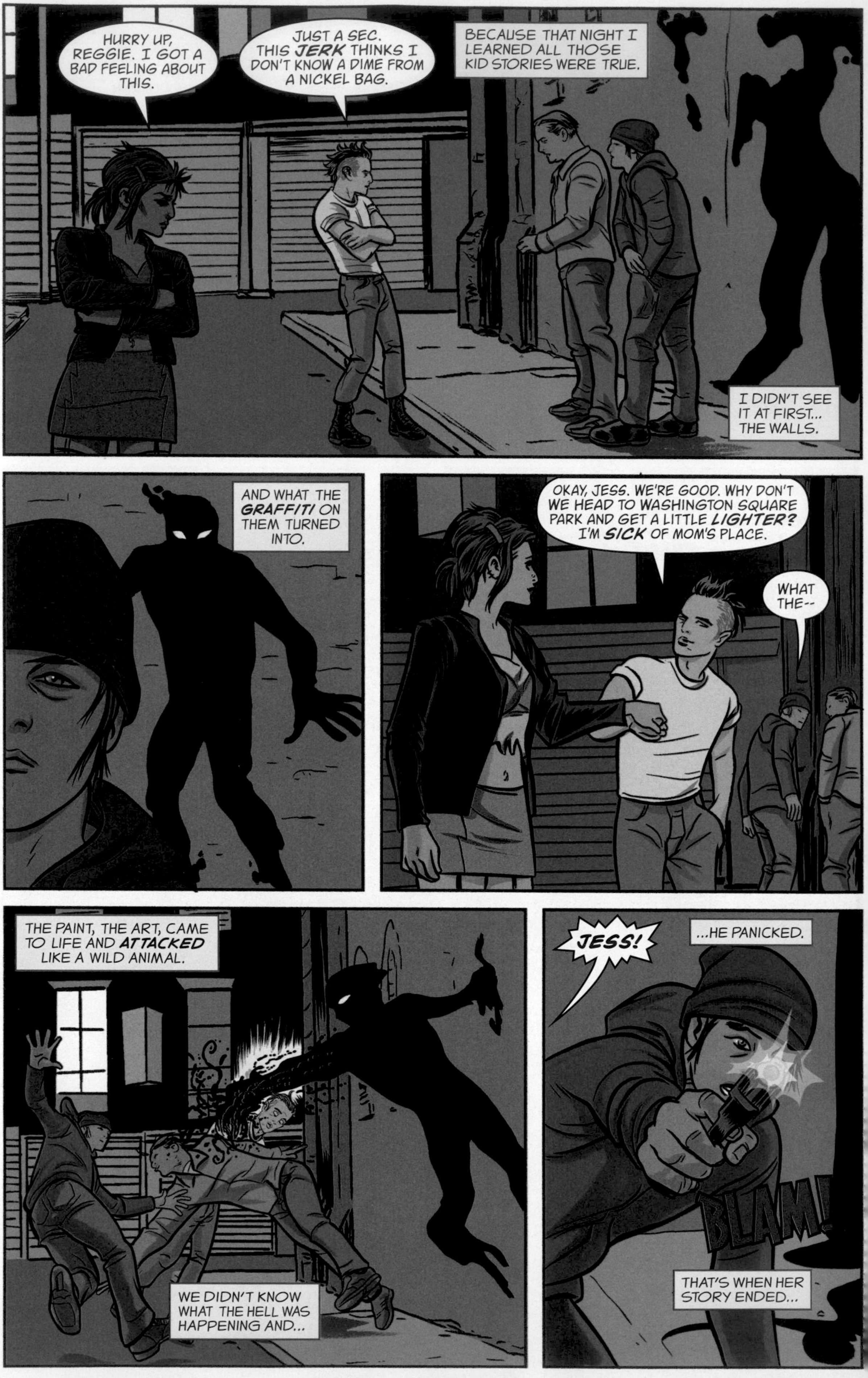
HURRY UP, REGGIE. I GOT A BAD FEELING ABOUT THIS.
JUST A SEC. THIS JERK THINKS I DON'T KNOW A DIME FROM A NICKEL BAG.
BECAUSE THAT NIGHT I LEARNED ALL THOSE KID STORIES WERE TRUE.
I DIDN'T SEE IT AT FIRST... THE WALLS.
AND WHAT THE GRAFFITI ON THEM TURNED INTO.
OKAY, JESS. WE'RE GOOD. WHY DON'T WE HEAD TO WASHINGTON SQUARE PARK AND GET A LITTLE LIGHTER? I'M SICK OF MOM'S PLACE.
WHAT THE--
THE PAINT, THE ART, CAME TO LIFE AND ATTACKED LIKE A WILD ANIMAL.
WE DIDN'T KNOW WHAT THE HELL WAS HAPPENING AND...
JESS!
...HE PANICKED.
BLAM!
THAT'S WHEN HER STORY ENDED...

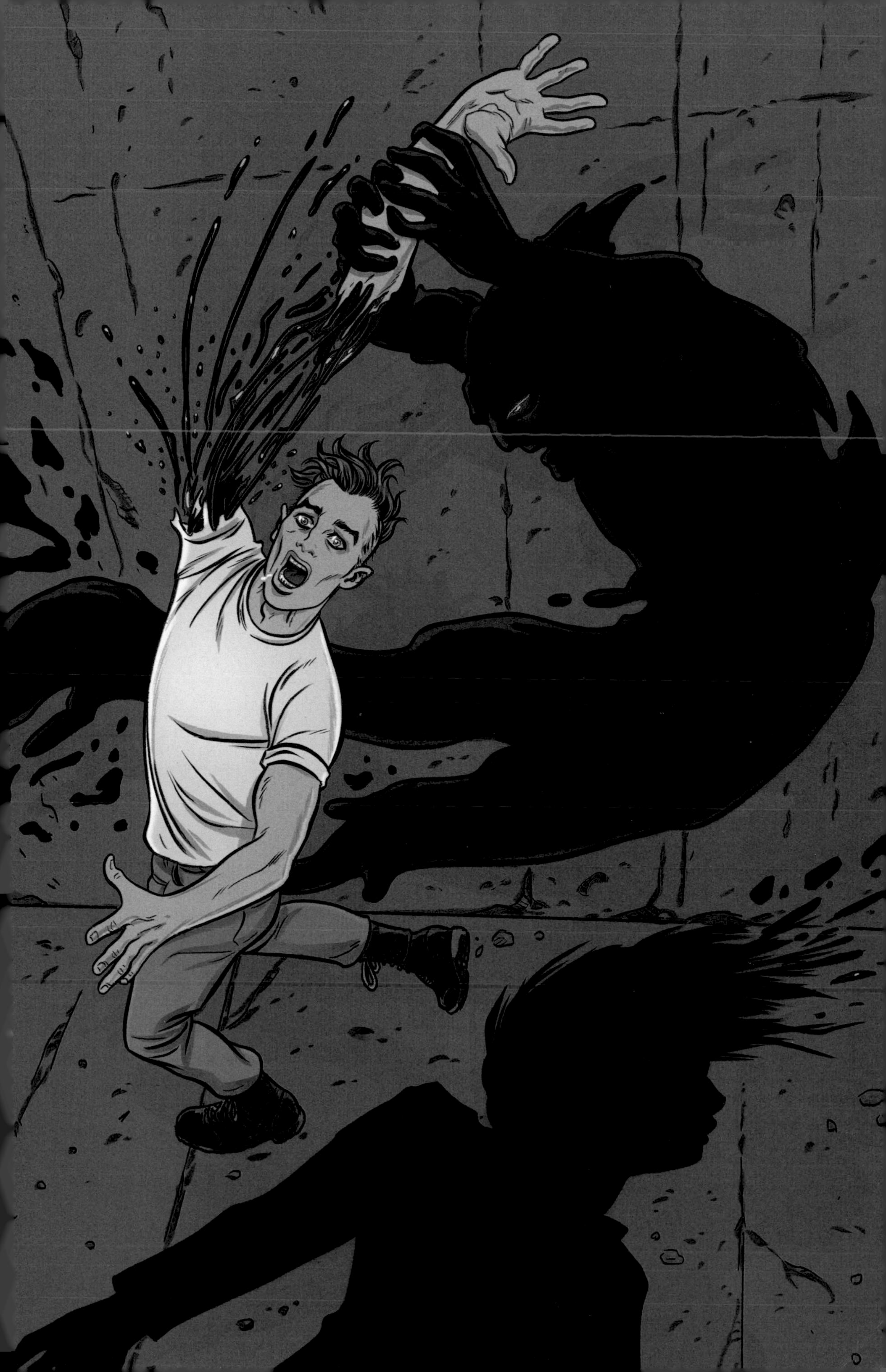

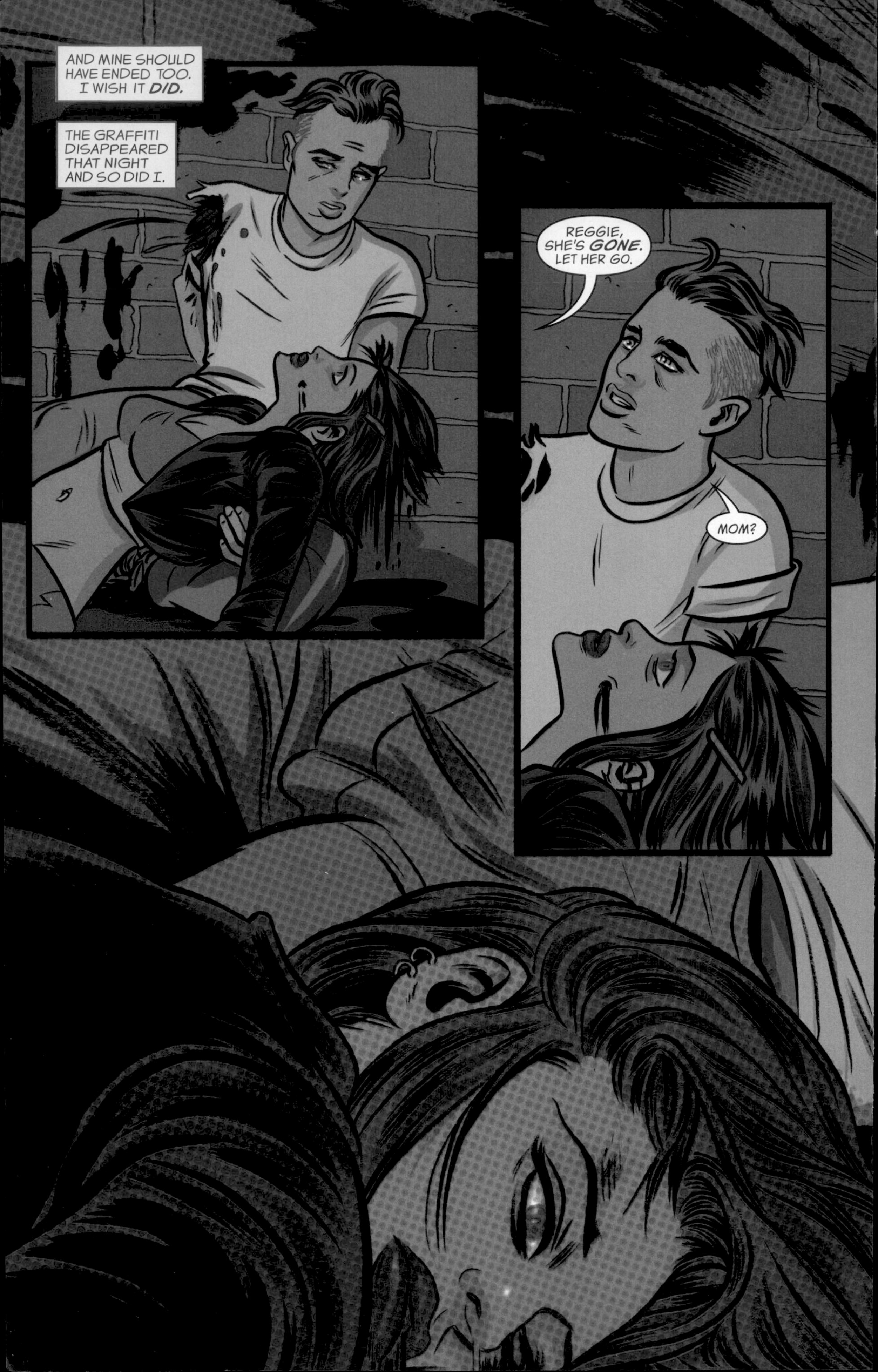
AND MINE SHOULD HAVE ENDED TOO. I WISH IT DID.
THE GRAFFITI DISAPPEARED THAT NIGHT AND SO DID I.
REGGIE, SHE'S GONE. LET HER GO.
MOM?

POLICE AND THIEVES
PART ONE OF HOW TO START A RIOT

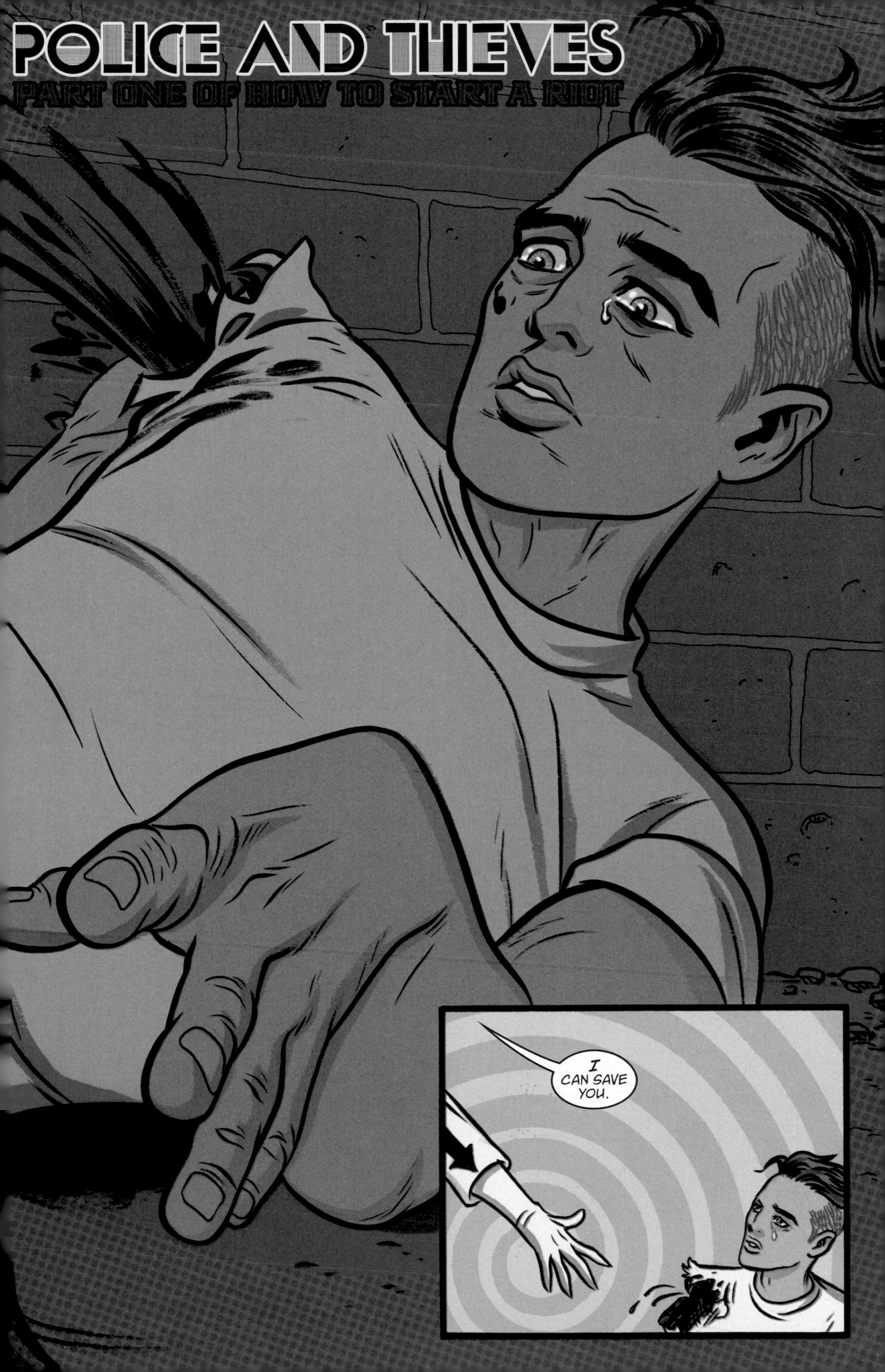
I CAN SAVE YOU.

ART
OPS

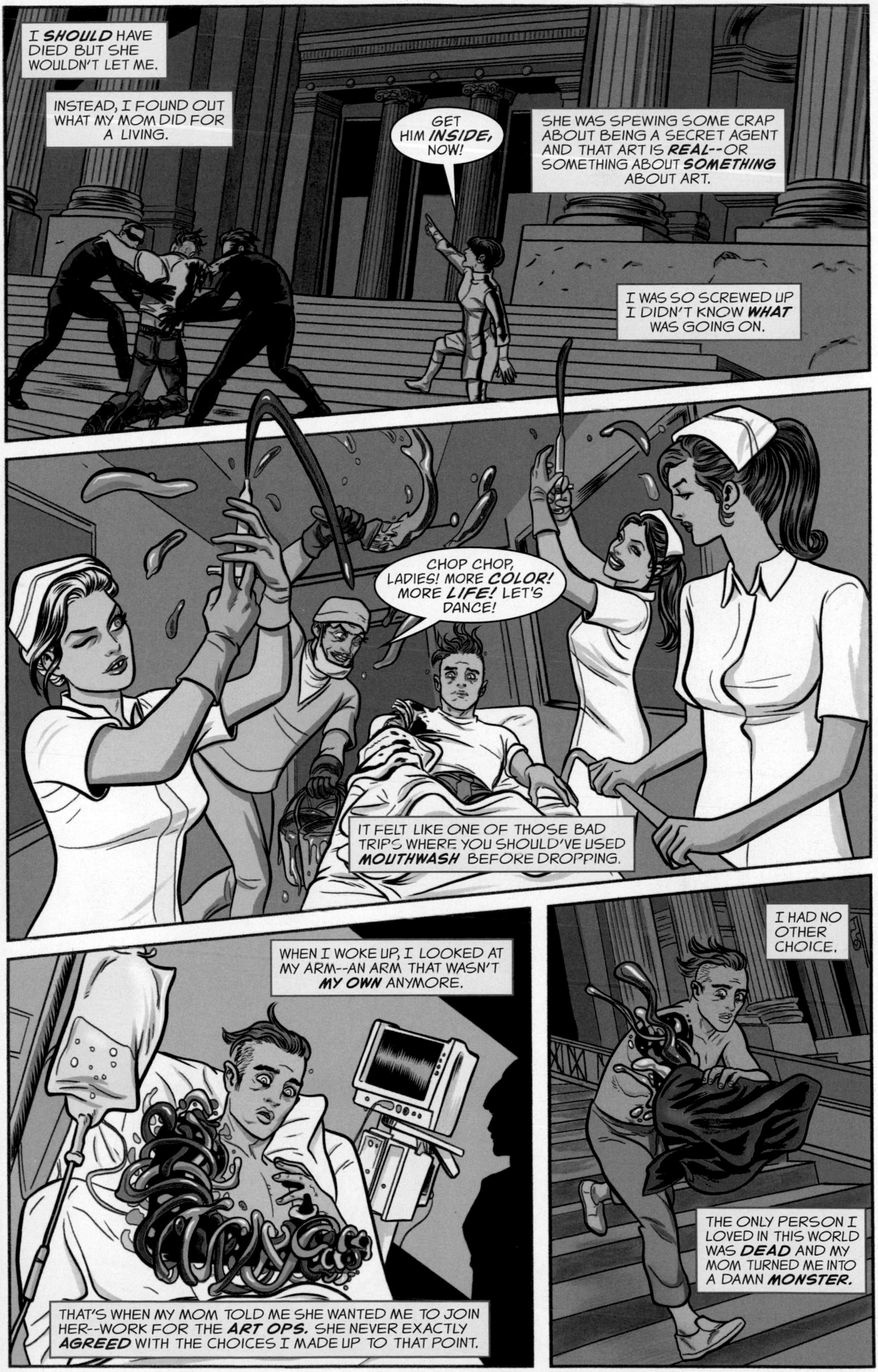
I SHOULD HAVE DIED BUT SHE WOULDN'T LET ME.
INSTEAD, I FOUND OUT WHAT MY MOM DID FOR A LIVING.
GET HIM INSIDE, NOW!
SHE WAS SPEWING SOME CRAP ABOUT BEING A SECRET AGENT AND THAT ART IS REAL--OR SOMETHING ABOUT SOMETHING ABOUT ART.
I WAS SO SCREWED UP I DIDN'T KNOW WHAT WAS GOING ON.
CHOP CHOP, LADIES! MORE COLOR! MORE LIFE! LET'S DANCE!
IT FELT LIKE ONE OF THOSE BAD TRIPS WHERE YOU SHOULD'VE USED MOUTHWASH BEFORE DROPPING.
WHEN I WOKE UP, I LOOKED AT MY ARM--AN ARM THAT WASN'T MY OWN ANYMORE.
THAT'S WHEN MY MOM TOLD ME SHE WANTED ME TO JOIN HER--WORK FOR THE ART OPS. SHE NEVER EXACTLY AGREED WITH THE CHOICES I MADE UP TO THAT POINT.
I HAD NO OTHER CHOICE.
THE ONLY PERSON I LOVED IN THIS WORLD WAS DEAD AND MY MOM TURNED ME INTO A DAMN MONSTER.

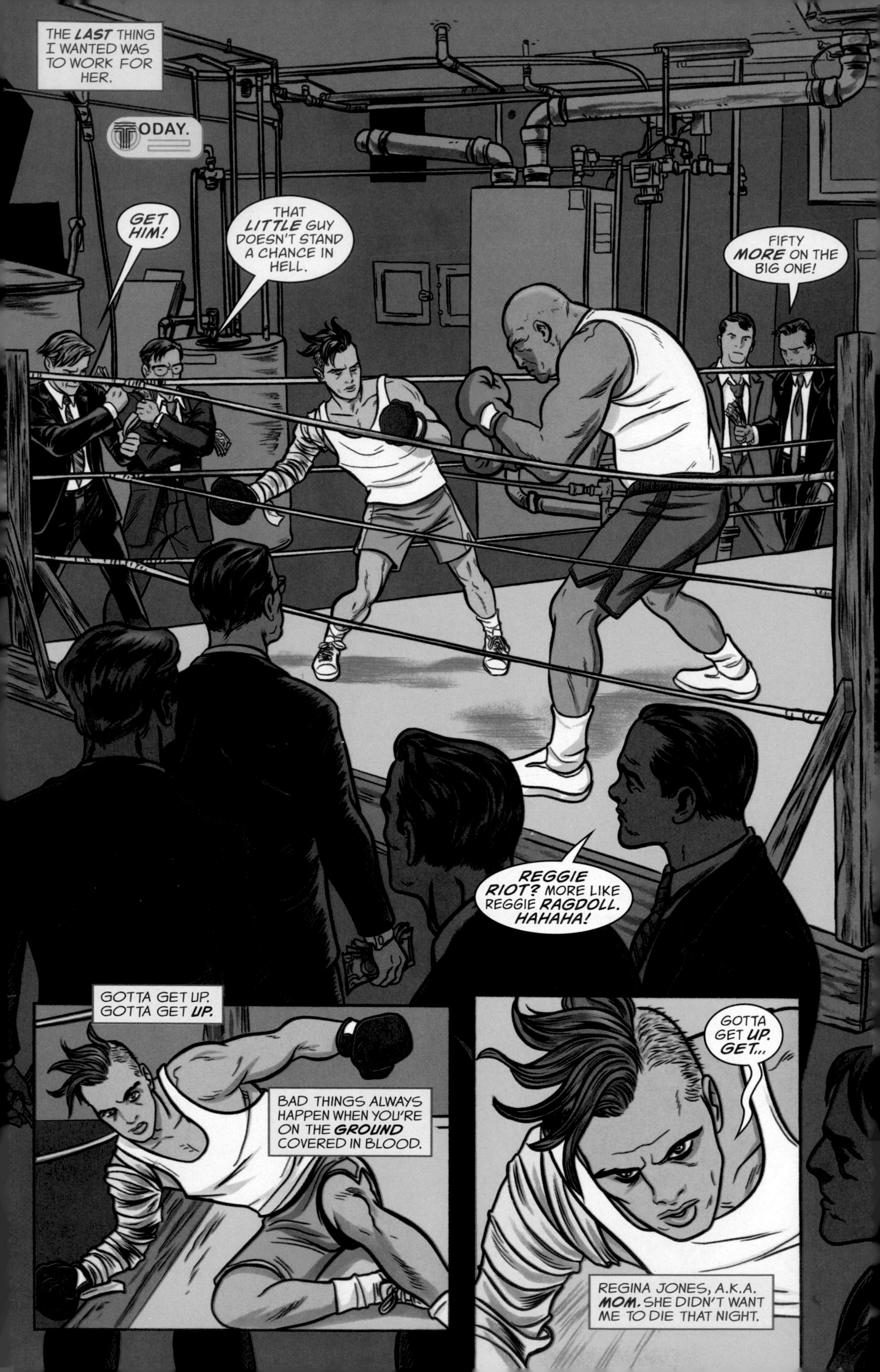
THE LAST THING I WANTED WAS TO WORK FOR HER.
TODAY.
GET HIM!
THAT LITTLE GUY DOESN'T STAND A CHANCE IN HELL.
FIFTY MORE ON THE BIG ONE!
REGGIE RIOT? MORE LIKE REGGIE RAGDOLL. HAHAHA!
GOTTA GET UP. GOTTA GET UP.
BAD THINGS ALWAYS HAPPEN WHEN YOU'RE ON THE GROUND COVERED IN BLOOD.
GOTTA GET UP. GET...
REGINA JONES, A.K.A. MOM. SHE DIDN'T WANT ME TO DIE THAT NIGHT.

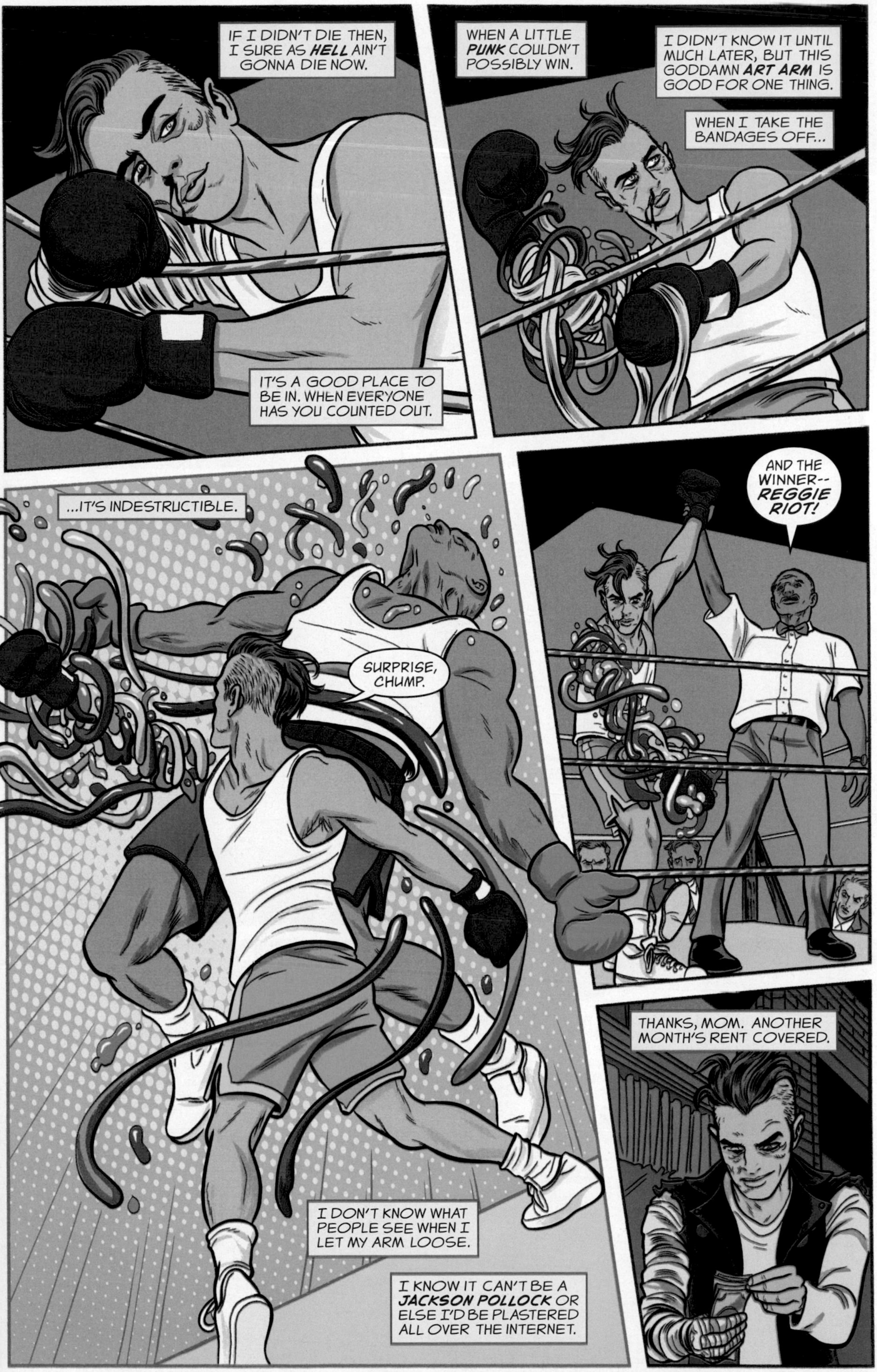
IF I DIDN'T DIE THEN, I SURE AS HELL AIN'T GONNA DIE NOW.
IT'S A GOOD PLACE TO BE IN. WHEN EVERYONE HAS YOU COUNTED OUT.
WHEN A LITTLE PUNK COULDN'T POSSIBLY WIN.
I DIDN'T KNOW IT UNTIL MUCH LATER, BUT THIS GODDAMN ART ARM IS GOOD FOR ONE THING.
WHEN I TAKE THE BANDAGES OFF...
...IT'S INDESTRUCTIBLE.
SURPRISE, CHUMP.
I DON'T KNOW WHAT PEOPLE SEE WHEN I LET MY ARM LOOSE.
I KNOW IT CAN'T BE A JACKSON POLLOCK OR ELSE I'D BE PLASTERED ALL OVER THE INTERNET.
AND THE WINNER-- REGGIE RIOT!
THANKS, MOM. ANOTHER MONTH'S RENT COVERED.

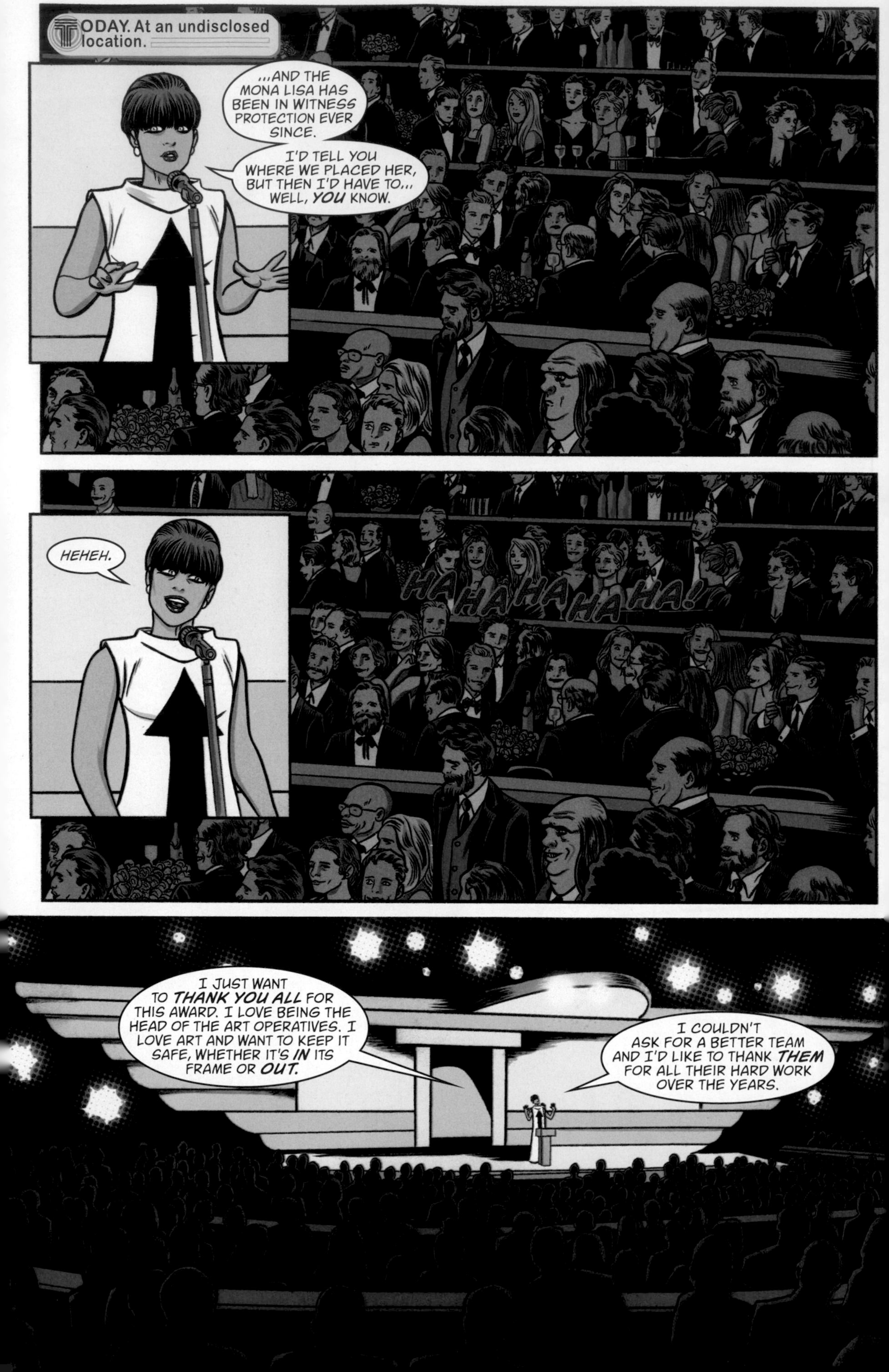
TODAY. At an undisclosed location.
...AND THE MONA LISA HAS BEEN IN WITNESS PROTECTION EVER SINCE.
I'D TELL YOU WHERE WE PLACED HER, BUT THEN I'D HAVE TO... WELL, YOU KNOW.
HEHEH.
HA HA HA HA HA HA!
I JUST WANT TO THANK YOU ALL FOR THIS AWARD. I LOVE BEING THE HEAD OF THE ART OPERATIVES. I LOVE ART AND WANT TO KEEP IT SAFE, WHETHER IT'S IN ITS FRAME OR OUT.
I COULDN'T ASK FOR A BETTER TEAM AND I'D LIKE TO THANK THEM FOR ALL THEIR HARD WORK OVER THE YEARS.

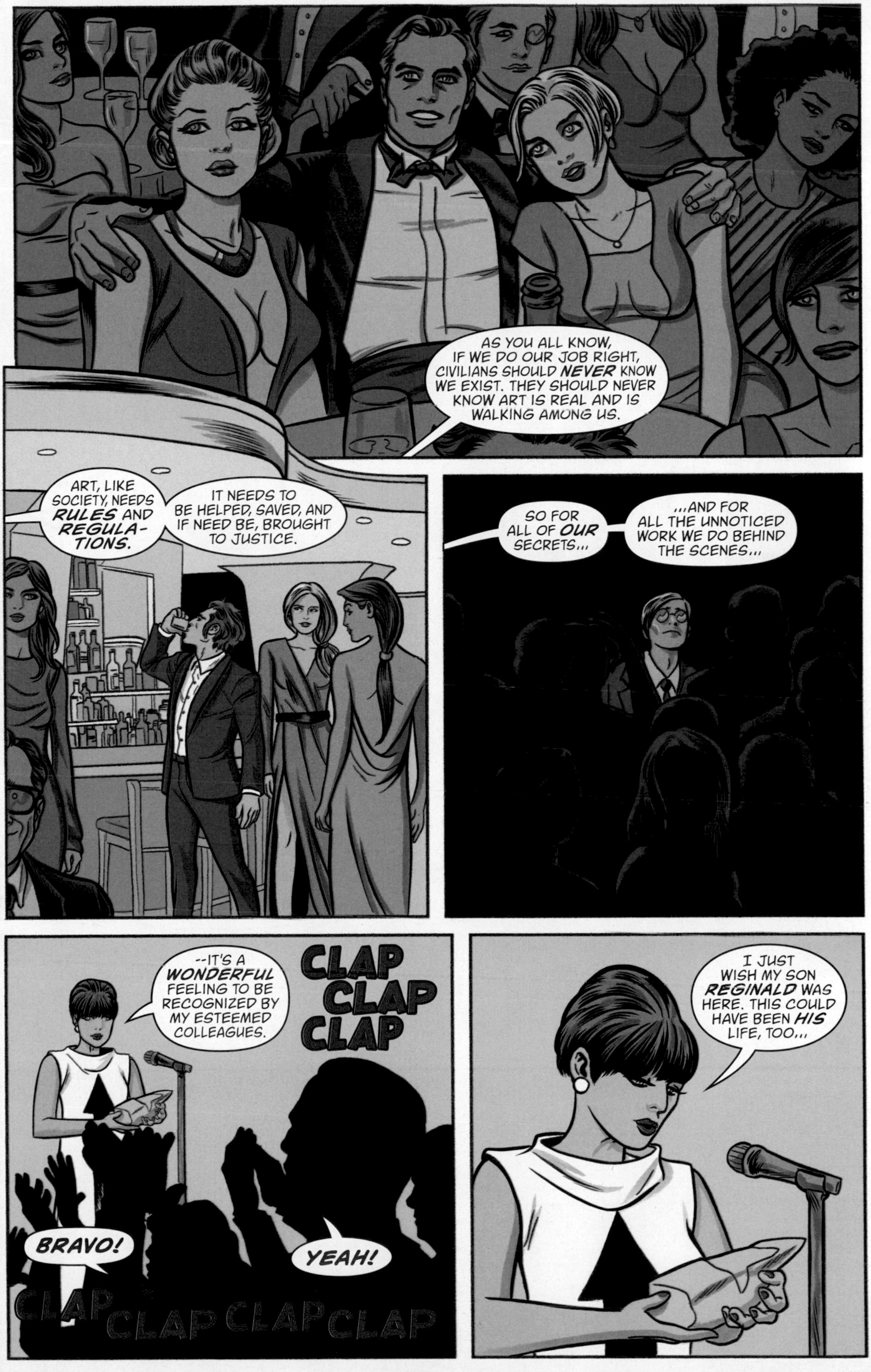
AS YOU ALL KNOW, IF WE DO OUR JOB RIGHT, CIVILIANS SHOULD NEVER KNOW WE EXIST. THEY SHOULD NEVER KNOW ART IS REAL AND IS WALKING AMONG US.
ART, LIKE SOCIETY, NEEDS RULES AND REGULA-TIONS.
IT NEEDS TO BE HELPED, SAVED, AND IF NEED BE, BROUGHT TO JUSTICE.
SO FOR ALL OF OUR SECRETS...
...AND FOR ALL THE UNNOTICED WORK WE DO BEHIND THE SCENES...
--IT'S A WONDERFUL FEELING TO BE RECOGNIZED BY MY ESTEEMED COLLEAGUES.
CLAP CLAP CLAP
BRAVO!
YEAH!
CLAP CLAP CLAP CLAP
I JUST WISH MY SON REGINALD WAS HERE. THIS COULD HAVE BEEN HIS LIFE, TOO...

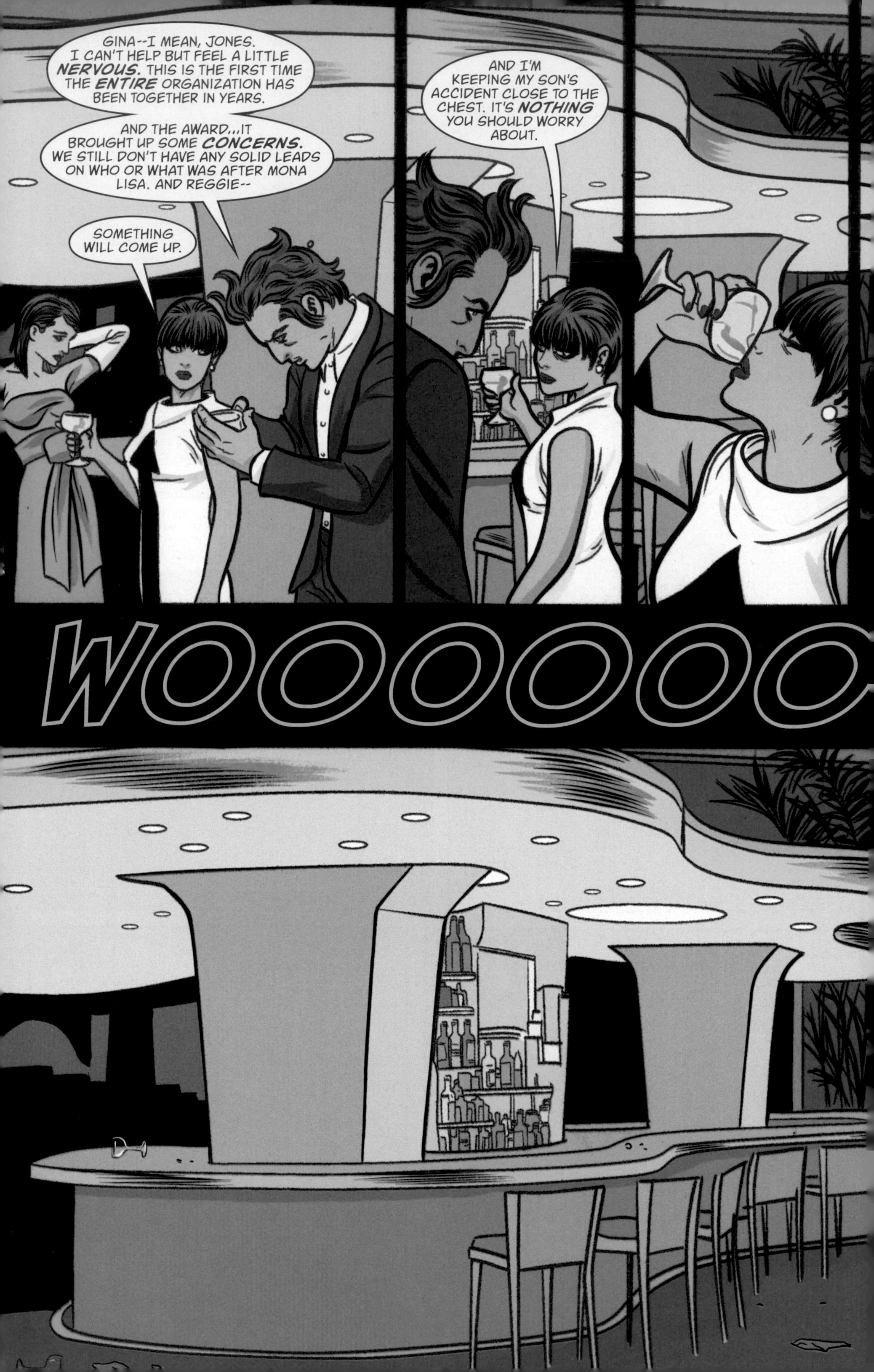
GINA--I MEAN, JONES. I CAN'T HELP BUT FEEL A LITTLE NERVOUS. THIS IS THE FIRST TIME THE ENTIRE ORGANIZATION HAS BEEN TOGETHER IN YEARS.
AND THE AWARD...IT BROUGHT UP SOME CONCERNS. WE STILL DON'T HAVE ANY SOLID LEADS ON WHO OR WHAT WAS AFTER MONA LISA. AND REGGIE--
SOMETHING WILL COME UP.
AND I'M KEEPING MY SON'S ACCIDENT CLOSE TO THE CHEST. IT'S NOTHING YOU SHOULD WORRY ABOUT.
WOOOOOO

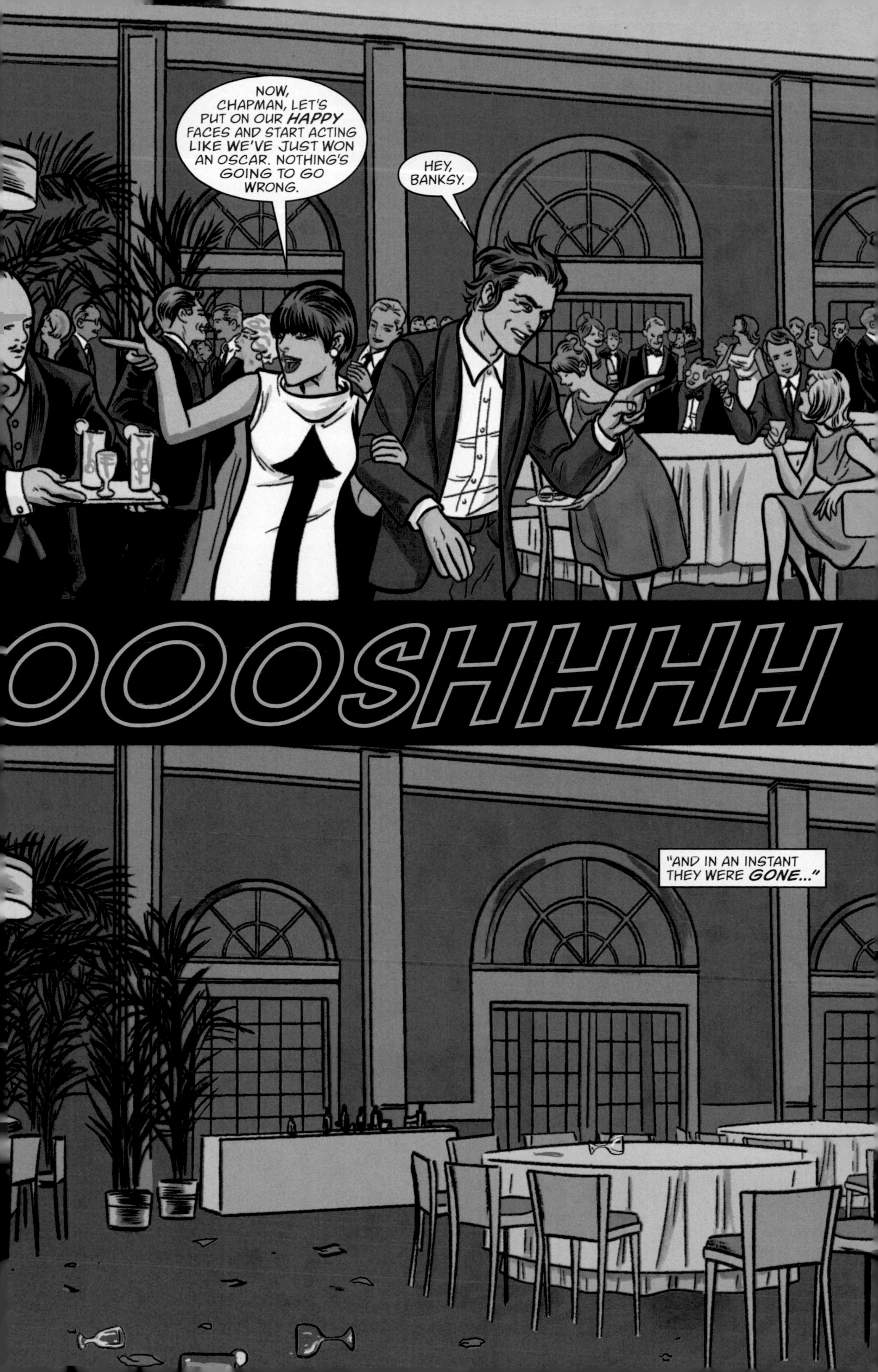
NOW, CHAPMAN, LET'S PUT ON OUR *HAPPY* FACES AND START ACTING LIKE WE'VE JUST WON AN OSCAR. NOTHING'S GOING TO GO WRONG.
HEY, BANKSY.
OOOSHHHH
"AND IN AN INSTANT THEY WERE *GONE...*"

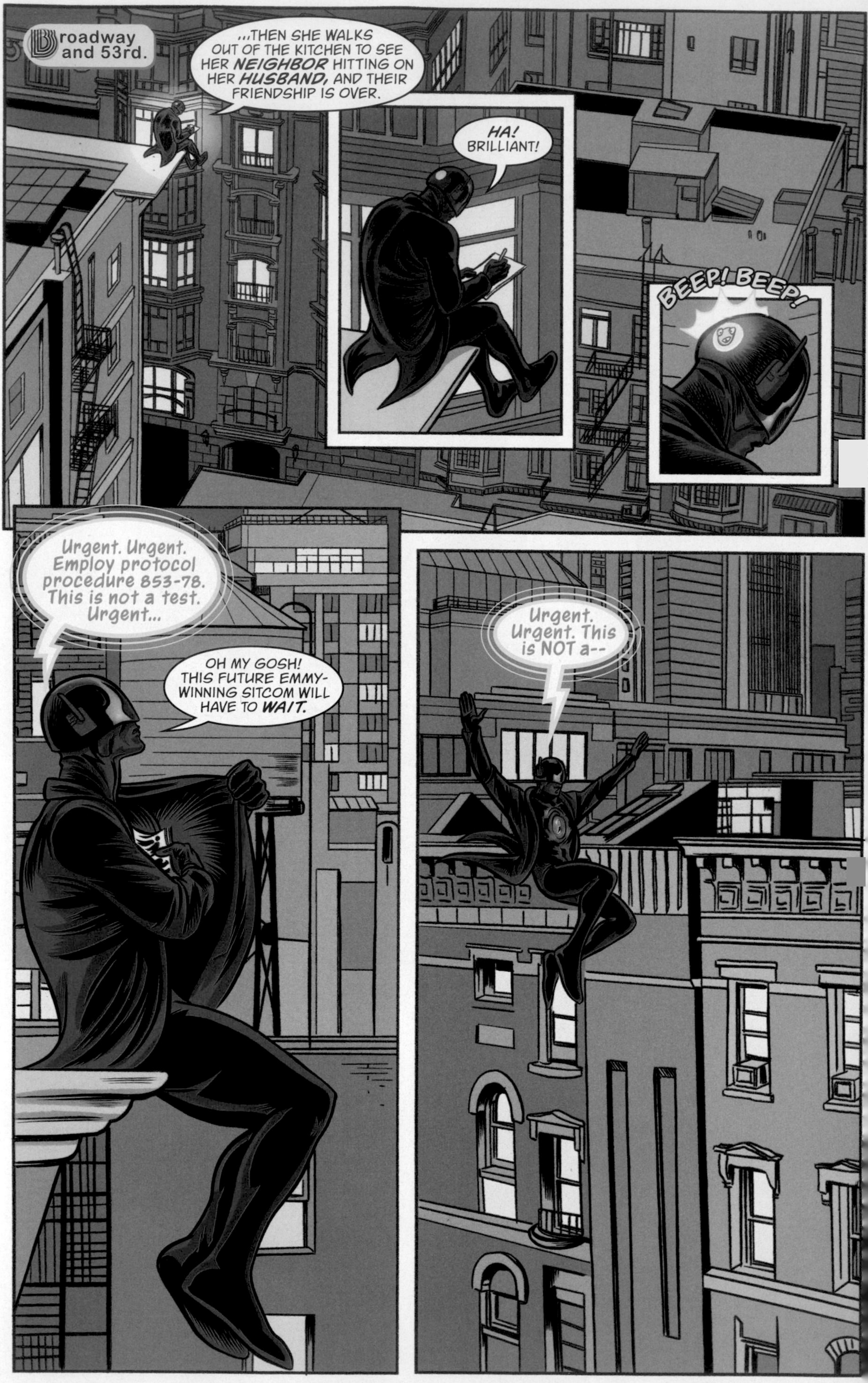

Broadway and 53rd.
...THEN SHE WALKS OUT OF THE KITCHEN TO SEE HER NEIGHBOR HITTING ON HER HUSBAND, AND THEIR FRIENDSHIP IS OVER.
HA! BRILLIANT!
BEEP! BEEP!
Urgent. Urgent. Employ protocol procedure 853-78. This is not a test. Urgent...
OH MY GOSH! THIS FUTURE EMMY-WINNING SITCOM WILL HAVE TO WAIT.
Urgent. Urgent. This is NOT a--

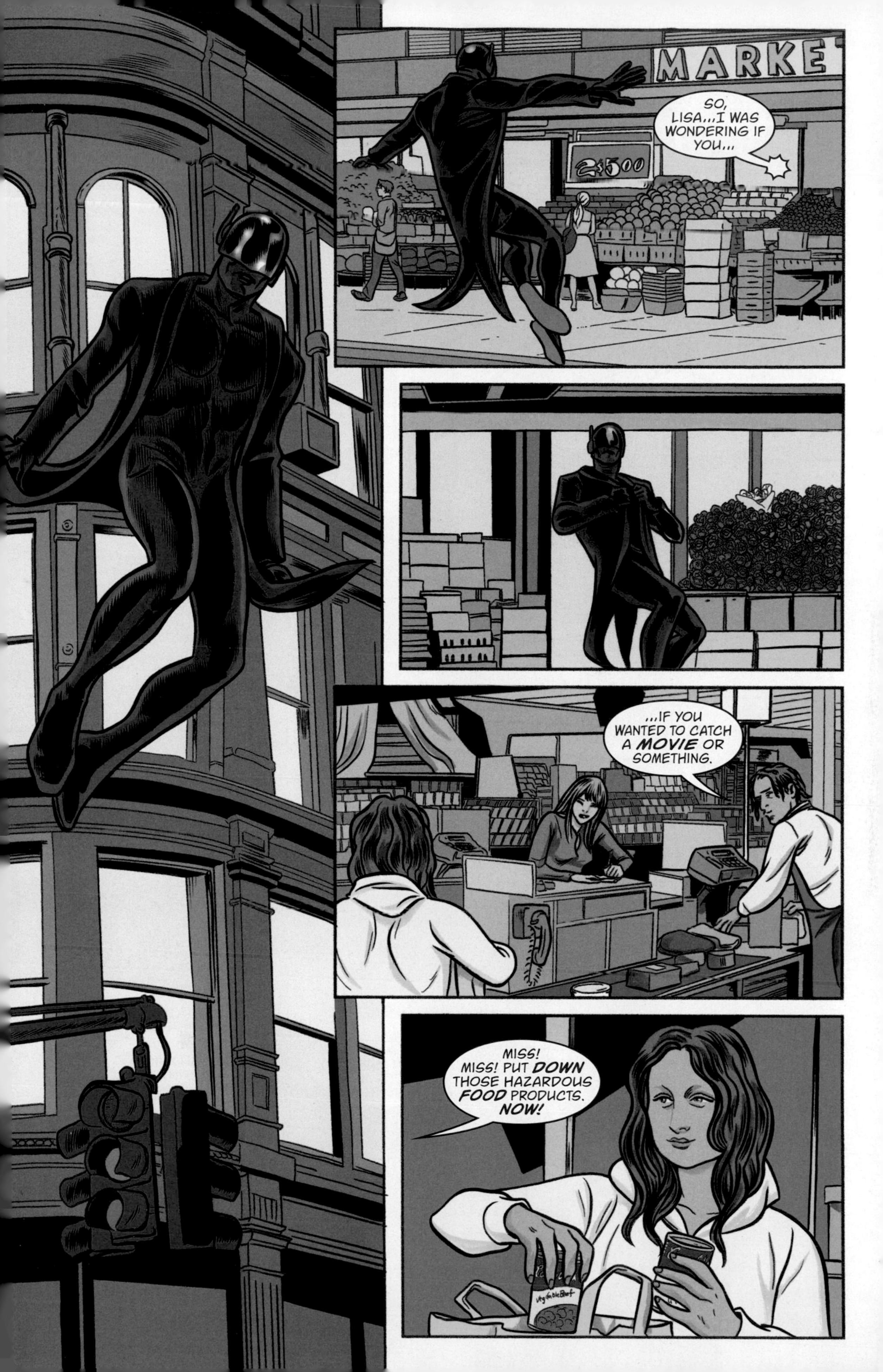
MARKE
SO, LISA...I WAS WONDERING IF YOU...
...IF YOU WANTED TO CATCH A **MOVIE** OR SOMETHING.
MISS! MISS! PUT **DOWN** THOSE HAZARDOUS **FOOD** PRODUCTS. **NOW!**

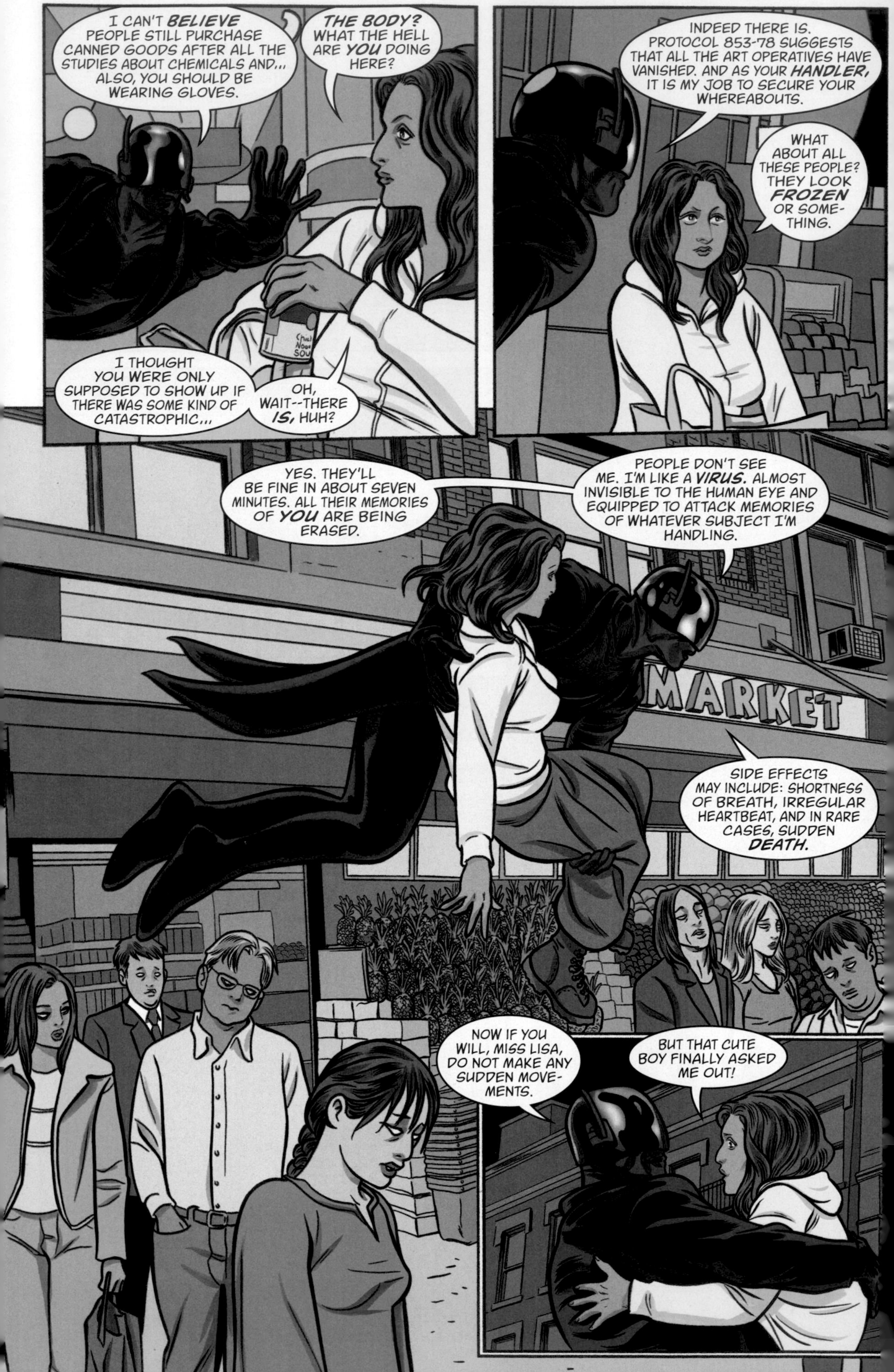
I CAN'T BELIEVE PEOPLE STILL PURCHASE CANNED GOODS AFTER ALL THE STUDIES ABOUT CHEMICALS AND... ALSO, YOU SHOULD BE WEARING GLOVES.
THE BODY? WHAT THE HELL ARE YOU DOING HERE?
I THOUGHT YOU WERE ONLY SUPPOSED TO SHOW UP IF THERE WAS SOME KIND OF CATASTROPHIC...
OH, WAIT--THERE IS, HUH?
INDEED THERE IS. PROTOCOL 853-78 SUGGESTS THAT ALL THE ART OPERATIVES HAVE VANISHED. AND AS YOUR HANDLER, IT IS MY JOB TO SECURE YOUR WHEREABOUTS.
WHAT ABOUT ALL THESE PEOPLE? THEY LOOK FROZEN OR SOME-THING.
YES. THEY'LL BE FINE IN ABOUT SEVEN MINUTES. ALL THEIR MEMORIES OF YOU ARE BEING ERASED.
PEOPLE DON'T SEE ME. I'M LIKE A VIRUS. ALMOST INVISIBLE TO THE HUMAN EYE AND EQUIPPED TO ATTACK MEMORIES OF WHATEVER SUBJECT I'M HANDLING.
MARKET
SIDE EFFECTS MAY INCLUDE: SHORTNESS OF BREATH, IRREGULAR HEARTBEAT, AND IN RARE CASES, SUDDEN DEATH.
NOW IF YOU WILL, MISS LISA, DO NOT MAKE ANY SUDDEN MOVE-MENTS.
BUT THAT CUTE BOY FINALLY ASKED ME OUT!

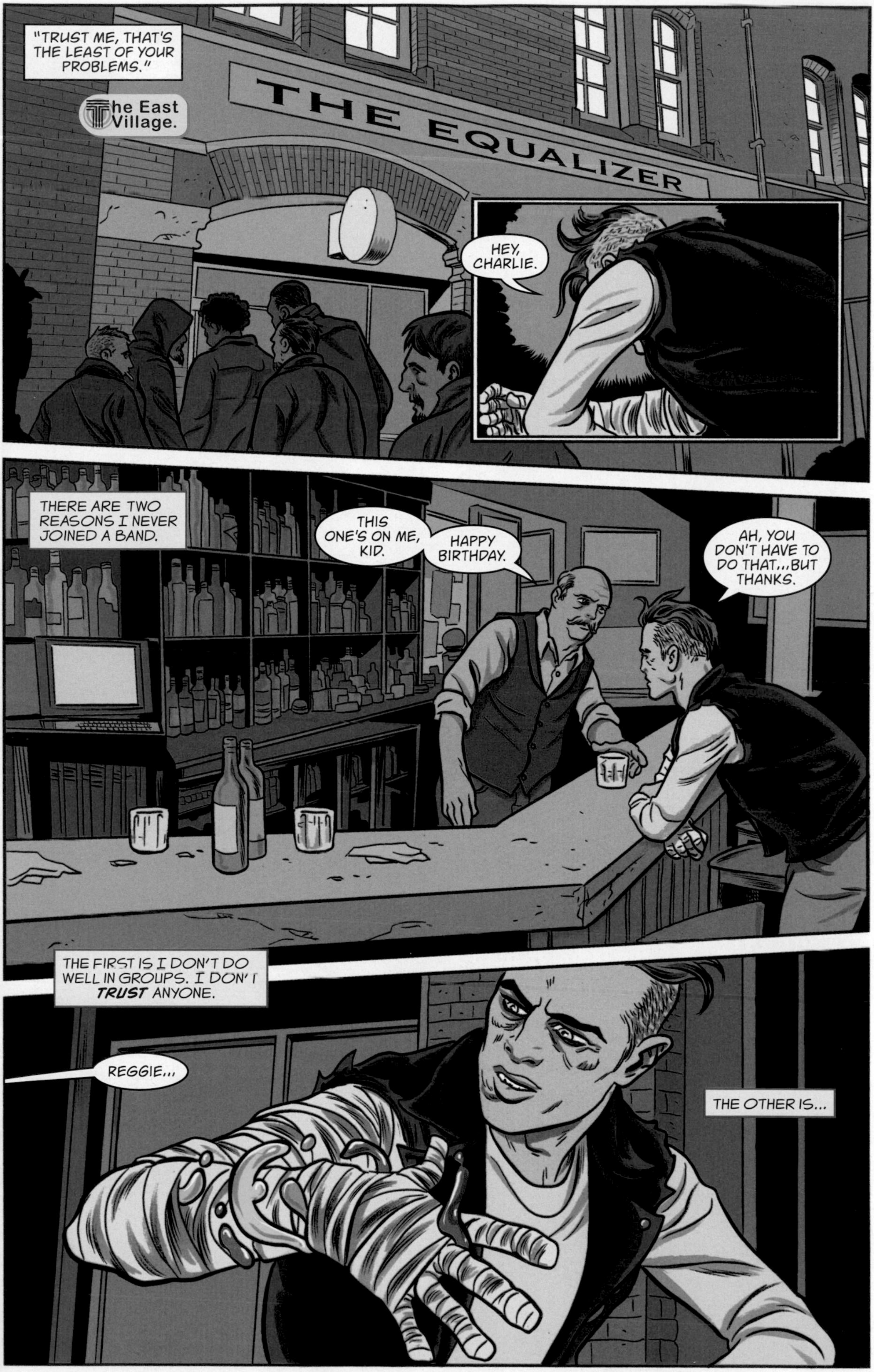
"TRUST ME, THAT'S THE LEAST OF YOUR PROBLEMS."
The East Village.
THE EQUALIZER
HEY, CHARLIE.
THERE ARE TWO REASONS I NEVER JOINED A BAND.
THIS ONE'S ON ME, KID.
HAPPY BIRTHDAY.
AH, YOU DON'T HAVE TO DO THAT...BUT THANKS.
THE FIRST IS I DON'T DO WELL IN GROUPS. I DON'T TRUST ANYONE.
REGGIE...
THE OTHER IS...

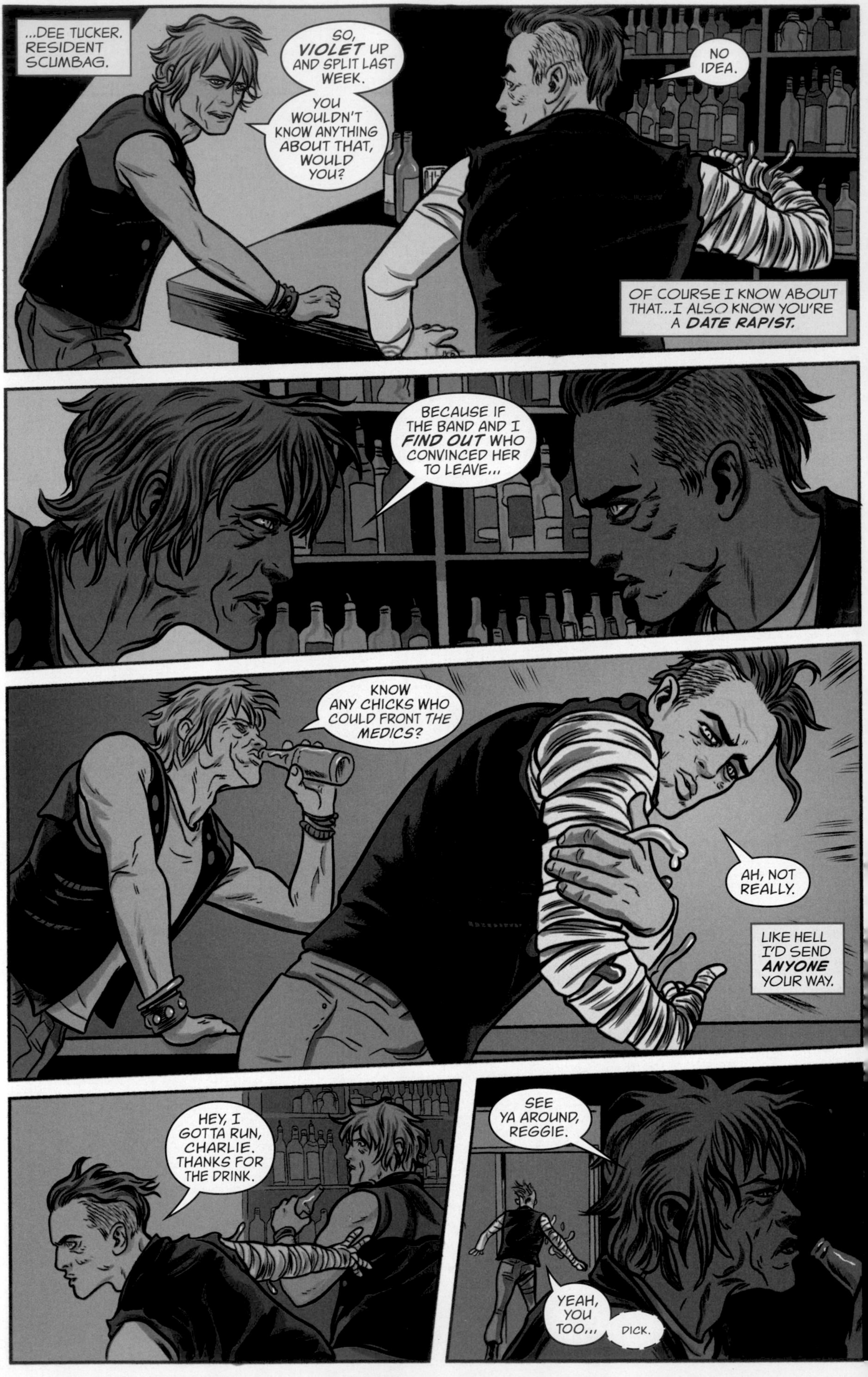
...DEE TUCKER. RESIDENT SCUMBAG.
SO, VIOLET UP AND SPLIT LAST WEEK.
YOU WOULDN'T KNOW ANYTHING ABOUT THAT, WOULD YOU?
NO IDEA.
OF COURSE I KNOW ABOUT THAT...I ALSO KNOW YOU'RE A DATE RAPIST.
BECAUSE IF THE BAND AND I FIND OUT WHO CONVINCED HER TO LEAVE...
KNOW ANY CHICKS WHO COULD FRONT THE MEDICS?
AH, NOT REALLY.
LIKE HELL I'D SEND ANYONE YOUR WAY.
HEY, I GOTTA RUN, CHARLIE. THANKS FOR THE DRINK.
SEE YA AROUND, REGGIE.
YEAH, YOU TOO...
DICK.

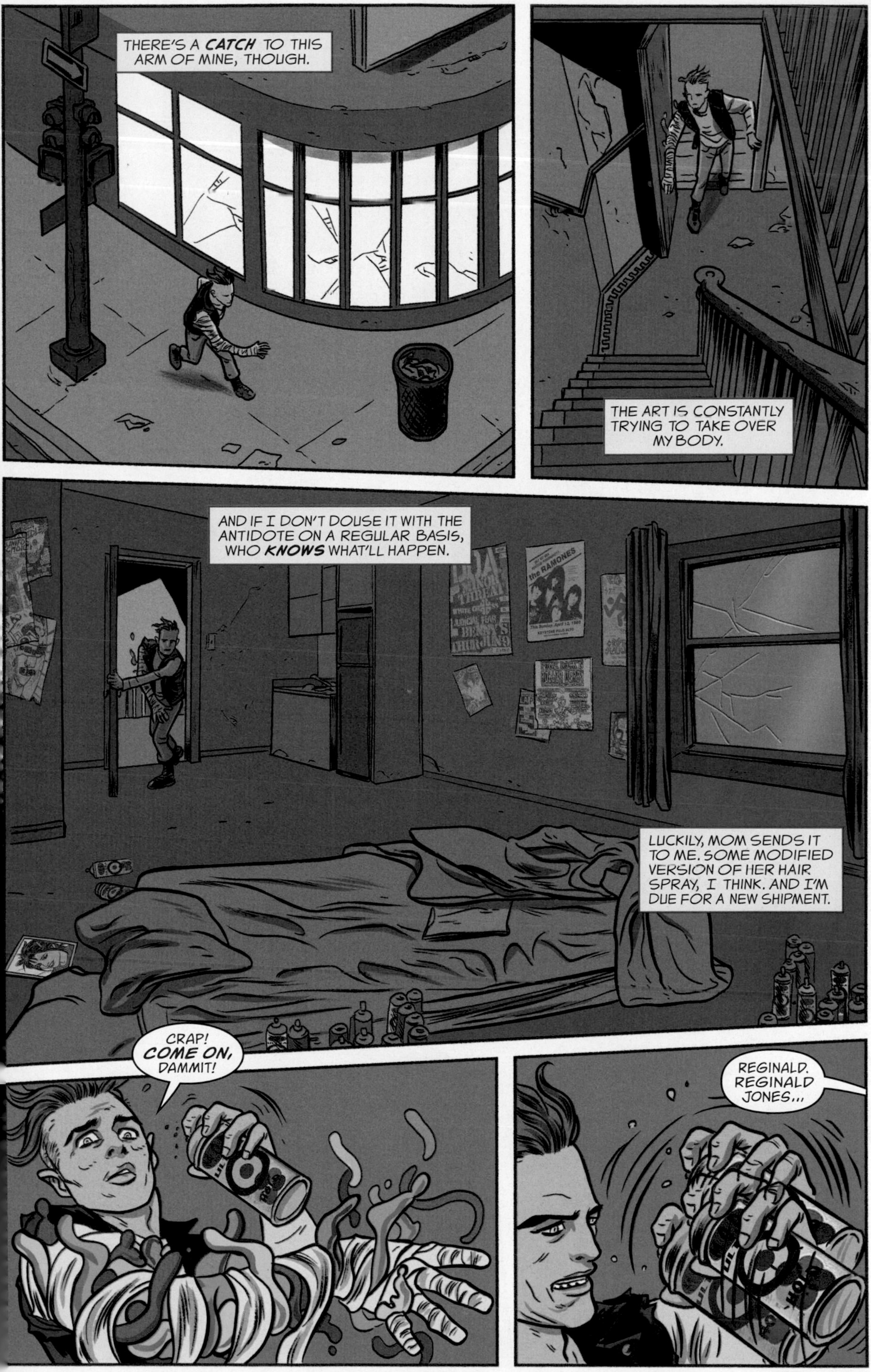

THERE'S A **CATCH** TO THIS ARM OF MINE, THOUGH.
THE ART IS CONSTANTLY TRYING TO TAKE OVER MY BODY.
AND IF I DON'T DOUSE IT WITH THE ANTIDOTE ON A REGULAR BASIS, WHO **KNOWS** WHAT'LL HAPPEN.
the RAMONES
LUCKILY, MOM SENDS IT TO ME. SOME MODIFIED VERSION OF HER HAIR SPRAY, I THINK. AND I'M DUE FOR A NEW SHIPMENT.
CRAP! **COME ON,** DAMMIT!
REGINALD. REGINALD JONES...

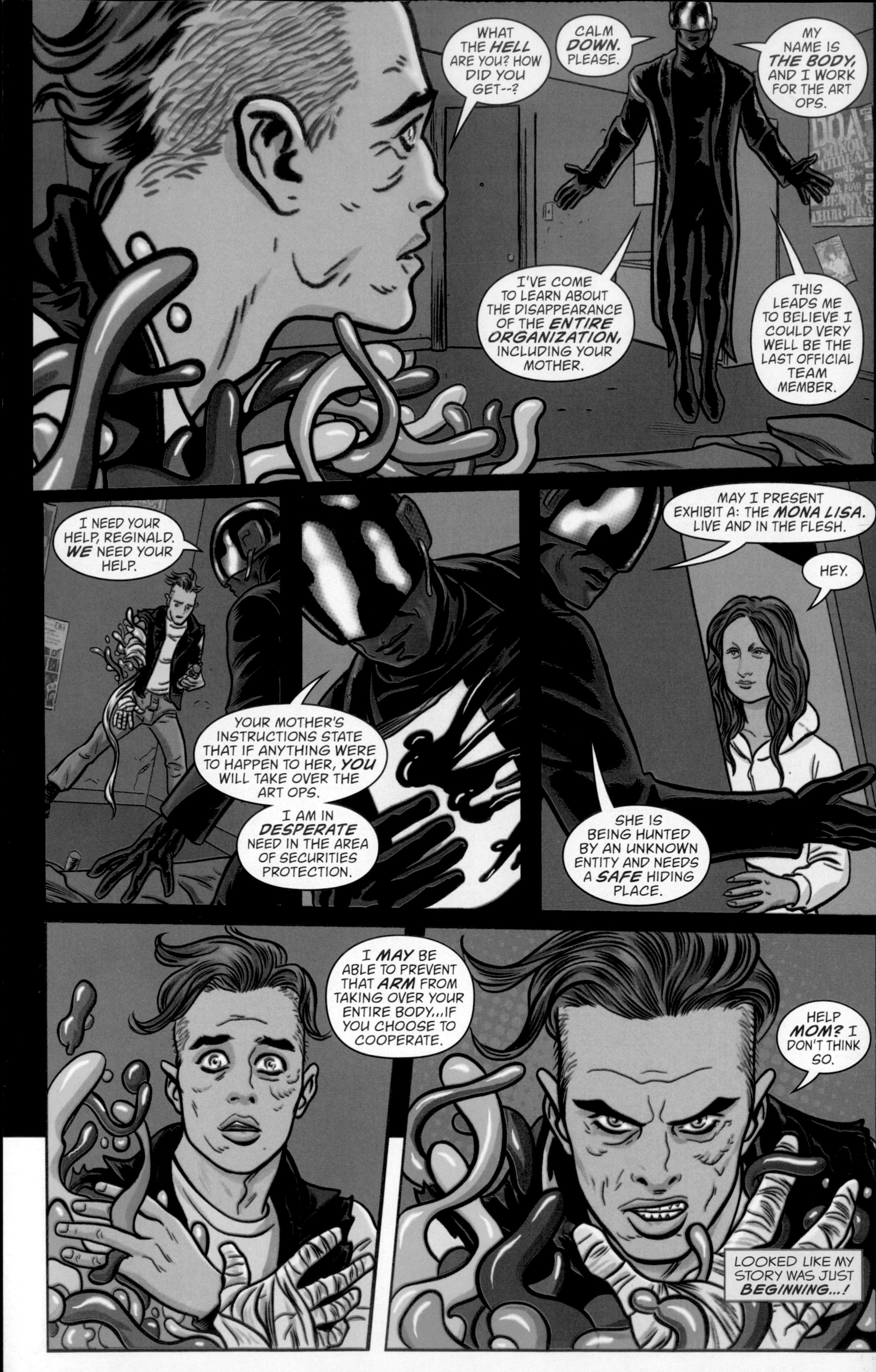
WHAT THE HELL ARE YOU? HOW DID YOU GET--?
CALM DOWN. PLEASE.
MY NAME IS THE BODY, AND I WORK FOR THE ART OPS.
I'VE COME TO LEARN ABOUT THE DISAPPEARANCE OF THE ENTIRE ORGANIZATION, INCLUDING YOUR MOTHER.
THIS LEADS ME TO BELIEVE I COULD VERY WELL BE THE LAST OFFICIAL TEAM MEMBER.
I NEED YOUR HELP, REGINALD. WE NEED YOUR HELP.
YOUR MOTHER'S INSTRUCTIONS STATE THAT IF ANYTHING WERE TO HAPPEN TO HER, YOU WILL TAKE OVER THE ART OPS.
I AM IN DESPERATE NEED IN THE AREA OF SECURITIES PROTECTION.
MAY I PRESENT EXHIBIT A: THE MONA LISA. LIVE AND IN THE FLESH.
HEY.
SHE IS BEING HUNTED BY AN UNKNOWN ENTITY AND NEEDS A SAFE HIDING PLACE.
I MAY BE ABLE TO PREVENT THAT ARM FROM TAKING OVER YOUR ENTIRE BODY...IF YOU CHOOSE TO COOPERATE.
HELP MOM? I DON'T THINK SO.
LOOKED LIKE MY STORY WAS JUST BEGINNING...!

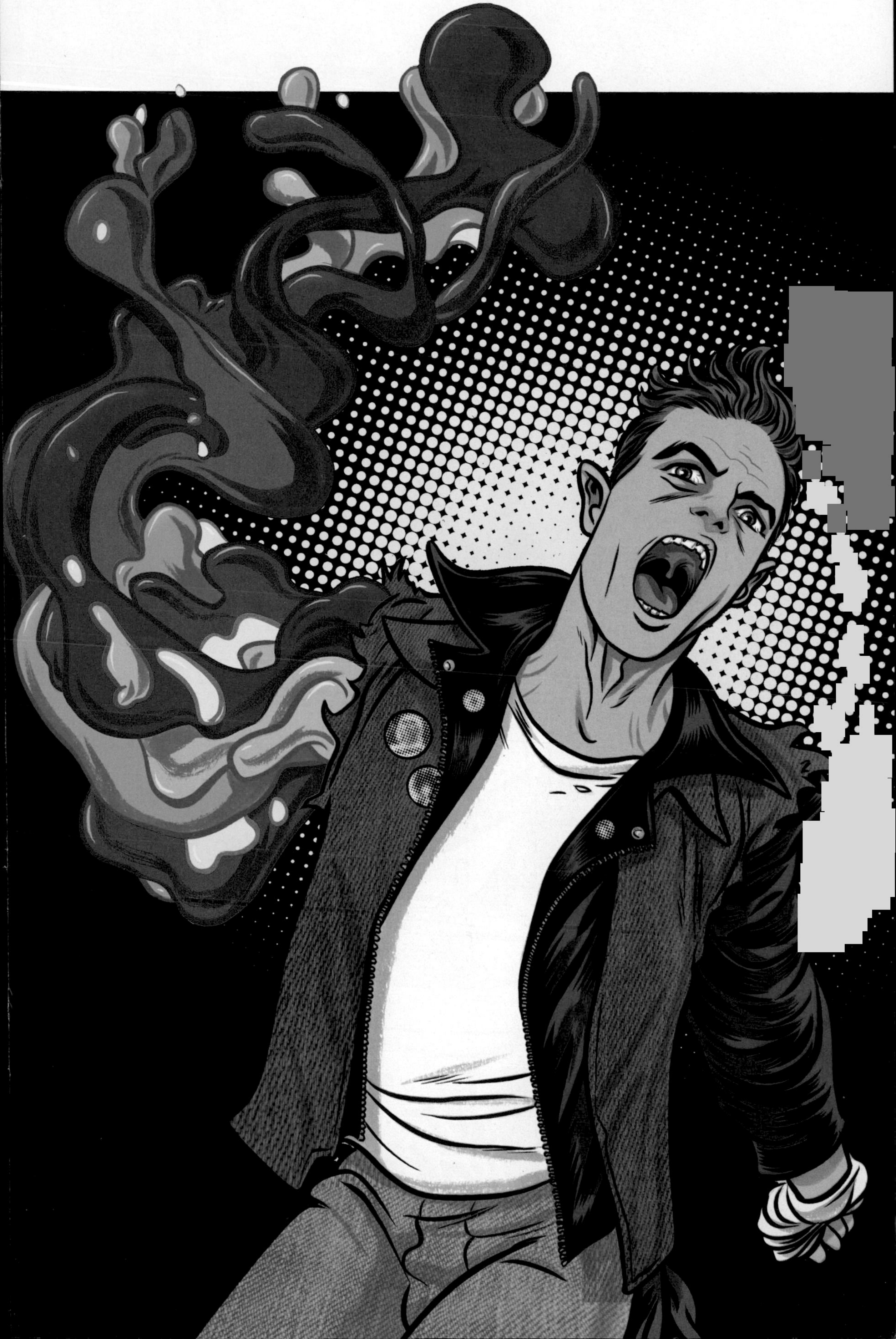

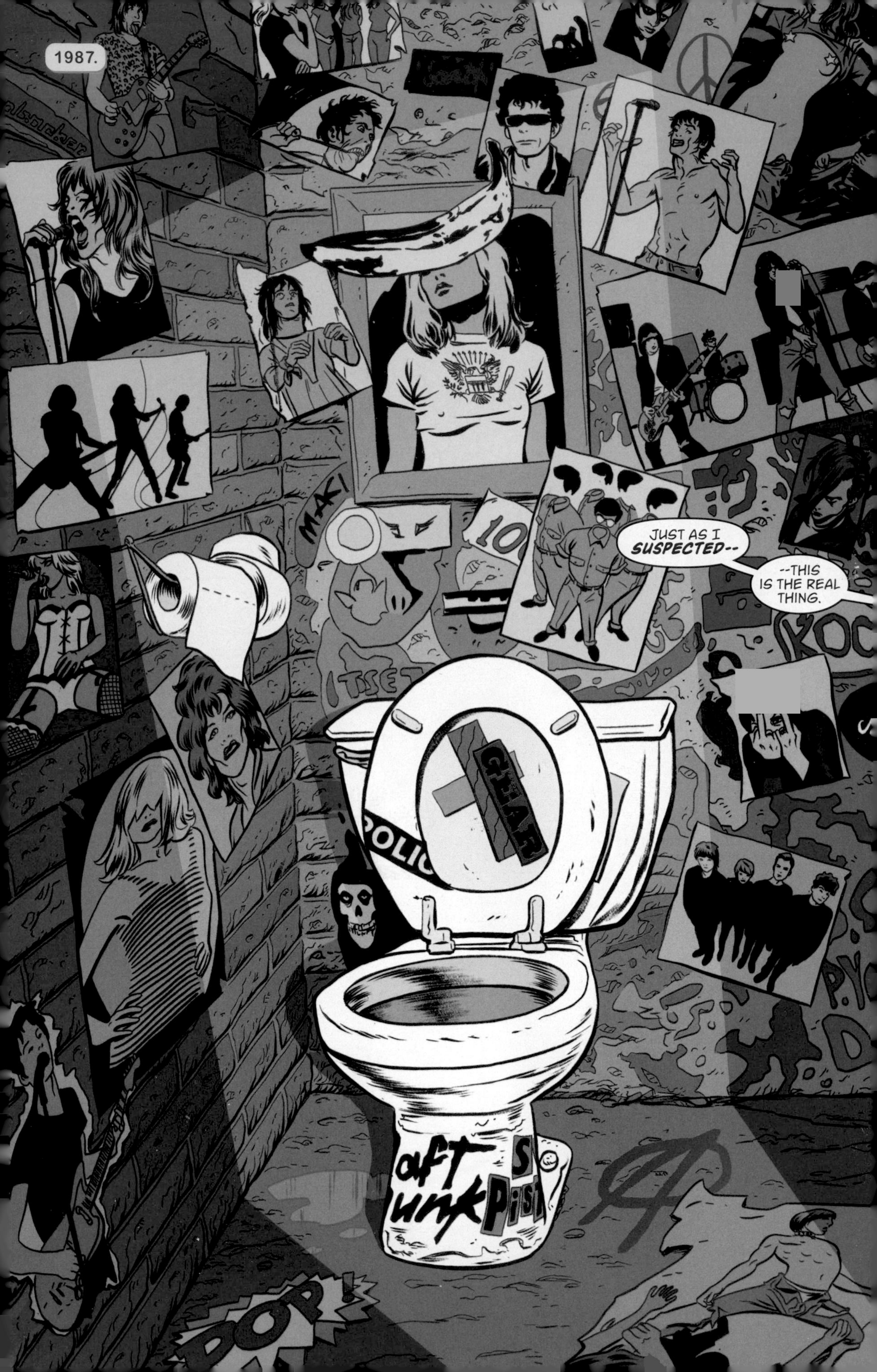
1987.
JUST AS I SUSPECTED--
--THIS IS THE REAL THING.

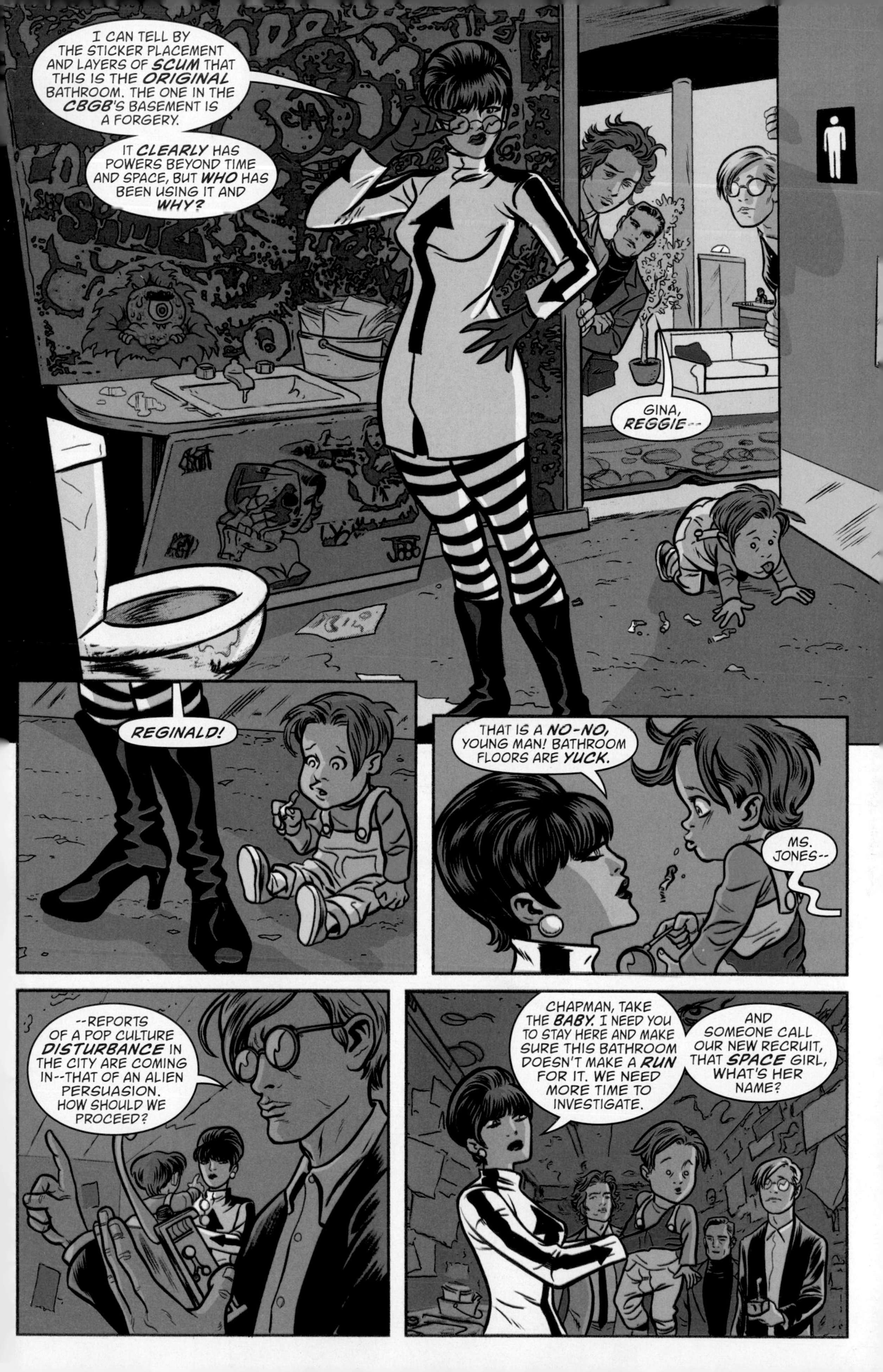
I CAN TELL BY THE STICKER PLACEMENT AND LAYERS OF SCUM THAT THIS IS THE ORIGINAL BATHROOM. THE ONE IN THE CBGB'S BASEMENT IS A FORGERY.
IT CLEARLY HAS POWERS BEYOND TIME AND SPACE, BUT WHO HAS BEEN USING IT AND WHY?
GINA, REGGIE--
REGINALD!
THAT IS A NO-NO, YOUNG MAN! BATHROOM FLOORS ARE YUCK.
MS. JONES--
--REPORTS OF A POP CULTURE DISTURBANCE IN THE CITY ARE COMING IN--THAT OF AN ALIEN PERSUASION. HOW SHOULD WE PROCEED?
CHAPMAN, TAKE THE BABY. I NEED YOU TO STAY HERE AND MAKE SURE THIS BATHROOM DOESN'T MAKE A RUN FOR IT. WE NEED MORE TIME TO INVESTIGATE.
AND SOMEONE CALL OUR NEW RECRUIT, THAT SPACE GIRL, WHAT'S HER NAME?

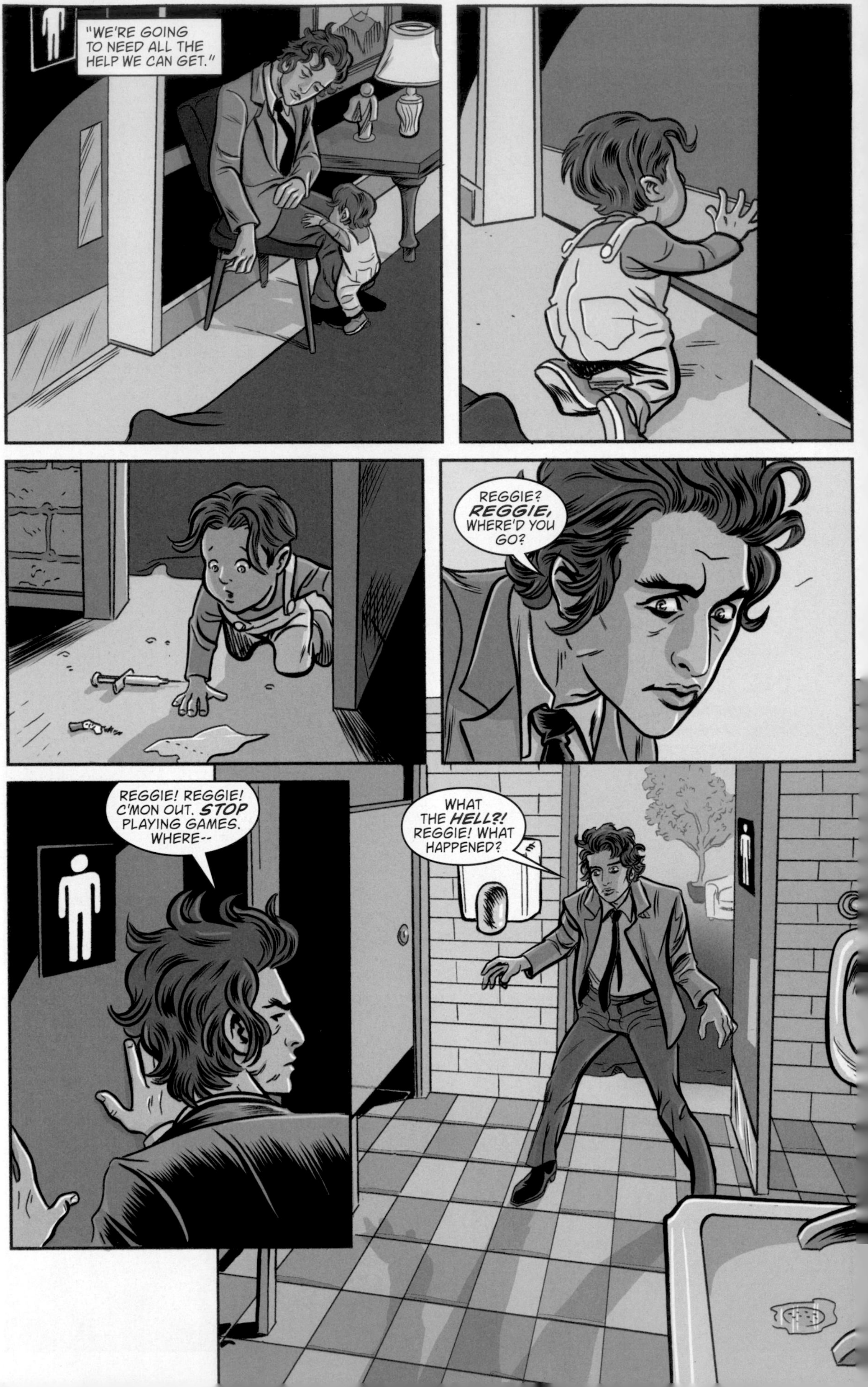
"WE'RE GOING TO NEED ALL THE HELP WE CAN GET."
REGGIE? REGGIE, WHERE'D YOU GO?
REGGIE! REGGIE! C'MON OUT. STOP PLAYING GAMES. WHERE--
WHAT THE HELL?! REGGIE! WHAT HAPPENED?

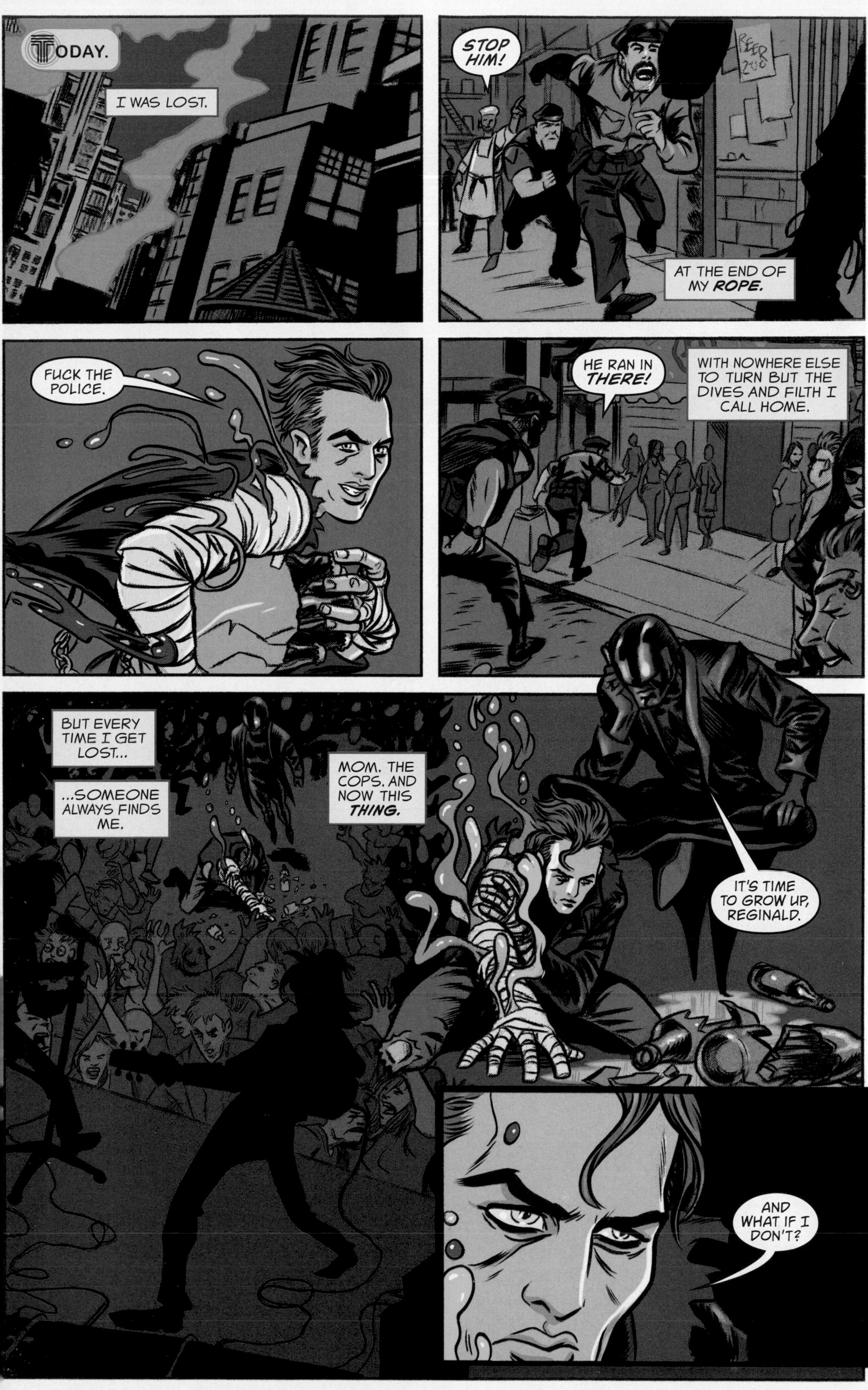
TODAY.
I WAS LOST.
STOP HIM!
AT THE END OF MY ROPE.
FUCK THE POLICE.
HE RAN IN THERE!
WITH NOWHERE ELSE TO TURN BUT THE DIVES AND FILTH I CALL HOME.
BUT EVERY TIME I GET LOST...
...SOMEONE ALWAYS FINDS ME.
MOM. THE COPS. AND NOW THIS THING.
IT'S TIME TO GROW UP, REGINALD.
AND WHAT IF I DON'T?

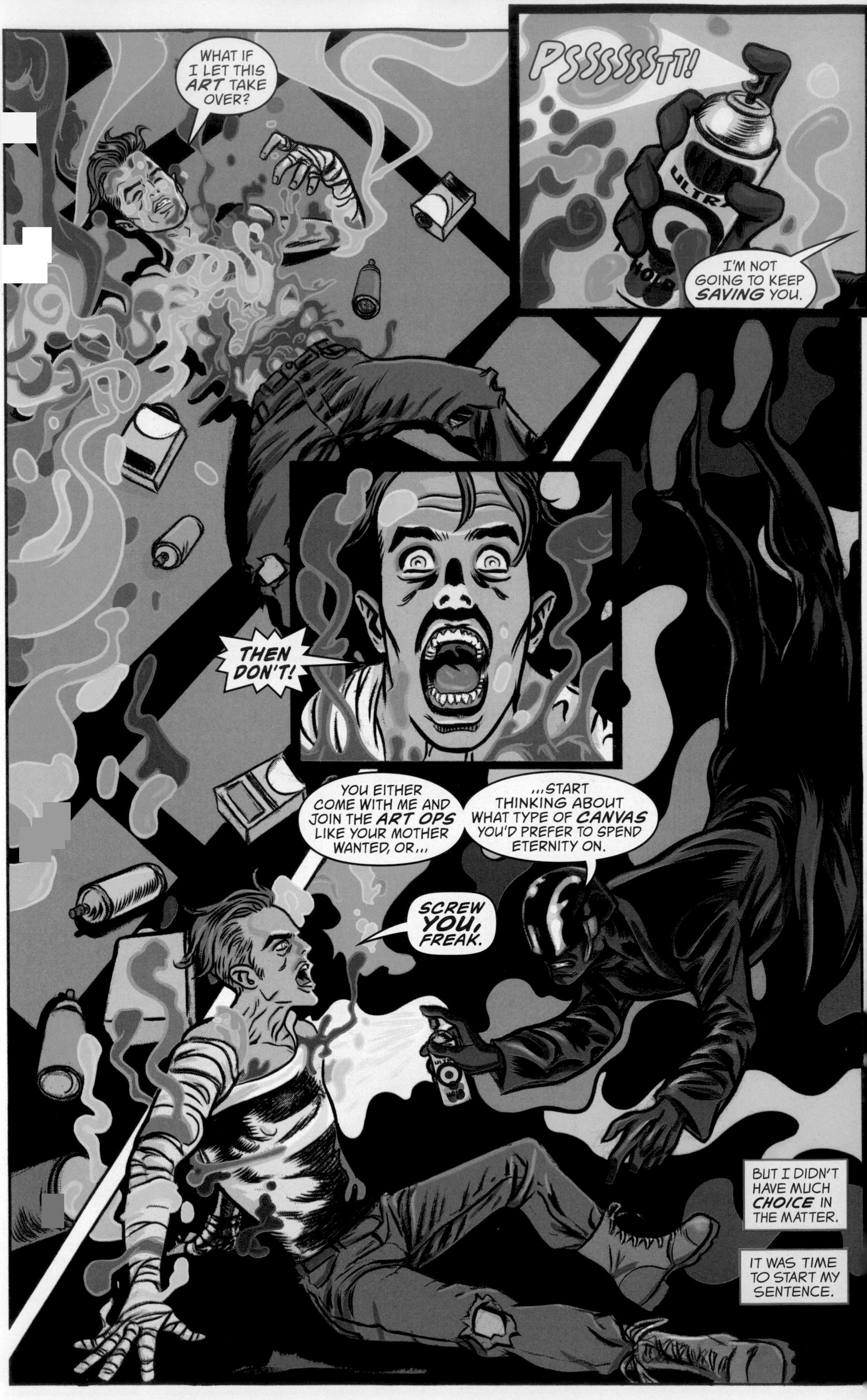
WHAT IF I LET THIS ART TAKE OVER?
PSSSSSSTT!
I'M NOT GOING TO KEEP SAVING YOU.
THEN DON'T!
YOU EITHER COME WITH ME AND JOIN THE ART OPS LIKE YOUR MOTHER WANTED, OR...
...START THINKING ABOUT WHAT TYPE OF CANVAS YOU'D PREFER TO SPEND ETERNITY ON.
SCREW YOU, FREAK.
BUT I DIDN'T HAVE MUCH CHOICE IN THE MATTER.
IT WAS TIME TO START MY SENTENCE.

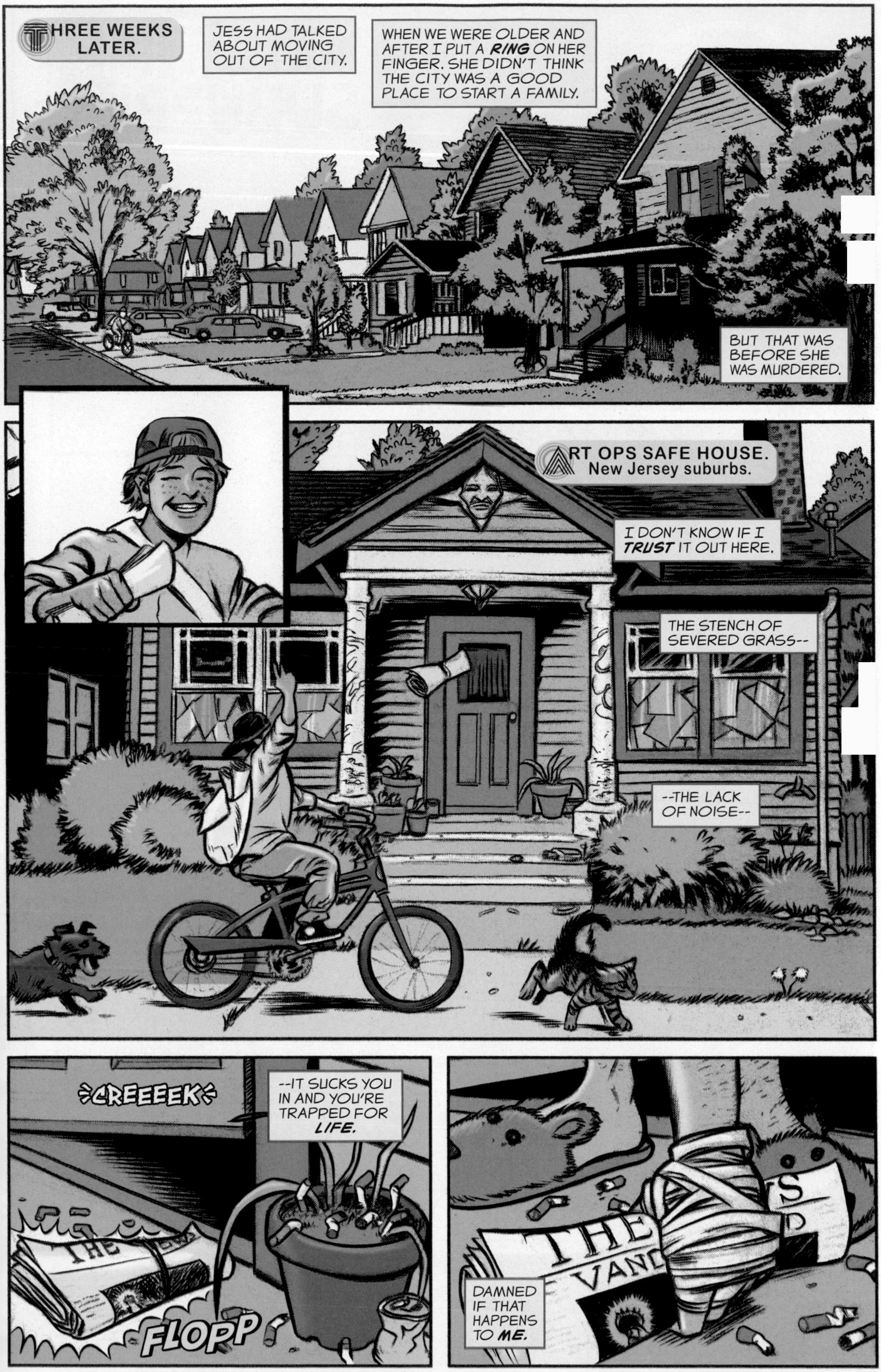
THREE WEEKS LATER.
JESS HAD TALKED ABOUT MOVING OUT OF THE CITY.
WHEN WE WERE OLDER AND AFTER I PUT A *RING* ON HER FINGER. SHE DIDN'T THINK THE CITY WAS A GOOD PLACE TO START A FAMILY.
BUT THAT WAS BEFORE SHE WAS MURDERED.
ART OPS SAFE HOUSE. New Jersey suburbs.
I DON'T KNOW IF I *TRUST* IT OUT HERE.
THE STENCH OF SEVERED GRASS--
--THE LACK OF NOISE--
CREEEEK
--IT SUCKS YOU IN AND YOU'RE TRAPPED FOR *LIFE.*
FLOPP
DAMNED IF THAT HAPPENS TO *ME.*

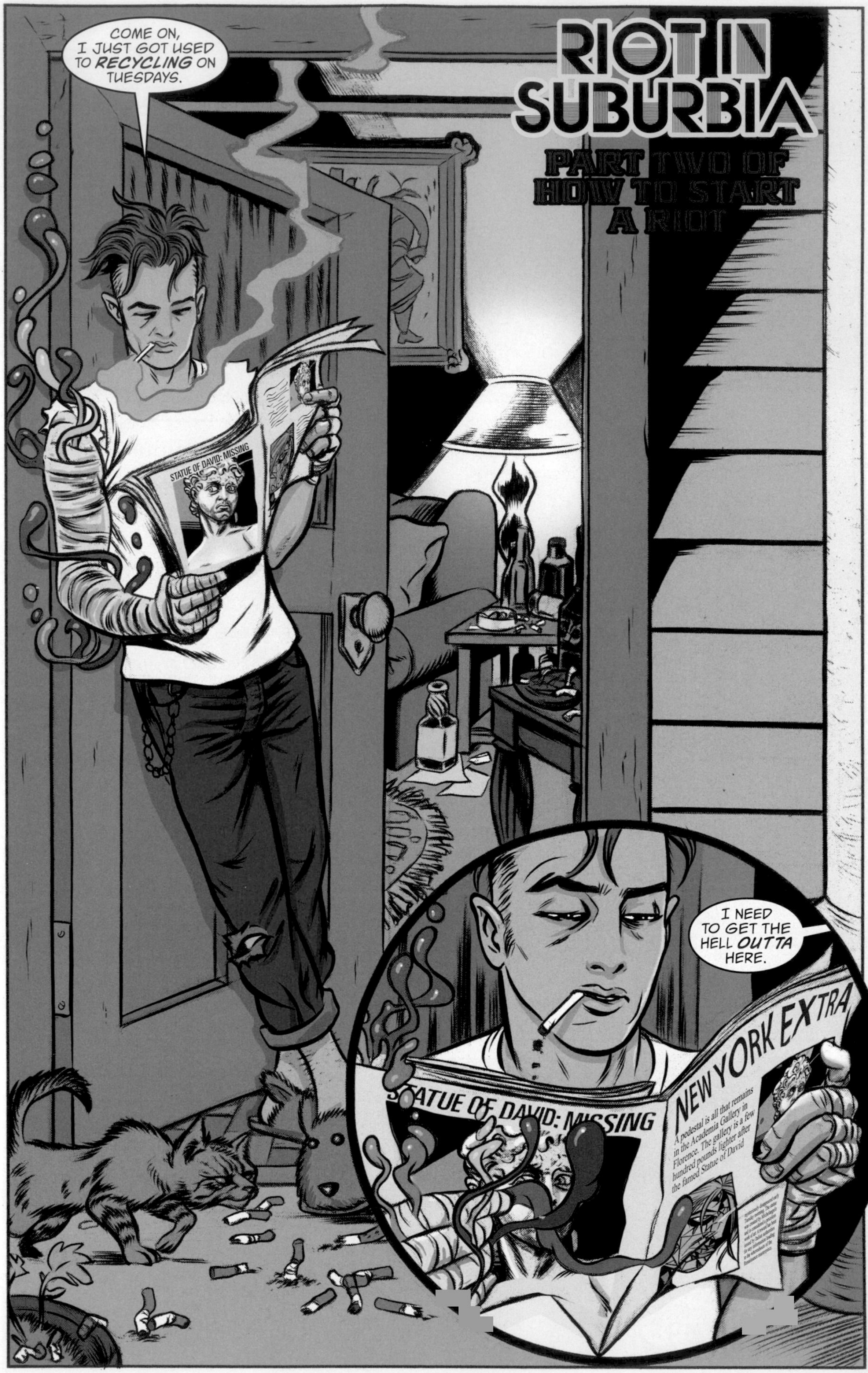
COME ON, I JUST GOT USED TO RECYCLING ON TUESDAYS.
RIOT IN SUBURBIA
PART TWO OF HOW TO START A RIOT
STATUE OF DAVID: MISSING
I NEED TO GET THE HELL OUTTA HERE.
NEW YORK EXTRA
STATUE OF DAVID: MISSING
A pedestal is all that remains in the Academia Gallery in Florence. The gallery is a few hundred pounds lighter after the famed Statue of David

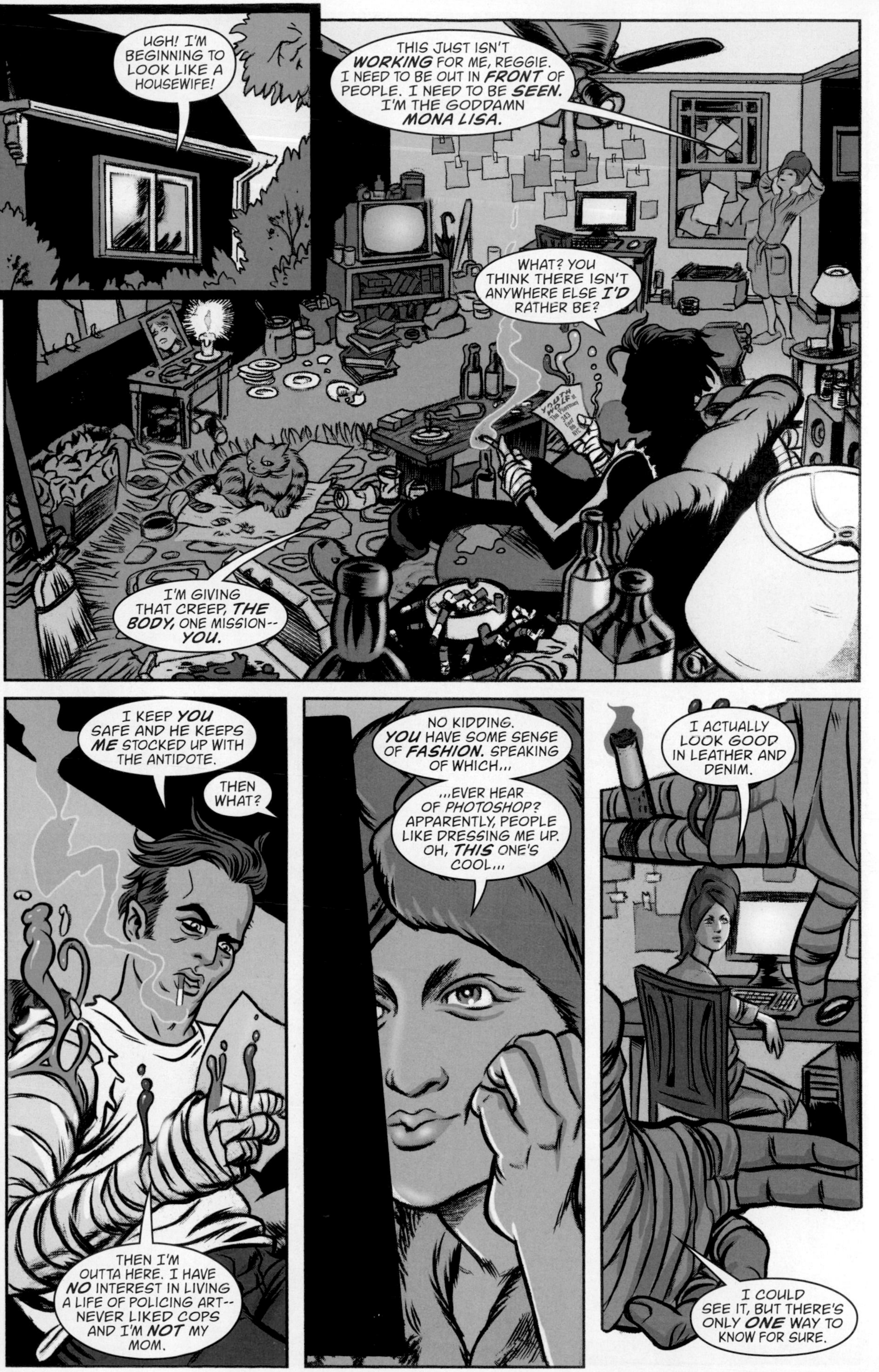
UGH! I'M BEGINNING TO LOOK LIKE A HOUSEWIFE!
THIS JUST ISN'T WORKING FOR ME, REGGIE. I NEED TO BE OUT IN FRONT OF PEOPLE. I NEED TO BE SEEN. I'M THE GODDAMN MONA LISA.
WHAT? YOU THINK THERE ISN'T ANYWHERE ELSE I'D RATHER BE?
I'M GIVING THAT CREEP, THE BODY, ONE MISSION-- YOU.
I KEEP YOU SAFE AND HE KEEPS ME STOCKED UP WITH THE ANTIDOTE.
THEN WHAT?
THEN I'M OUTTA HERE. I HAVE NO INTEREST IN LIVING A LIFE OF POLICING ART-- NEVER LIKED COPS AND I'M NOT MY MOM.
NO KIDDING. YOU HAVE SOME SENSE OF FASHION. SPEAKING OF WHICH...
...EVER HEAR OF PHOTOSHOP? APPARENTLY, PEOPLE LIKE DRESSING ME UP. OH, THIS ONE'S COOL...
I ACTUALLY LOOK GOOD IN LEATHER AND DENIM.
I COULD SEE IT, BUT THERE'S ONLY ONE WAY TO KNOW FOR SURE.

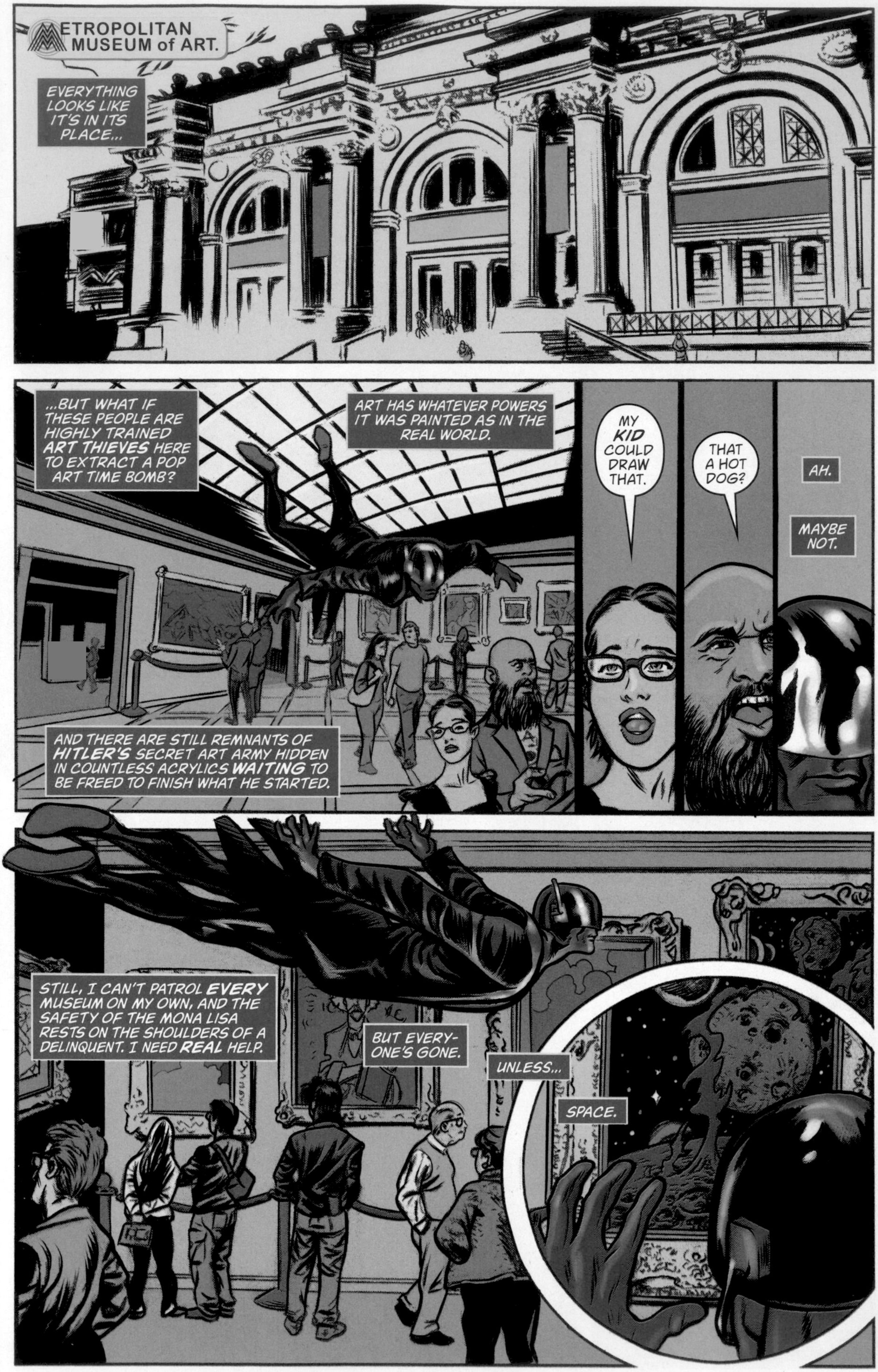
METROPOLITAN MUSEUM of ART.
EVERYTHING LOOKS LIKE IT'S IN ITS PLACE...
...BUT WHAT IF THESE PEOPLE ARE HIGHLY TRAINED ART THIEVES HERE TO EXTRACT A POP ART TIME BOMB?
ART HAS WHATEVER POWERS IT WAS PAINTED AS IN THE REAL WORLD.
AND THERE ARE STILL REMNANTS OF HITLER'S SECRET ART ARMY HIDDEN IN COUNTLESS ACRYLICS WAITING TO BE FREED TO FINISH WHAT HE STARTED.
MY KID COULD DRAW THAT.
THAT A HOT DOG?
AH.
MAYBE NOT.
STILL, I CAN'T PATROL EVERY MUSEUM ON MY OWN, AND THE SAFETY OF THE MONA LISA RESTS ON THE SHOULDERS OF A DELINQUENT. I NEED REAL HELP.
BUT EVERY-ONE'S GONE.
UNLESS...
SPACE.

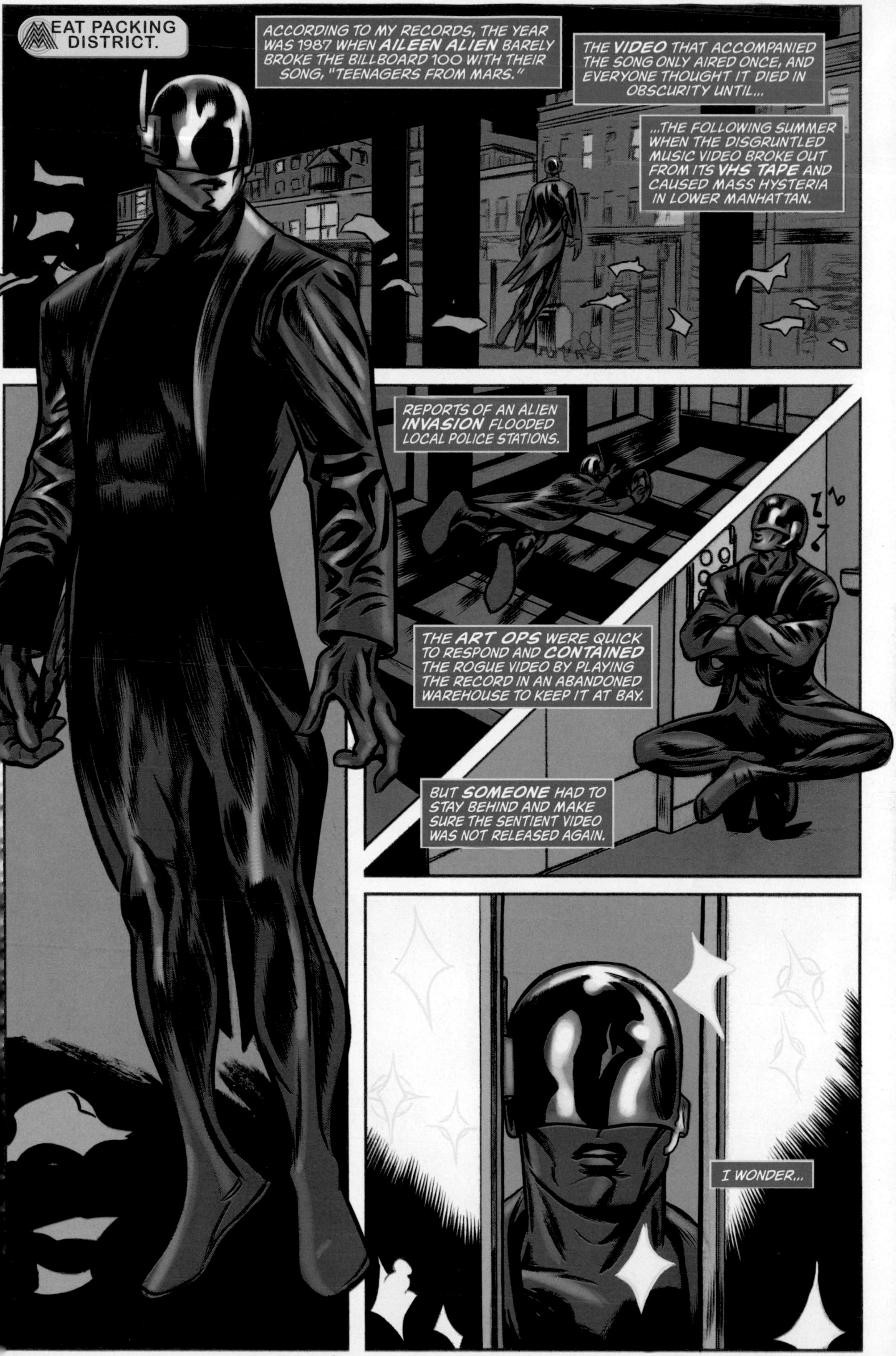
MEAT PACKING DISTRICT.
ACCORDING TO MY RECORDS, THE YEAR WAS 1987 WHEN AILEEN ALIEN BARELY BROKE THE BILLBOARD 100 WITH THEIR SONG, "TEENAGERS FROM MARS."
THE VIDEO THAT ACCOMPANIED THE SONG ONLY AIRED ONCE, AND EVERYONE THOUGHT IT DIED IN OBSCURITY UNTIL...
...THE FOLLOWING SUMMER WHEN THE DISGRUNTLED MUSIC VIDEO BROKE OUT FROM ITS VHS TAPE AND CAUSED MASS HYSTERIA IN LOWER MANHATTAN.
REPORTS OF AN ALIEN INVASION FLOODED LOCAL POLICE STATIONS.
THE ART OPS WERE QUICK TO RESPOND AND CONTAINED THE ROGUE VIDEO BY PLAYING THE RECORD IN AN ABANDONED WAREHOUSE TO KEEP IT AT BAY.
BUT SOMEONE HAD TO STAY BEHIND AND MAKE SURE THE SENTIENT VIDEO WAS NOT RELEASED AGAIN.
I WONDER...

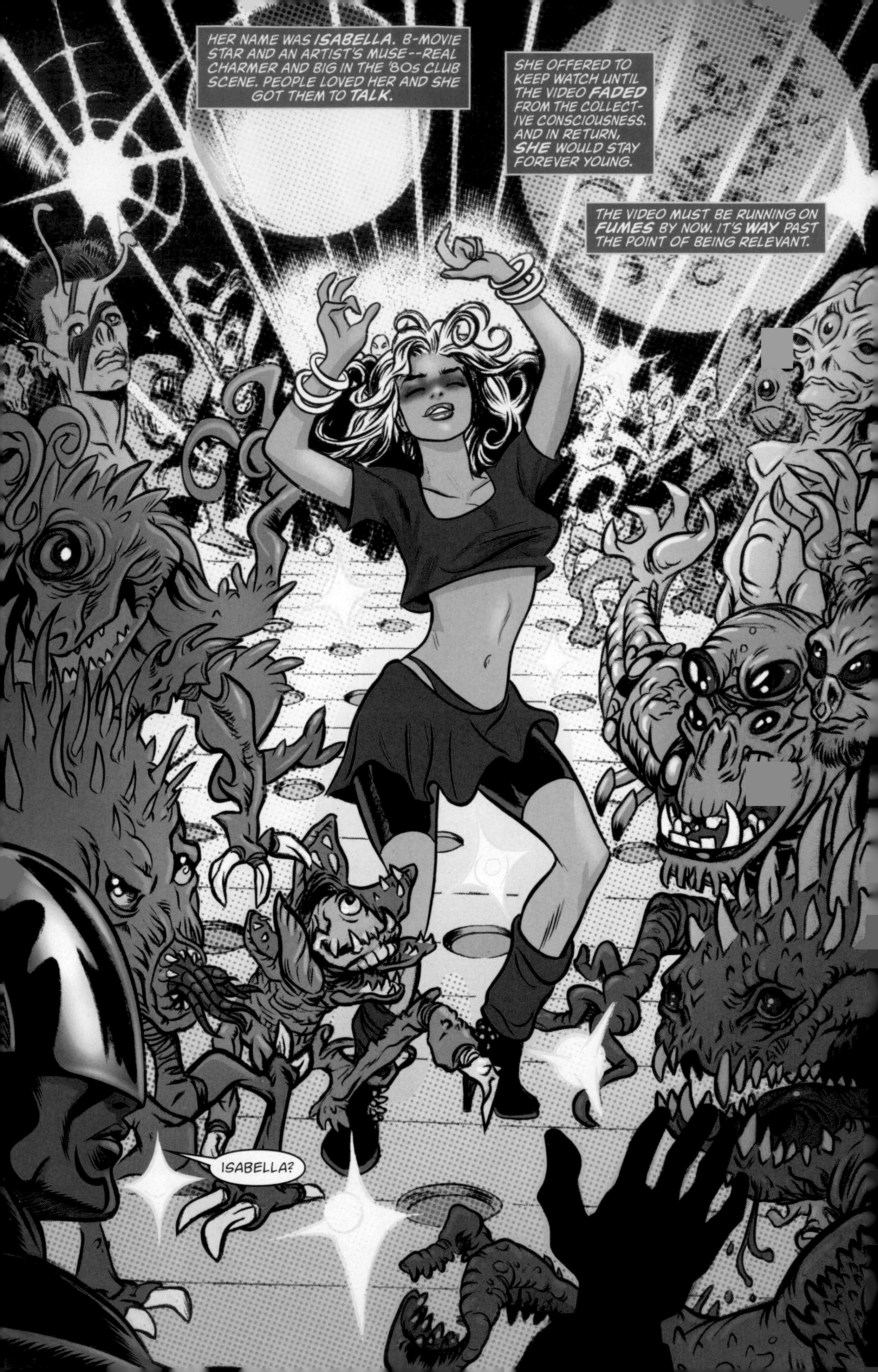
HER NAME WAS ISABELLA. B-MOVIE STAR AND AN ARTIST'S MUSE--REAL CHARMER AND BIG IN THE '80s CLUB SCENE. PEOPLE LOVED HER AND SHE GOT THEM TO TALK.
SHE OFFERED TO KEEP WATCH UNTIL THE VIDEO FADED FROM THE COLLECTIVE CONSCIOUSNESS. AND IN RETURN, SHE WOULD STAY FOREVER YOUNG.
THE VIDEO MUST BE RUNNING ON FUMES BY NOW. IT'S WAY PAST THE POINT OF BEING RELEVANT.
ISABELLA?

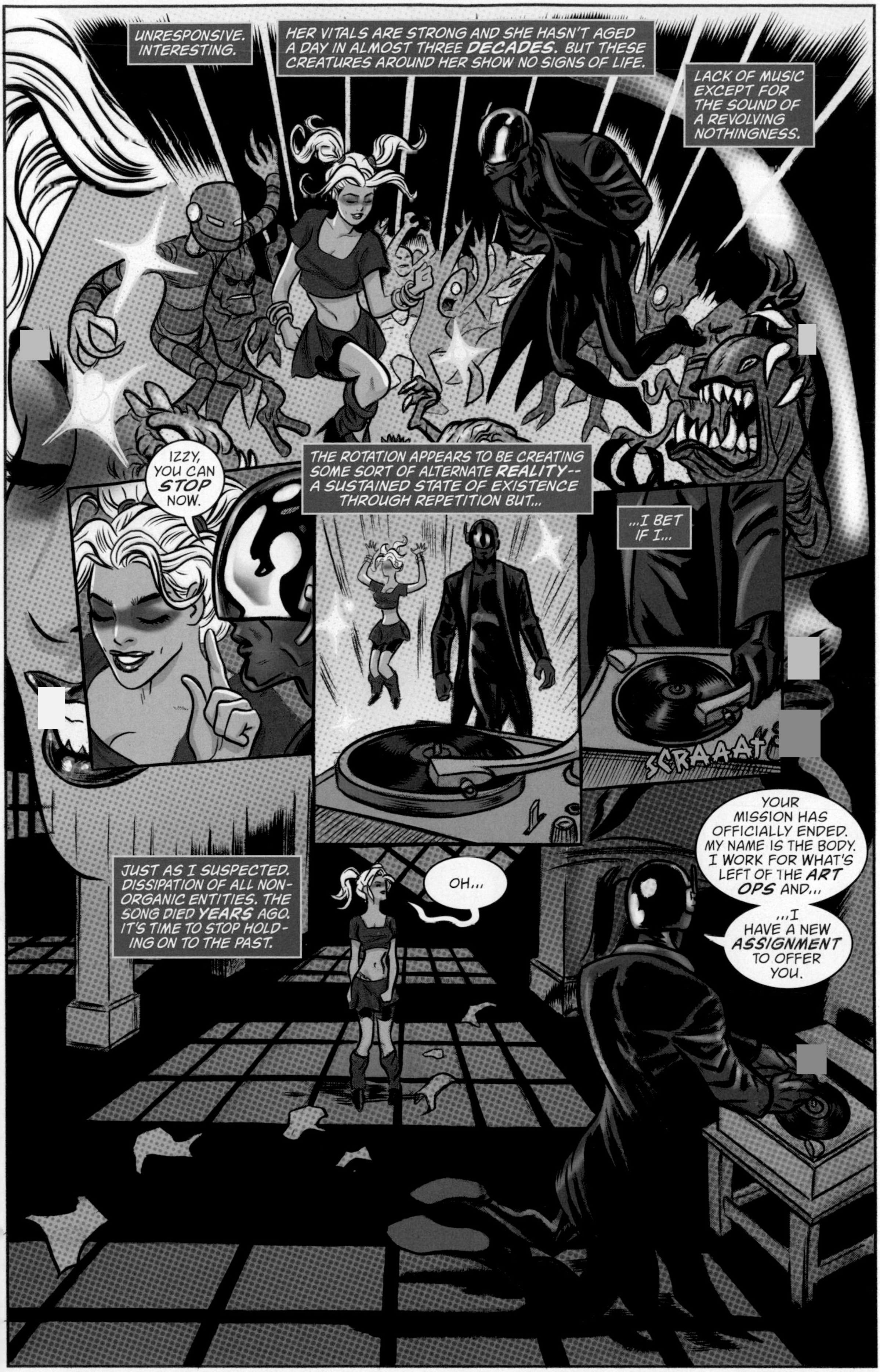
UNRESPONSIVE. INTERESTING.
HER VITALS ARE STRONG AND SHE HASN'T AGED A DAY IN ALMOST THREE DECADES. BUT THESE CREATURES AROUND HER SHOW NO SIGNS OF LIFE.
LACK OF MUSIC EXCEPT FOR THE SOUND OF A REVOLVING NOTHINGNESS.
IZZY, YOU CAN STOP NOW.
THE ROTATION APPEARS TO BE CREATING SOME SORT OF ALTERNATE REALITY-- A SUSTAINED STATE OF EXISTENCE THROUGH REPETITION BUT...
...I BET IF I...
SCRAAAT
JUST AS I SUSPECTED. DISSIPATION OF ALL NON-ORGANIC ENTITIES. THE SONG DIED YEARS AGO. IT'S TIME TO STOP HOLDING ON TO THE PAST.
OH...
YOUR MISSION HAS OFFICIALLY ENDED. MY NAME IS THE BODY. I WORK FOR WHAT'S LEFT OF THE ART OPS AND...
...I HAVE A NEW ASSIGNMENT TO OFFER YOU.

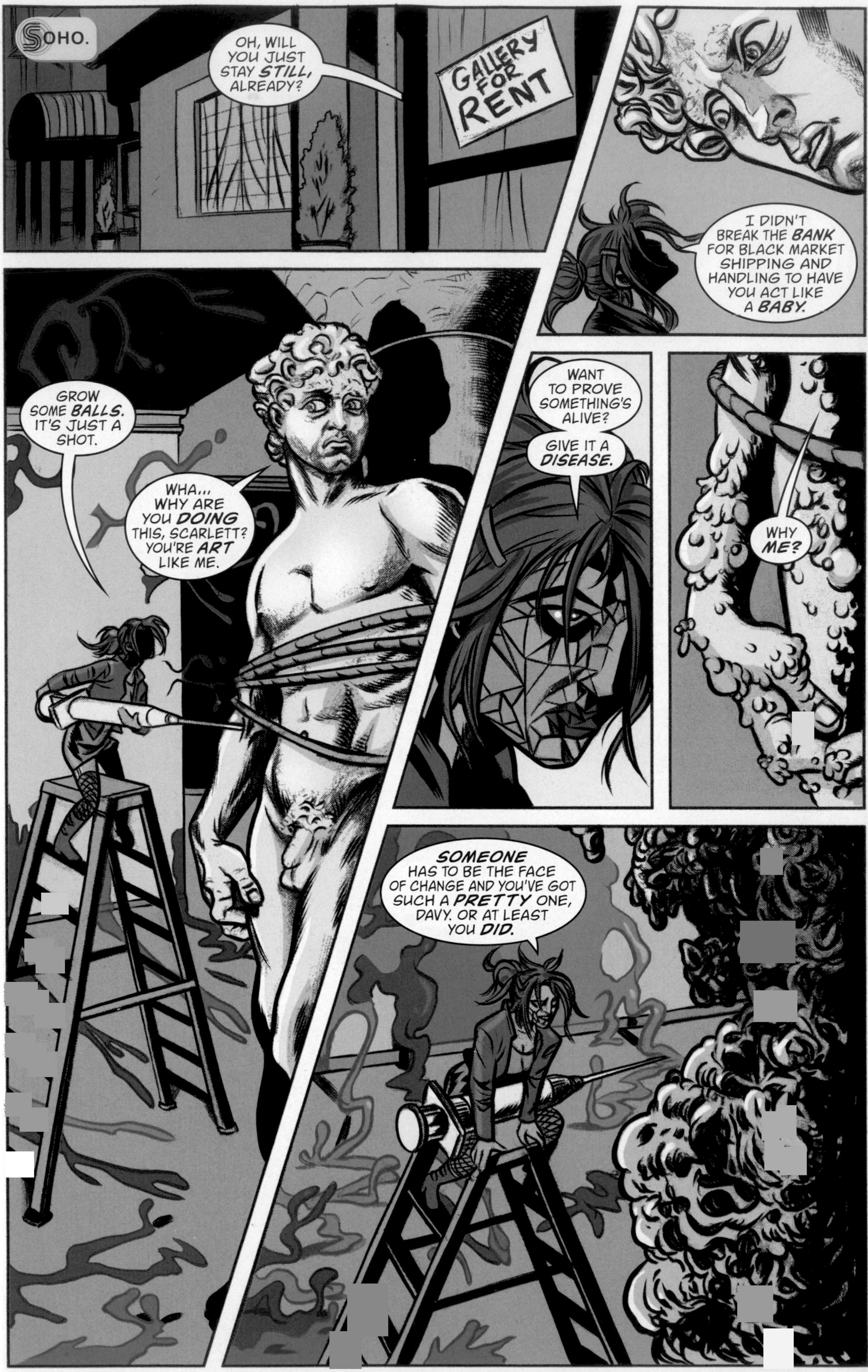
SOHO.
OH, WILL YOU JUST STAY STILL, ALREADY?
GALLERY FOR RENT
I DIDN'T BREAK THE BANK FOR BLACK MARKET SHIPPING AND HANDLING TO HAVE YOU ACT LIKE A BABY.
GROW SOME BALLS. IT'S JUST A SHOT.
WHA... WHY ARE YOU DOING THIS, SCARLETT? YOU'RE ART LIKE ME.
WANT TO PROVE SOMETHING'S ALIVE?
GIVE IT A DISEASE.
WHY ME?
SOMEONE HAS TO BE THE FACE OF CHANGE AND YOU'VE GOT SUCH A PRETTY ONE, DAVY. OR AT LEAST YOU DID.

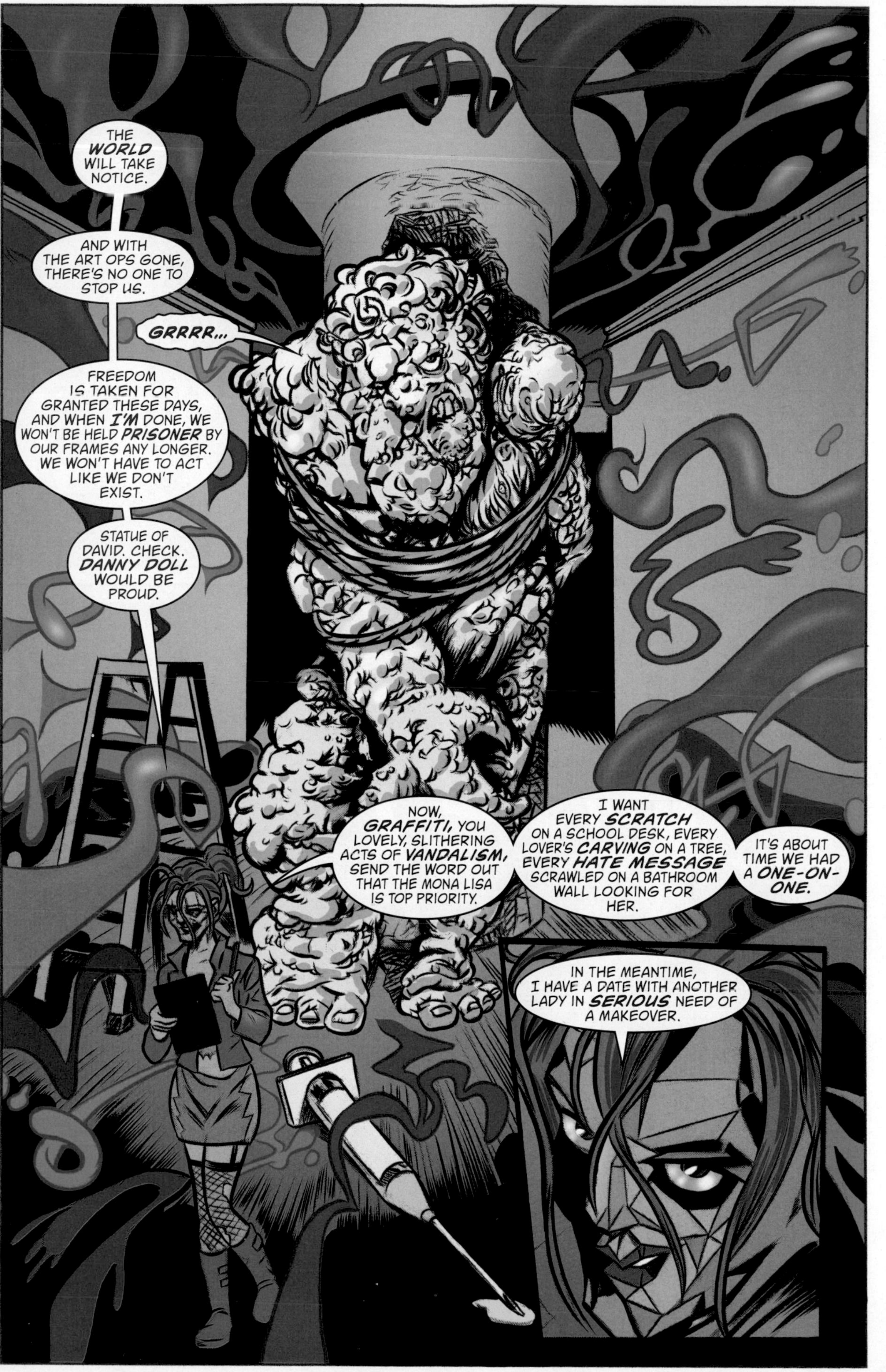
THE WORLD WILL TAKE NOTICE.
AND WITH THE ART OPS GONE, THERE'S NO ONE TO STOP US.
GRRRR...
FREEDOM IS TAKEN FOR GRANTED THESE DAYS, AND WHEN I'M DONE, WE WON'T BE HELD PRISONER BY OUR FRAMES ANY LONGER. WE WON'T HAVE TO ACT LIKE WE DON'T EXIST.
STATUE OF DAVID. CHECK. DANNY DOLL WOULD BE PROUD.
NOW, GRAFFITI, YOU LOVELY, SLITHERING ACTS OF VANDALISM, SEND THE WORD OUT THAT THE MONA LISA IS TOP PRIORITY.
I WANT EVERY SCRATCH ON A SCHOOL DESK, EVERY LOVER'S CARVING ON A TREE, EVERY HATE MESSAGE SCRAWLED ON A BATHROOM WALL LOOKING FOR HER.
IT'S ABOUT TIME WE HAD A ONE-ON-ONE.
IN THE MEANTIME, I HAVE A DATE WITH ANOTHER LADY IN SERIOUS NEED OF A MAKEOVER.

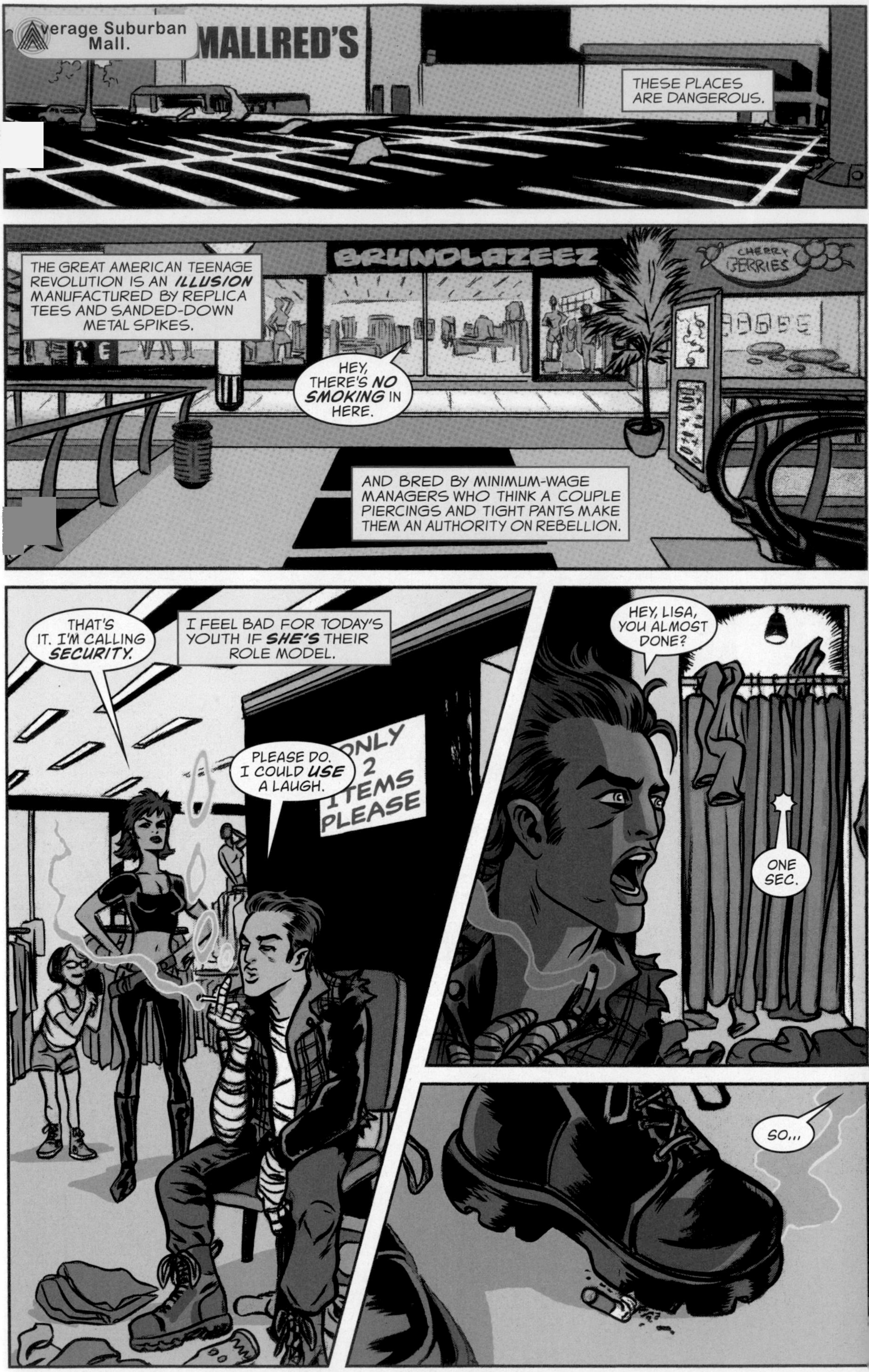
Average Suburban Mall.
MALLRED'S
THESE PLACES ARE DANGEROUS.
BRUNDLAZEEZ
CHERRY BERRIES
THE GREAT AMERICAN TEENAGE REVOLUTION IS AN ILLUSION MANUFACTURED BY REPLICA TEES AND SANDED-DOWN METAL SPIKES.
HEY, THERE'S NO SMOKING IN HERE.
AND BRED BY MINIMUM-WAGE MANAGERS WHO THINK A COUPLE PIERCINGS AND TIGHT PANTS MAKE THEM AN AUTHORITY ON REBELLION.
THAT'S IT. I'M CALLING SECURITY.
I FEEL BAD FOR TODAY'S YOUTH IF SHE'S THEIR ROLE MODEL.
PLEASE DO. I COULD USE A LAUGH.
ONLY 2 ITEMS PLEASE
HEY, LISA, YOU ALMOST DONE?
ONE SEC.
SO...

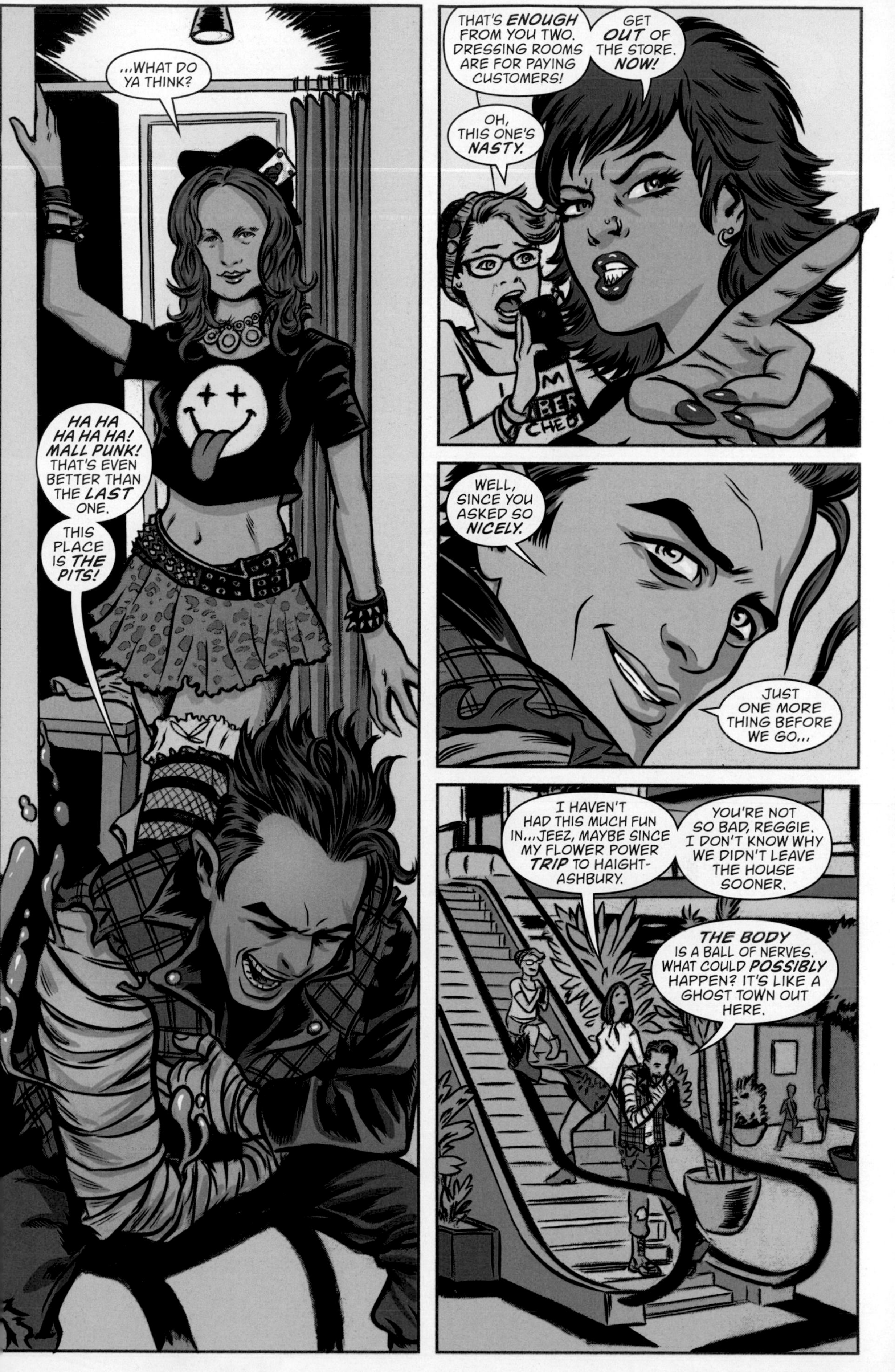
...WHAT DO YA THINK?
HA HA HA HA HA! MALL PUNK! THAT'S EVEN BETTER THAN THE LAST ONE.
THIS PLACE IS THE PITS!
THAT'S ENOUGH FROM YOU TWO. DRESSING ROOMS ARE FOR PAYING CUSTOMERS!
GET OUT OF THE STORE. NOW!
OH, THIS ONE'S NASTY.
WELL, SINCE YOU ASKED SO NICELY.
JUST ONE MORE THING BEFORE WE GO...
I HAVEN'T HAD THIS MUCH FUN IN...JEEZ, MAYBE SINCE MY FLOWER POWER TRIP TO HAIGHT-ASHBURY.
YOU'RE NOT SO BAD, REGGIE. I DON'T KNOW WHY WE DIDN'T LEAVE THE HOUSE SOONER.
THE BODY IS A BALL OF NERVES. WHAT COULD POSSIBLY HAPPEN? IT'S LIKE A GHOST TOWN OUT HERE.

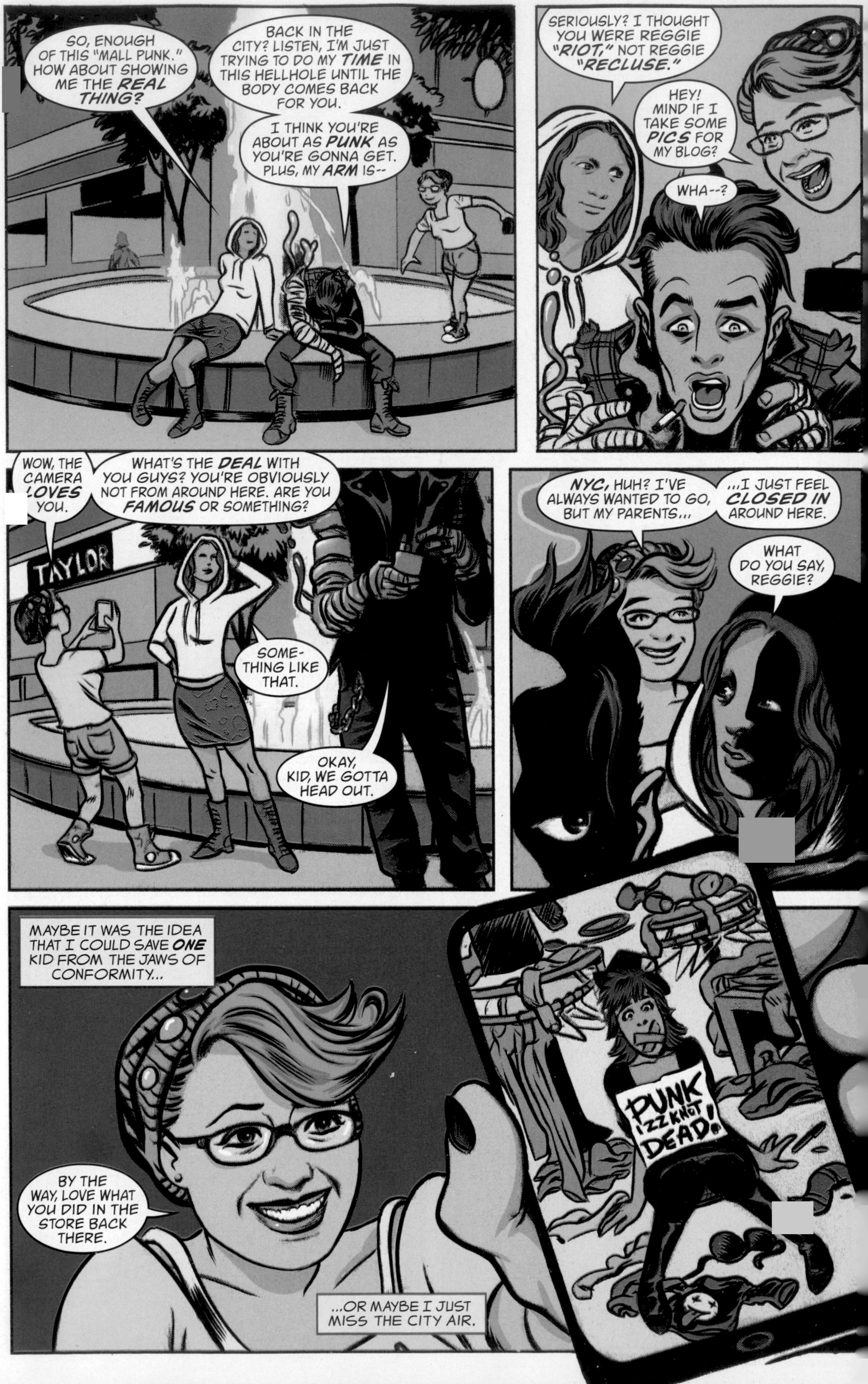
SO, ENOUGH OF THIS "MALL PUNK." HOW ABOUT SHOWING ME THE REAL THING?
BACK IN THE CITY? LISTEN, I'M JUST TRYING TO DO MY TIME IN THIS HELLHOLE UNTIL THE BODY COMES BACK FOR YOU.
I THINK YOU'RE ABOUT AS PUNK AS YOU'RE GONNA GET. PLUS, MY ARM IS--
SERIOUSLY? I THOUGHT YOU WERE REGGIE "RIOT," NOT REGGIE "RECLUSE."
HEY! MIND IF I TAKE SOME PICS FOR MY BLOG?
WHA--?
WOW, THE CAMERA LOVES YOU.
WHAT'S THE DEAL WITH YOU GUYS? YOU'RE OBVIOUSLY NOT FROM AROUND HERE. ARE YOU FAMOUS OR SOMETHING?
TAYLOR
SOMETHING LIKE THAT.
OKAY, KID, WE GOTTA HEAD OUT.
NYC, HUH? I'VE ALWAYS WANTED TO GO, BUT MY PARENTS...
...I JUST FEEL CLOSED IN AROUND HERE.
WHAT DO YOU SAY, REGGIE?
MAYBE IT WAS THE IDEA THAT I COULD SAVE ONE KID FROM THE JAWS OF CONFORMITY...
BY THE WAY, LOVE WHAT YOU DID IN THE STORE BACK THERE.
PUNK IZZ KNOT DEAD!
...OR MAYBE I JUST MISS THE CITY AIR.

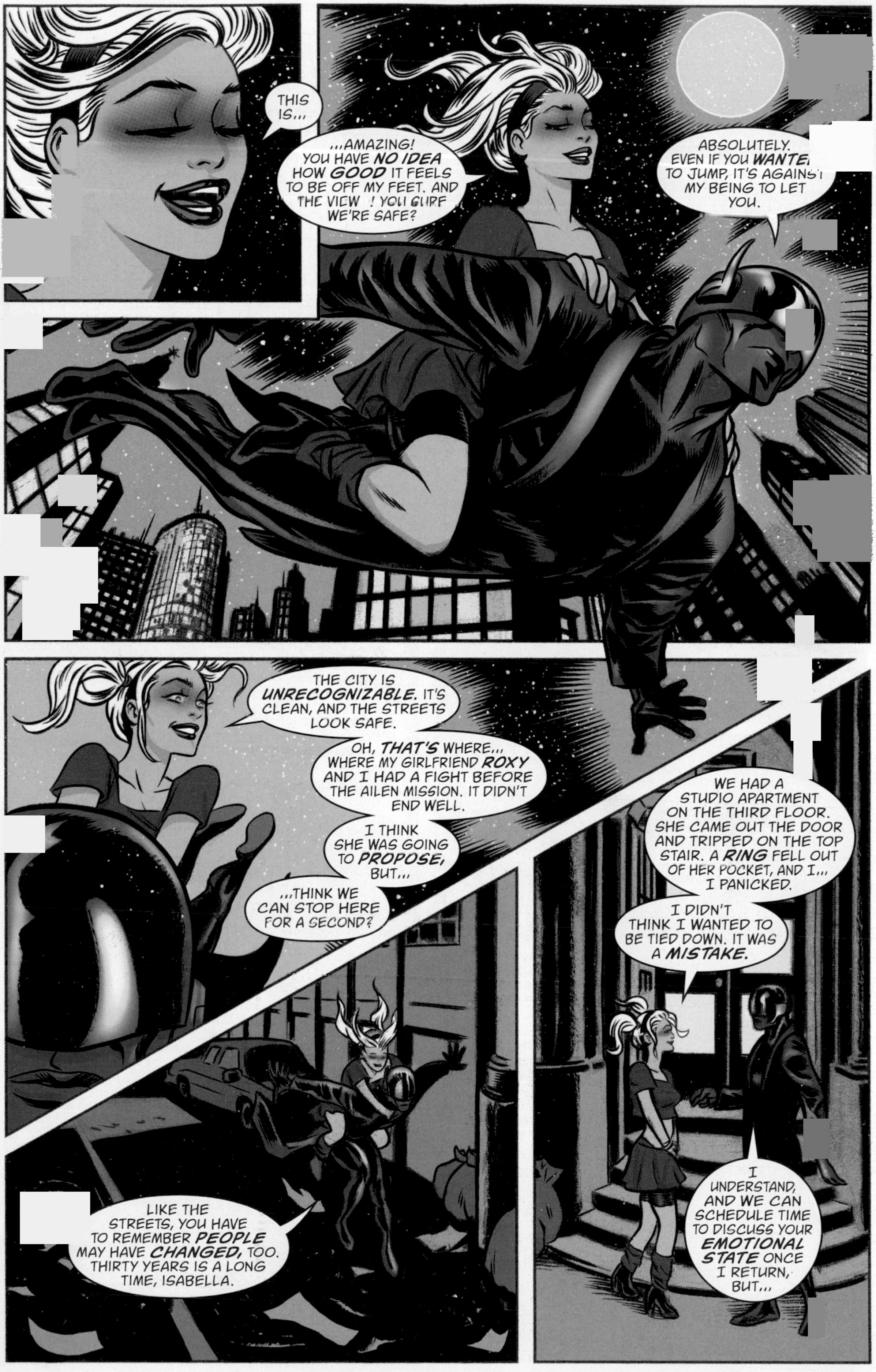
THIS IS...
...AMAZING! YOU HAVE NO IDEA HOW GOOD IT FEELS TO BE OFF MY FEET. AND THE VIEW ! YOU SURE WE'RE SAFE?
ABSOLUTELY. EVEN IF YOU WANTE TO JUMP, IT'S AGAINS MY BEING TO LET YOU.
THE CITY IS UNRECOGNIZABLE. IT'S CLEAN, AND THE STREETS LOOK SAFE.
OH, THAT'S WHERE... WHERE MY GIRLFRIEND ROXY AND I HAD A FIGHT BEFORE THE AILEN MISSION. IT DIDN'T END WELL.
I THINK SHE WAS GOING TO PROPOSE, BUT...
...THINK WE CAN STOP HERE FOR A SECOND?
LIKE THE STREETS, YOU HAVE TO REMEMBER PEOPLE MAY HAVE CHANGED, TOO. THIRTY YEARS IS A LONG TIME, ISABELLA.
WE HAD A STUDIO APARTMENT ON THE THIRD FLOOR. SHE CAME OUT THE DOOR AND TRIPPED ON THE TOP STAIR. A RING FELL OUT OF HER POCKET, AND I... I PANICKED.
I DIDN'T THINK I WANTED TO BE TIED DOWN. IT WAS A MISTAKE.
I UNDERSTAND, AND WE CAN SCHEDULE TIME TO DISCUSS YOUR EMOTIONAL STATE ONCE I RETURN, BUT...

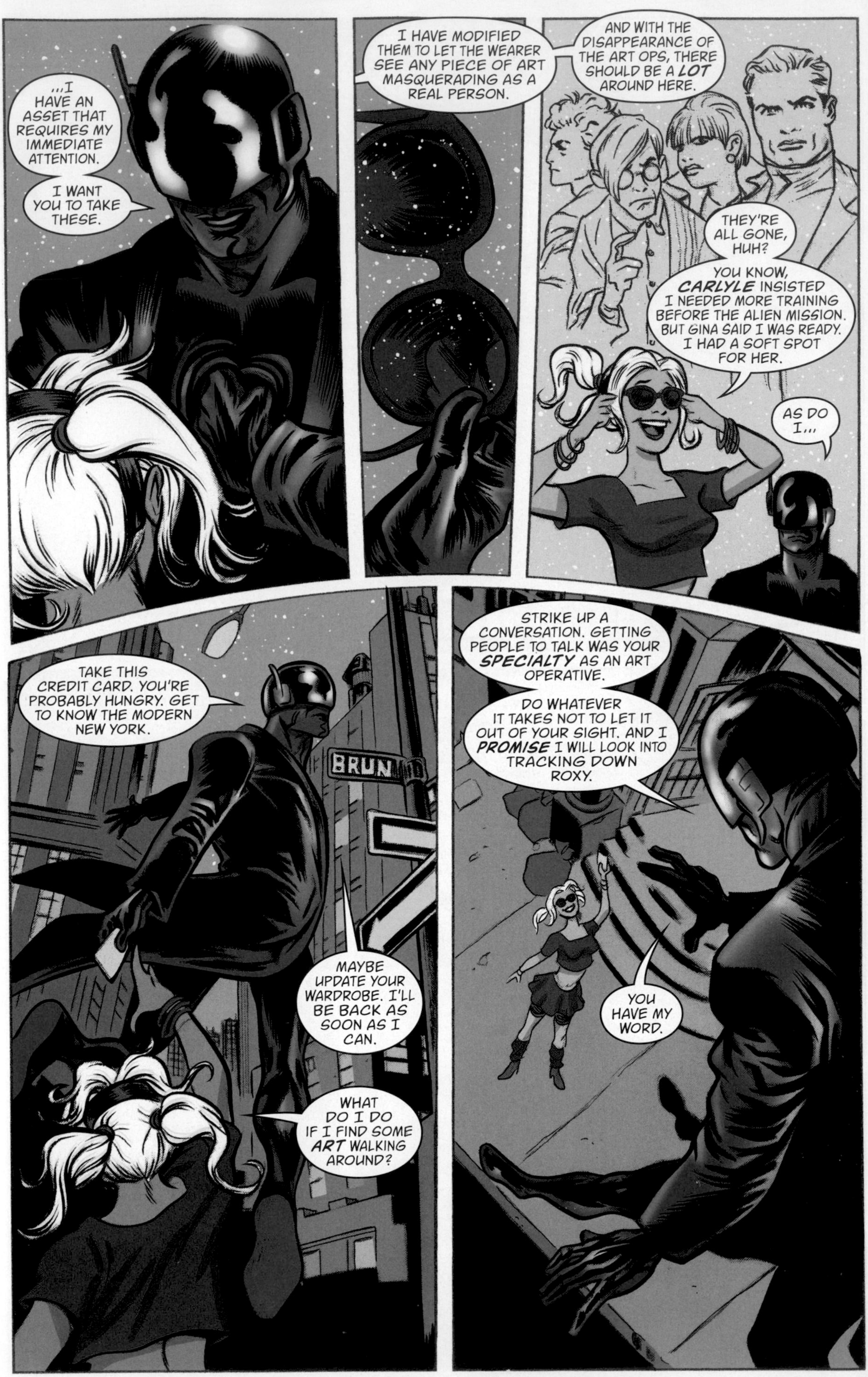
...I HAVE AN ASSET THAT REQUIRES MY IMMEDIATE ATTENTION.
I WANT YOU TO TAKE THESE.
I HAVE MODIFIED THEM TO LET THE WEARER SEE ANY PIECE OF ART MASQUERADING AS A REAL PERSON.
AND WITH THE DISAPPEARANCE OF THE ART OPS, THERE SHOULD BE A LOT AROUND HERE.
THEY'RE ALL GONE, HUH?
YOU KNOW, CARLYLE INSISTED I NEEDED MORE TRAINING BEFORE THE ALIEN MISSION. BUT GINA SAID I WAS READY. I HAD A SOFT SPOT FOR HER.
AS DO I...
TAKE THIS CREDIT CARD. YOU'RE PROBABLY HUNGRY. GET TO KNOW THE MODERN NEW YORK.
BRUN
MAYBE UPDATE YOUR WARDROBE. I'LL BE BACK AS SOON AS I CAN.
WHAT DO I DO IF I FIND SOME ART WALKING AROUND?
STRIKE UP A CONVERSATION. GETTING PEOPLE TO TALK WAS YOUR SPECIALTY AS AN ART OPERATIVE.
DO WHATEVER IT TAKES NOT TO LET IT OUT OF YOUR SIGHT. AND I PROMISE I WILL LOOK INTO TRACKING DOWN ROXY.
YOU HAVE MY WORD.

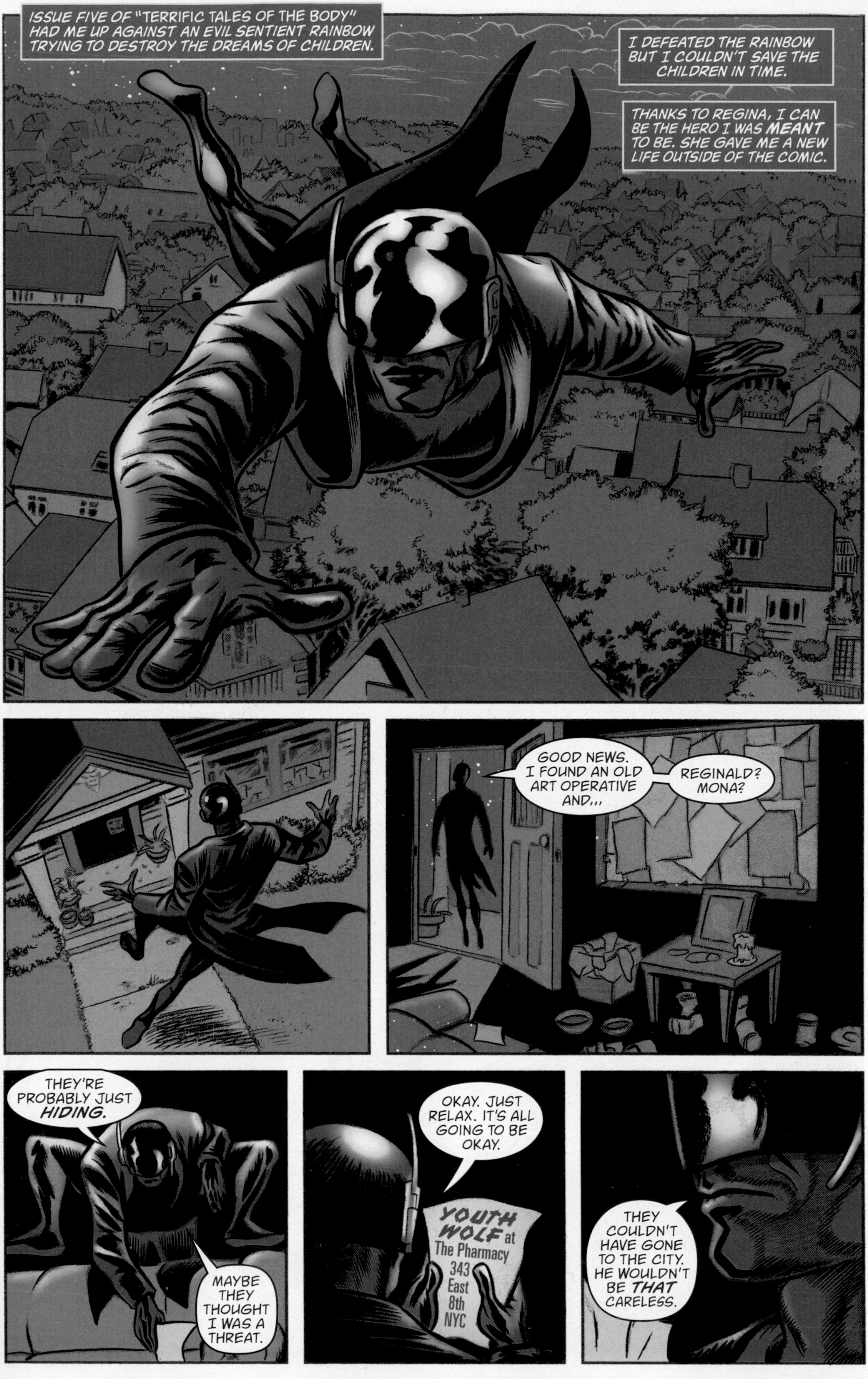
ISSUE FIVE OF "TERRIFIC TALES OF THE BODY" HAD ME UP AGAINST AN EVIL SENTIENT RAINBOW TRYING TO DESTROY THE DREAMS OF CHILDREN.
I DEFEATED THE RAINBOW BUT I COULDN'T SAVE THE CHILDREN IN TIME.
THANKS TO REGINA, I CAN BE THE HERO I WAS MEANT TO BE. SHE GAVE ME A NEW LIFE OUTSIDE OF THE COMIC.
GOOD NEWS. I FOUND AN OLD ART OPERATIVE AND...
REGINALD? MONA?
THEY'RE PROBABLY JUST HIDING.
MAYBE THEY THOUGHT I WAS A THREAT.
OKAY. JUST RELAX. IT'S ALL GOING TO BE OKAY.
YOUTH WOLF at The Pharmacy 343 East 8th NYC
THEY COULDN'T HAVE GONE TO THE CITY. HE WOULDN'T BE THAT CARELESS.

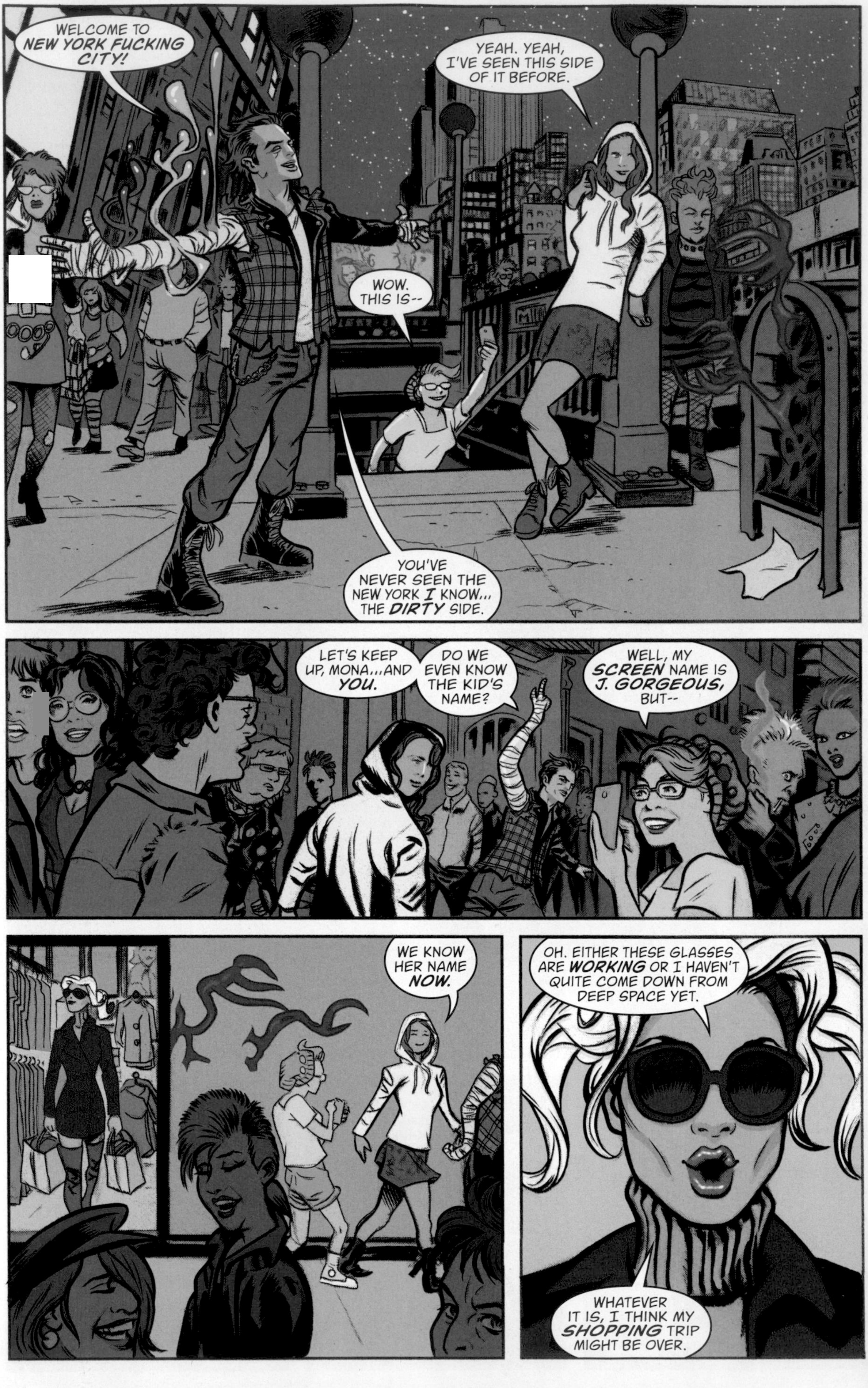
WELCOME TO NEW YORK FUCKING CITY!
YEAH. YEAH, I'VE SEEN THIS SIDE OF IT BEFORE.
WOW. THIS IS--
YOU'VE NEVER SEEN THE NEW YORK I KNOW... THE DIRTY SIDE.
LET'S KEEP UP, MONA...AND YOU.
DO WE EVEN KNOW THE KID'S NAME?
WELL, MY SCREEN NAME IS J. GORGEOUS, BUT--
WE KNOW HER NAME NOW.
OH. EITHER THESE GLASSES ARE WORKING OR I HAVEN'T QUITE COME DOWN FROM DEEP SPACE YET.
WHATEVER IT IS, I THINK MY SHOPPING TRIP MIGHT BE OVER.

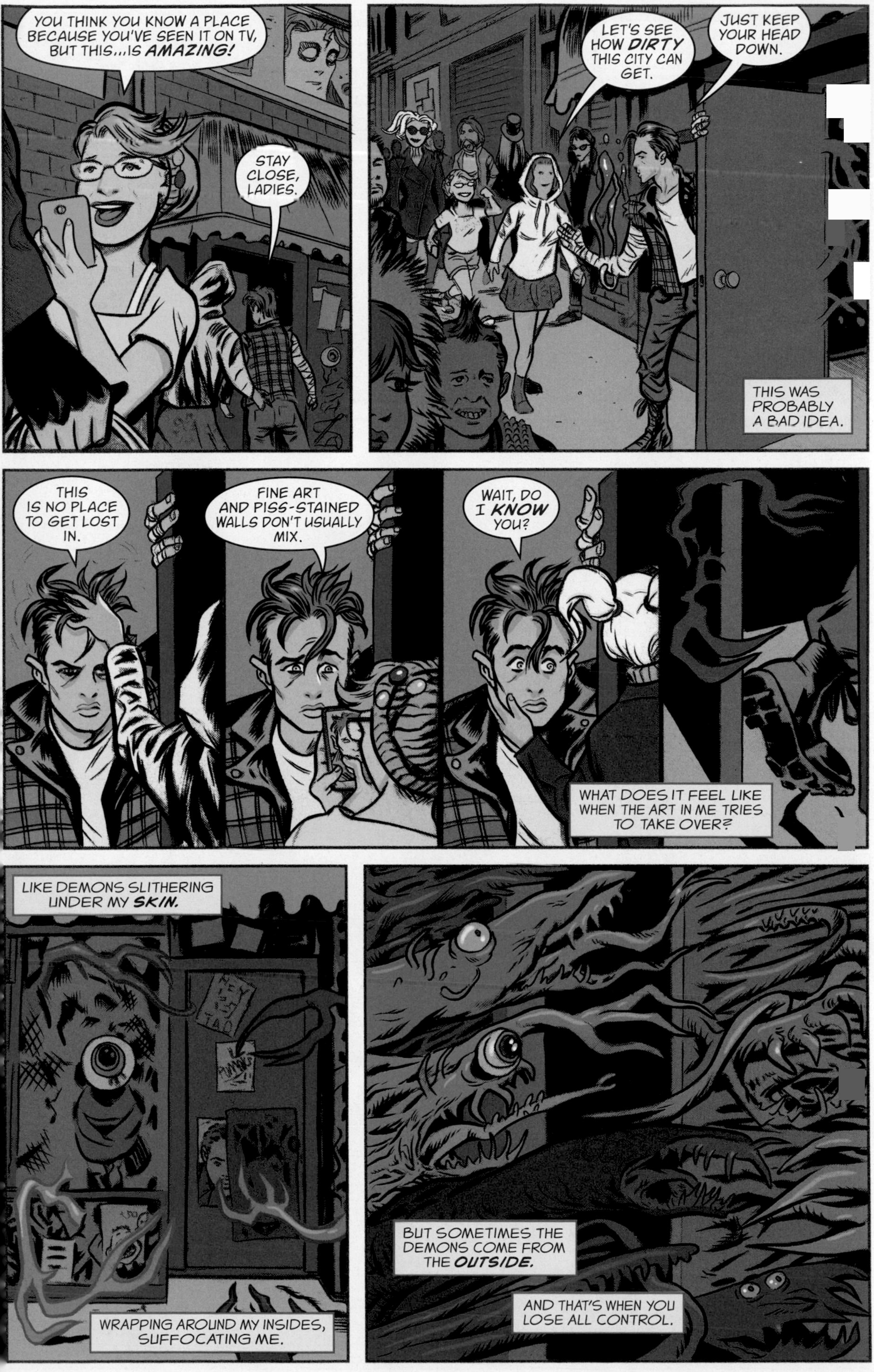
YOU THINK YOU KNOW A PLACE BECAUSE YOU'VE SEEN IT ON TV, BUT THIS...IS *AMAZING!*
STAY CLOSE, LADIES.
LET'S SEE HOW *DIRTY* THIS CITY CAN GET.
JUST KEEP YOUR HEAD DOWN.
THIS WAS PROBABLY A BAD IDEA.
THIS IS NO PLACE TO GET LOST IN.
FINE ART AND PISS-STAINED WALLS DON'T USUALLY MIX.
WAIT, DO I *KNOW* YOU?
WHAT DOES IT FEEL LIKE WHEN THE ART IN ME TRIES TO TAKE OVER?
LIKE DEMONS SLITHERING UNDER MY *SKIN.*
WRAPPING AROUND MY INSIDES, SUFFOCATING ME.
BUT SOMETIMES THE DEMONS COME FROM THE *OUTSIDE.*
AND THAT'S WHEN YOU LOSE ALL CONTROL.

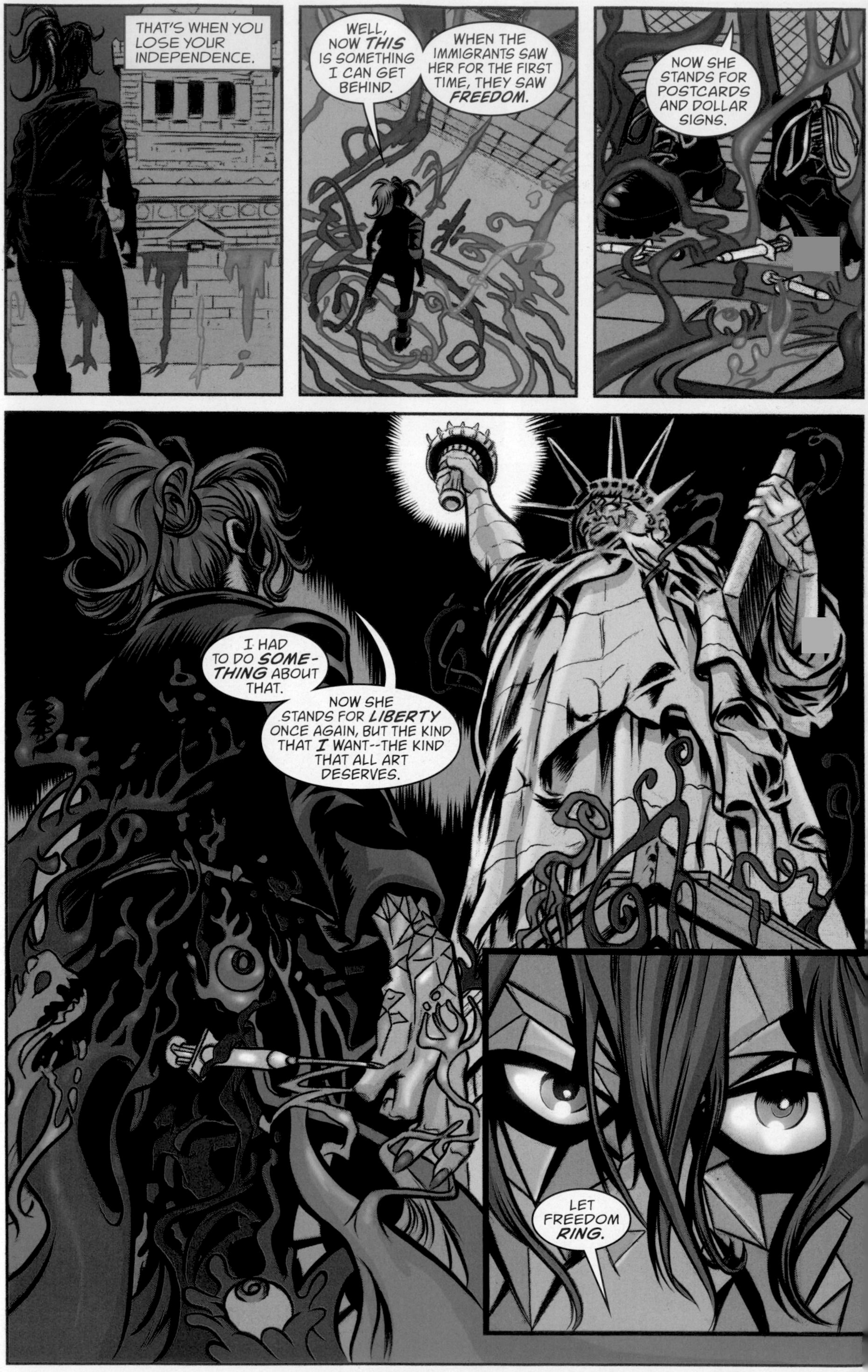
THAT'S WHEN YOU LOSE YOUR INDEPENDENCE.
WELL, NOW THIS IS SOMETHING I CAN GET BEHIND.
WHEN THE IMMIGRANTS SAW HER FOR THE FIRST TIME, THEY SAW FREEDOM.
NOW SHE STANDS FOR POSTCARDS AND DOLLAR SIGNS.
I HAD TO DO SOME-THING ABOUT THAT.
NOW SHE STANDS FOR LIBERTY ONCE AGAIN, BUT THE KIND THAT I WANT--THE KIND THAT ALL ART DESERVES.
LET FREEDOM RING.

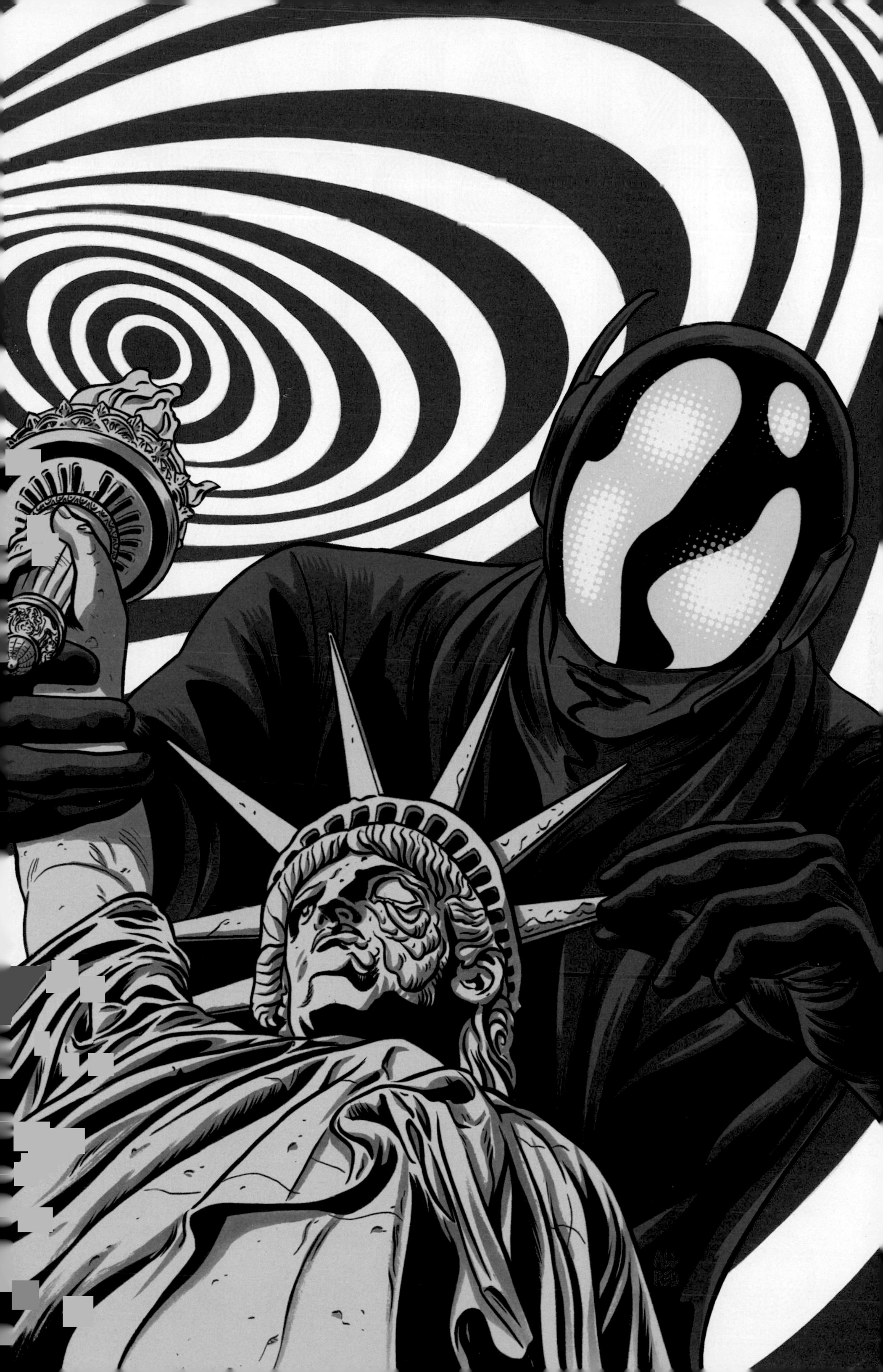

ART ART ART
OPS OPS OPS
ART ART ART
OPS OPS OPS
ART ART ART
OPS OPS OPS
ART ART ART
OPS OPS OPS
ART ART ART
OPS OPS OPS
ART ART ART
OPS OPS OPS

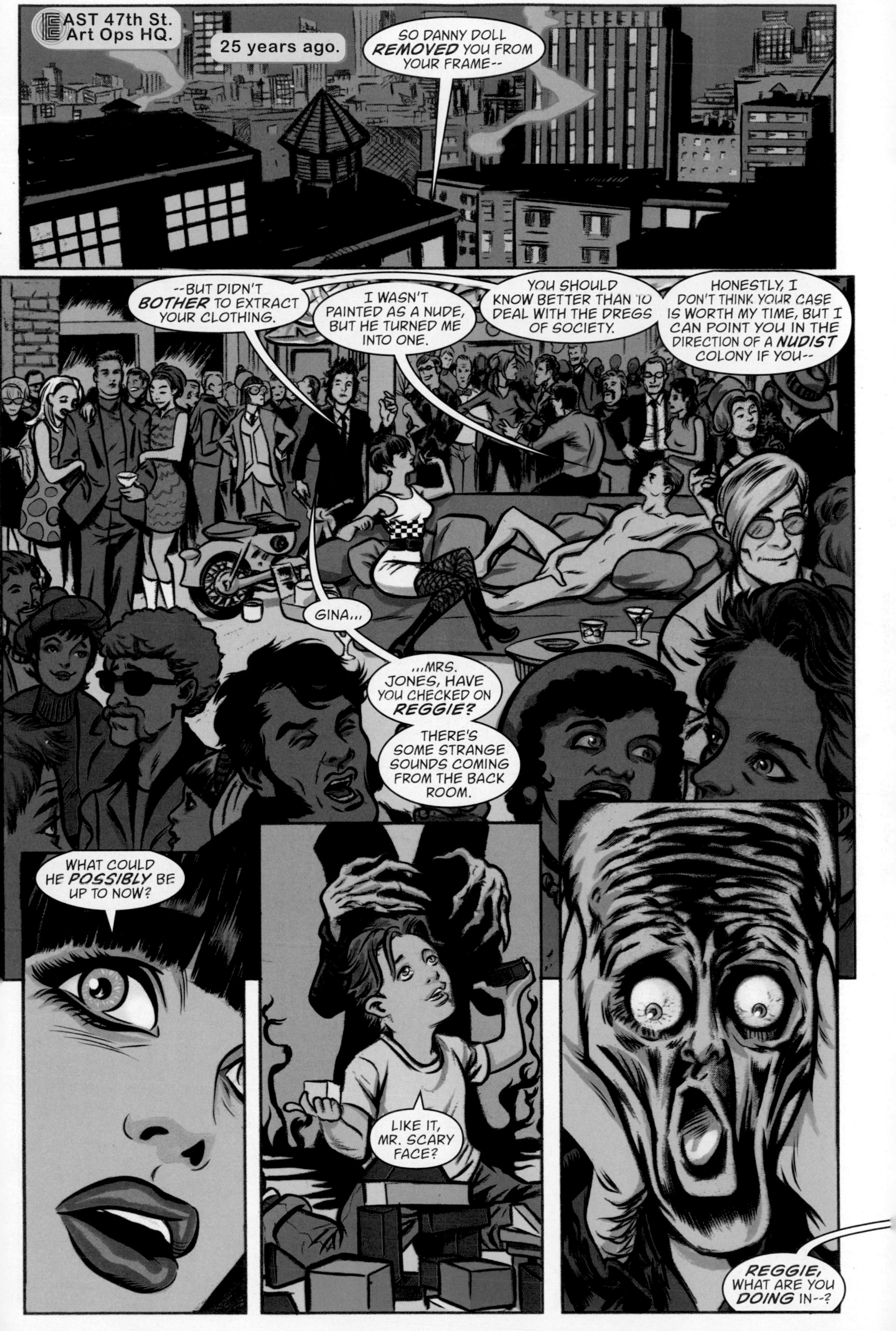
EAST 47th St. Art Ops HQ.
25 years ago.
SO DANNY DOLL REMOVED YOU FROM YOUR FRAME--
--BUT DIDN'T BOTHER TO EXTRACT YOUR CLOTHING.
I WASN'T PAINTED AS A NUDE, BUT HE TURNED ME INTO ONE.
YOU SHOULD KNOW BETTER THAN TO DEAL WITH THE DREGS OF SOCIETY.
HONESTLY, I DON'T THINK YOUR CASE IS WORTH MY TIME, BUT I CAN POINT YOU IN THE DIRECTION OF A NUDIST COLONY IF YOU--
GINA...
...MRS. JONES, HAVE YOU CHECKED ON REGGIE?
THERE'S SOME STRANGE SOUNDS COMING FROM THE BACK ROOM.
WHAT COULD HE POSSIBLY BE UP TO NOW?
LIKE IT, MR. SCARY FACE?
REGGIE, WHAT ARE YOU DOING IN--?

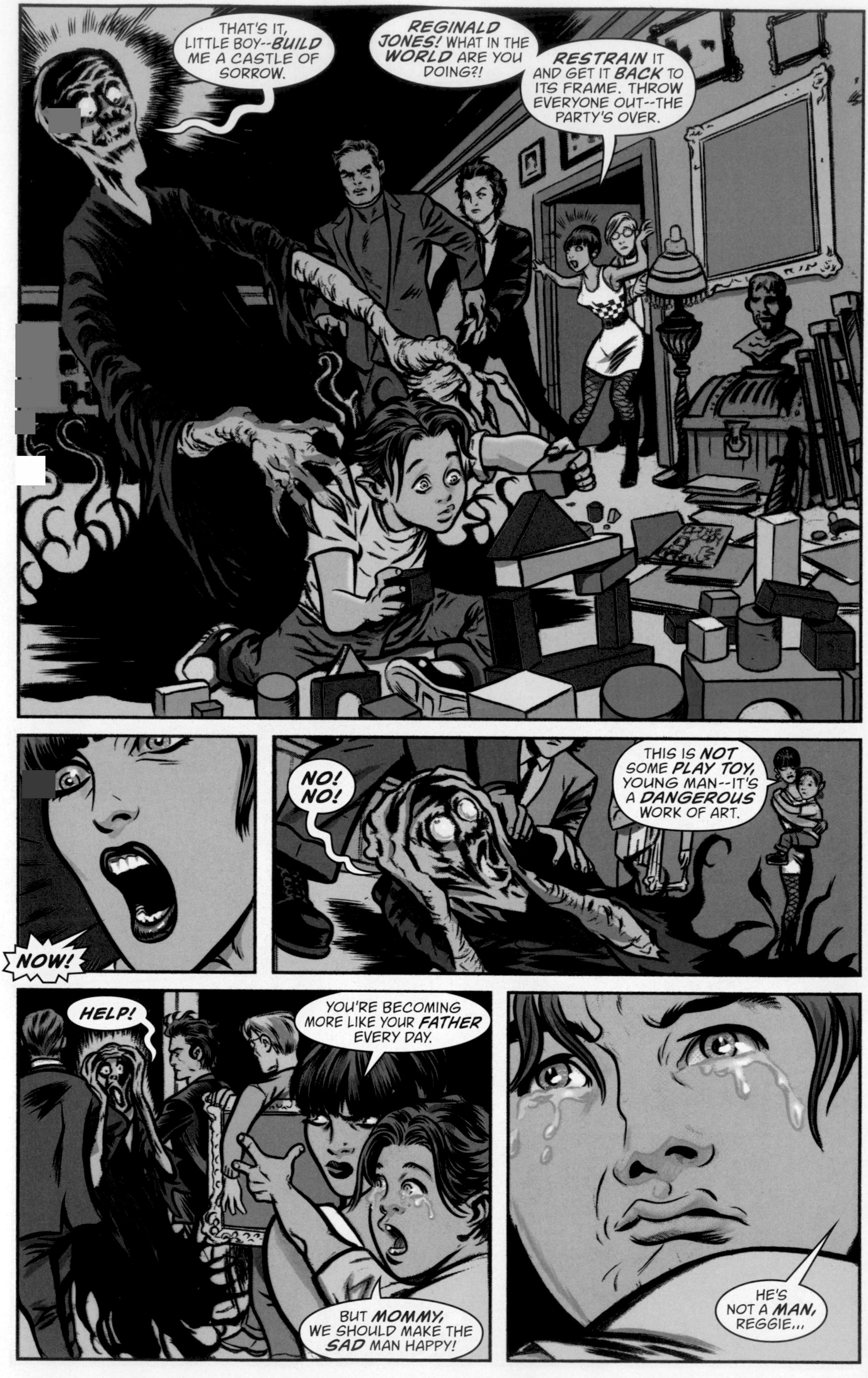
THAT'S IT, LITTLE BOY--BUILD ME A CASTLE OF SORROW.
REGINALD JONES! WHAT IN THE WORLD ARE YOU DOING?!
RESTRAIN IT AND GET IT BACK TO ITS FRAME. THROW EVERYONE OUT--THE PARTY'S OVER.
NOW!
NO! NO!
THIS IS NOT SOME PLAY TOY, YOUNG MAN--IT'S A DANGEROUS WORK OF ART.
HELP!
YOU'RE BECOMING MORE LIKE YOUR FATHER EVERY DAY.
BUT MOMMY, WE SHOULD MAKE THE SAD MAN HAPPY!
HE'S NOT A MAN, REGGIE...

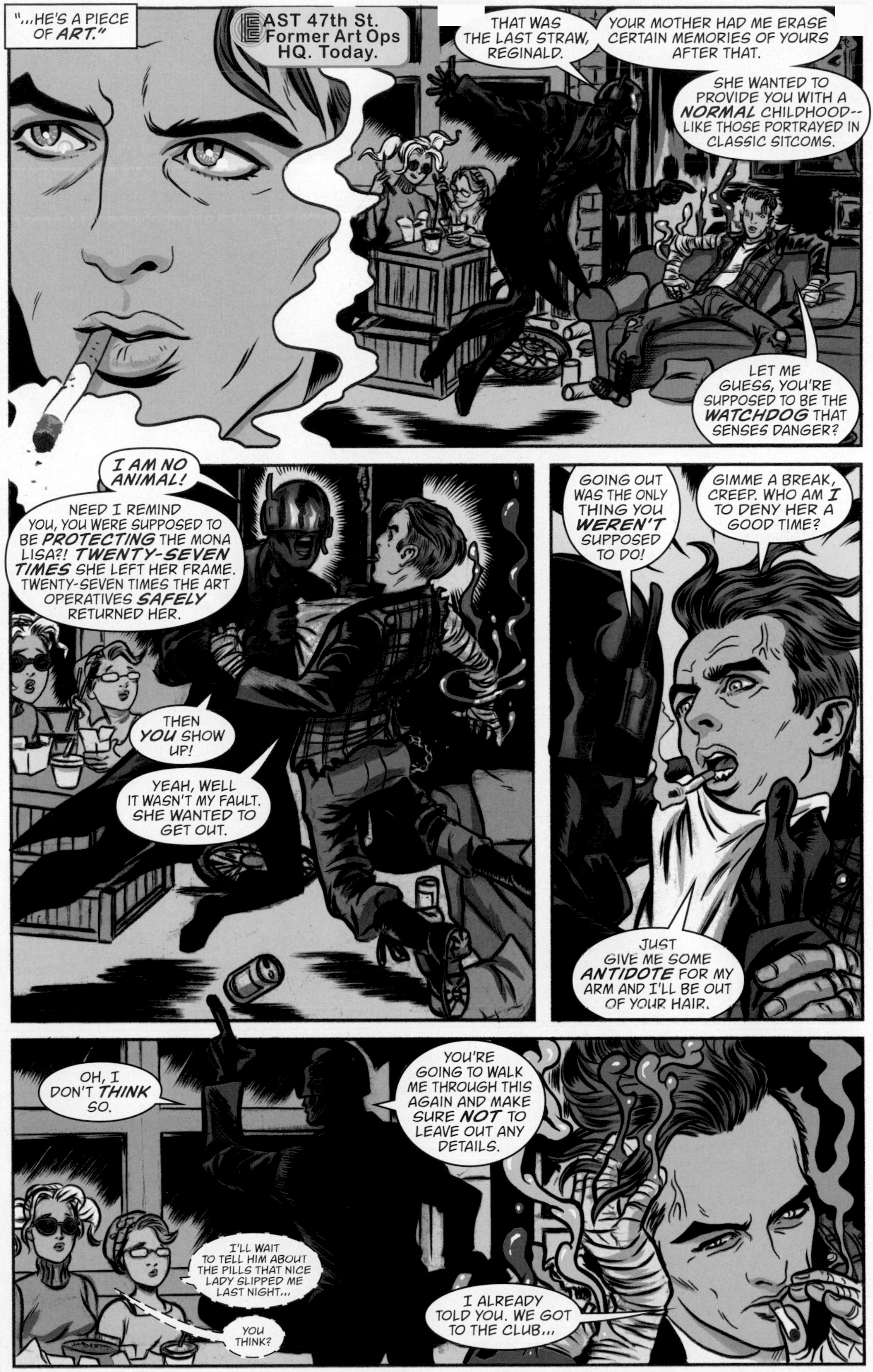
"...HE'S A PIECE OF ART."
EAST 47th St. Former Art Ops HQ. Today.
THAT WAS THE LAST STRAW, REGINALD.
YOUR MOTHER HAD ME ERASE CERTAIN MEMORIES OF YOURS AFTER THAT.
SHE WANTED TO PROVIDE YOU WITH A NORMAL CHILDHOOD-- LIKE THOSE PORTRAYED IN CLASSIC SITCOMS.
LET ME GUESS, YOU'RE SUPPOSED TO BE THE WATCHDOG THAT SENSES DANGER?
I AM NO ANIMAL!
NEED I REMIND YOU, YOU WERE SUPPOSED TO BE PROTECTING THE MONA LISA?! TWENTY-SEVEN TIMES SHE LEFT HER FRAME. TWENTY-SEVEN TIMES THE ART OPERATIVES SAFELY RETURNED HER.
THEN YOU SHOW UP!
YEAH, WELL IT WASN'T MY FAULT. SHE WANTED TO GET OUT.
GOING OUT WAS THE ONLY THING YOU WEREN'T SUPPOSED TO DO!
GIMME A BREAK, CREEP. WHO AM I TO DENY HER A GOOD TIME?
JUST GIVE ME SOME ANTIDOTE FOR MY ARM AND I'LL BE OUT OF YOUR HAIR.
OH, I DON'T THINK SO.
YOU'RE GOING TO WALK ME THROUGH THIS AGAIN AND MAKE SURE NOT TO LEAVE OUT ANY DETAILS.
I'LL WAIT TO TELL HIM ABOUT THE PILLS THAT NICE LADY SLIPPED ME LAST NIGHT...
YOU THINK?
I ALREADY TOLD YOU. WE GOT TO THE CLUB...

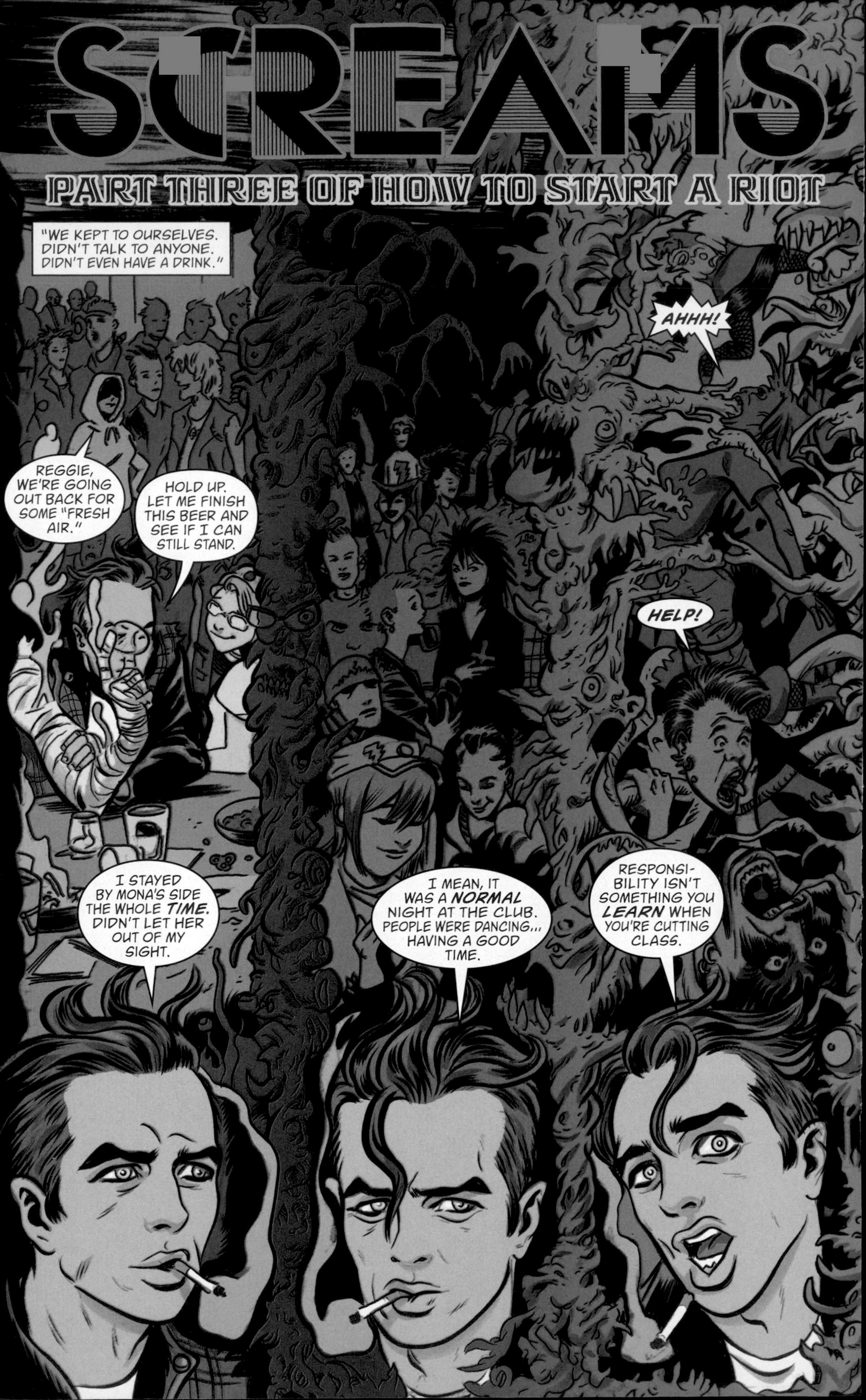
SCREAMS
PART THREE OF HOW TO START A RIOT
"WE KEPT TO OURSELVES. DIDN'T TALK TO ANYONE. DIDN'T EVEN HAVE A DRINK."
AHHH!
REGGIE, WE'RE GOING OUT BACK FOR SOME "FRESH AIR."
HOLD UP. LET ME FINISH THIS BEER AND SEE IF I CAN STILL STAND.
HELP!
I STAYED BY MONA'S SIDE THE WHOLE *TIME*. DIDN'T LET HER OUT OF MY SIGHT.
I MEAN, IT WAS A *NORMAL* NIGHT AT THE CLUB. PEOPLE WERE DANCING... HAVING A GOOD TIME.
RESPONSI-BILITY ISN'T SOMETHING YOU *LEARN* WHEN YOU'RE CUTTING CLASS.

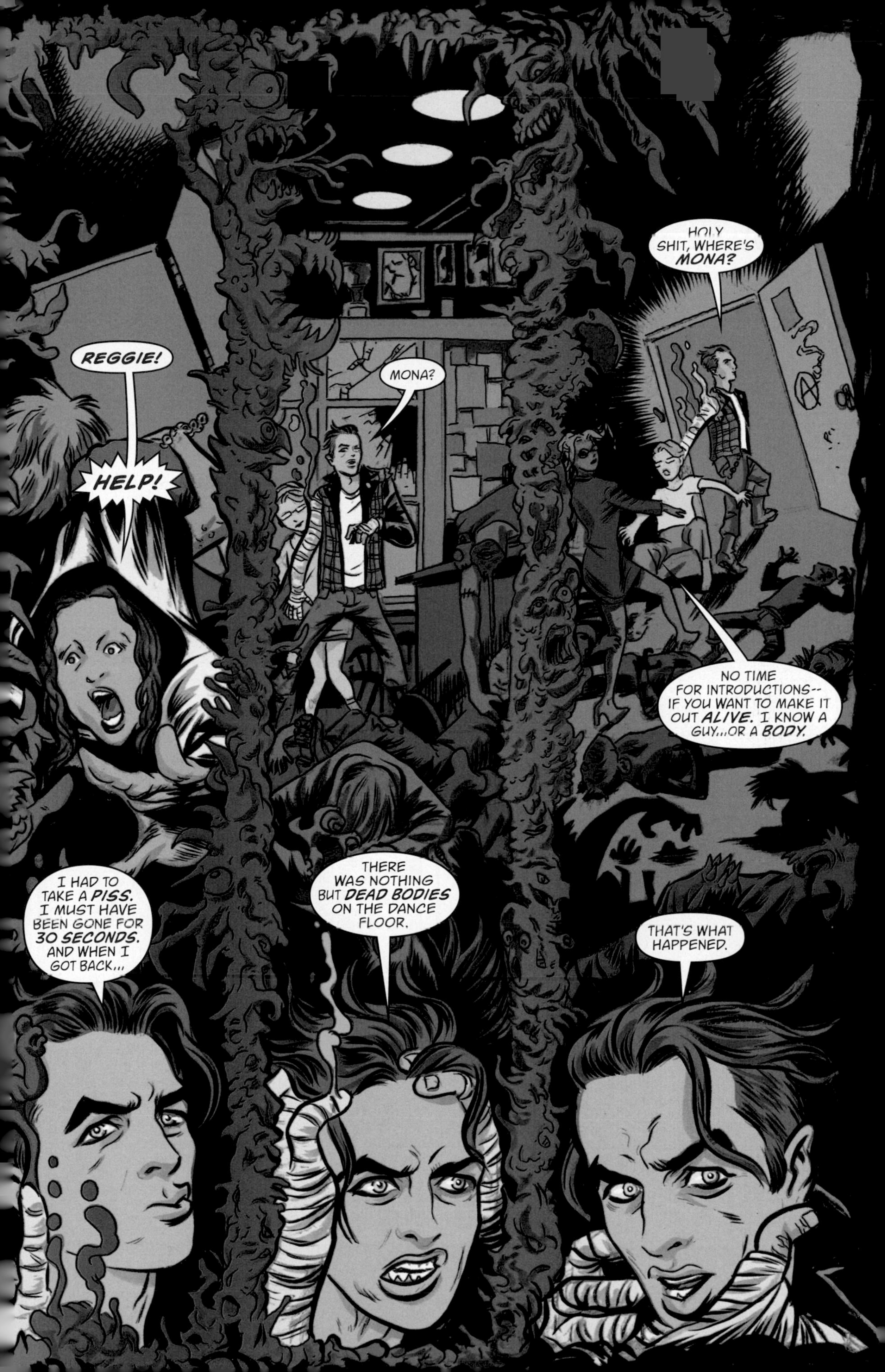
REGGIE!
HELP!
MONA?
HOLY SHIT, WHERE'S MONA?
NO TIME FOR INTRODUCTIONS-- IF YOU WANT TO MAKE IT OUT ALIVE. I KNOW A GUY...OR A BODY.
I HAD TO TAKE A PISS. I MUST HAVE BEEN GONE FOR 30 SECONDS. AND WHEN I GOT BACK...
THERE WAS NOTHING BUT DEAD BODIES ON THE DANCE FLOOR.
THAT'S WHAT HAPPENED.

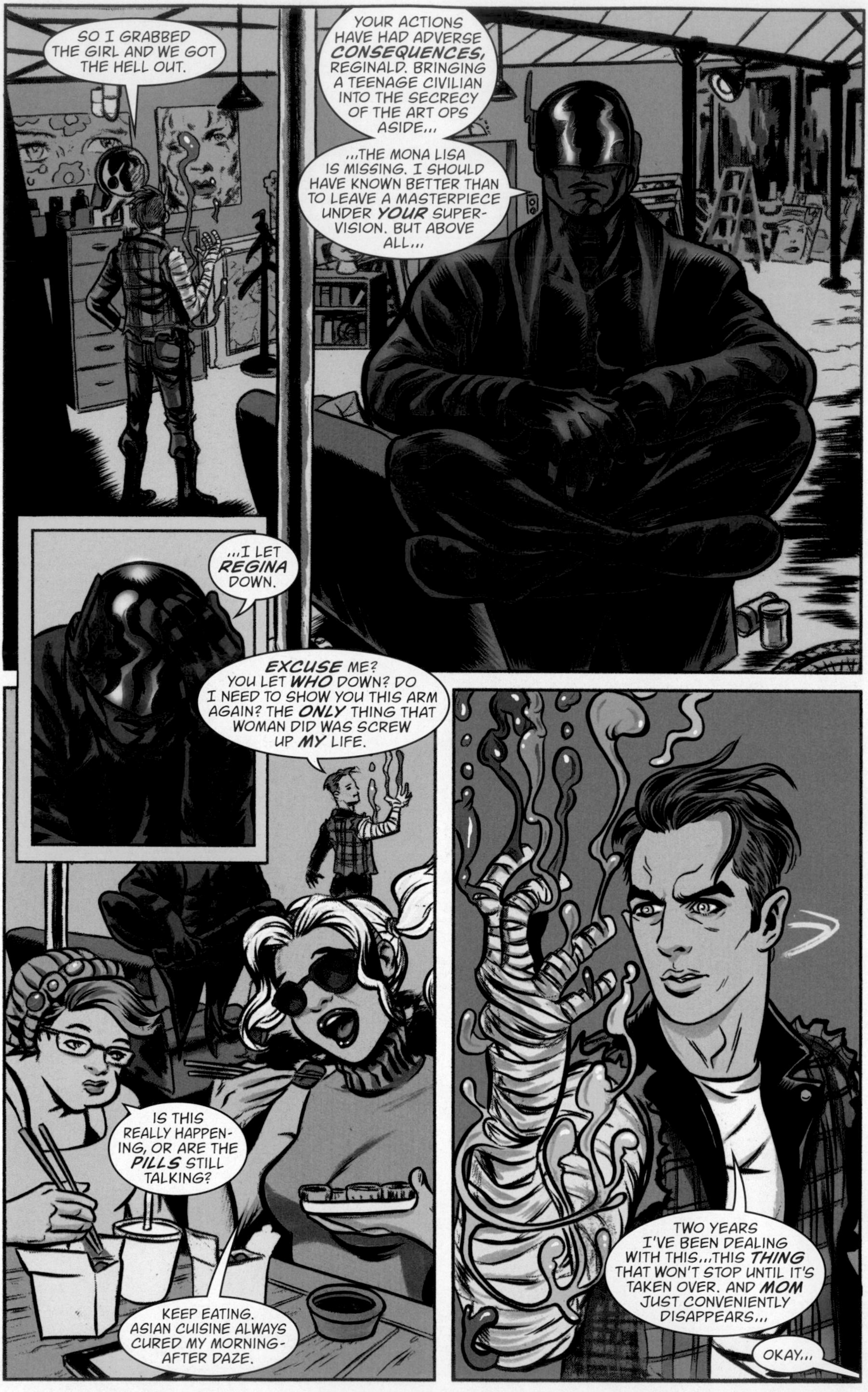
SO I GRABBED THE GIRL AND WE GOT THE HELL OUT.
YOUR ACTIONS HAVE HAD ADVERSE CONSEQUENCES, REGINALD. BRINGING A TEENAGE CIVILIAN INTO THE SECRECY OF THE ART OPS ASIDE...
...THE MONA LISA IS MISSING. I SHOULD HAVE KNOWN BETTER THAN TO LEAVE A MASTERPIECE UNDER YOUR SUPER-VISION. BUT ABOVE ALL...
...I LET REGINA DOWN.
EXCUSE ME? YOU LET WHO DOWN? DO I NEED TO SHOW YOU THIS ARM AGAIN? THE ONLY THING THAT WOMAN DID WAS SCREW UP MY LIFE.
IS THIS REALLY HAPPEN-ING, OR ARE THE PILLS STILL TALKING?
KEEP EATING. ASIAN CUISINE ALWAYS CURED MY MORNING-AFTER DAZE.
TWO YEARS I'VE BEEN DEALING WITH THIS...THIS THING THAT WON'T STOP UNTIL IT'S TAKEN OVER. AND MOM JUST CONVENIENTLY DISAPPEARS...
OKAY...

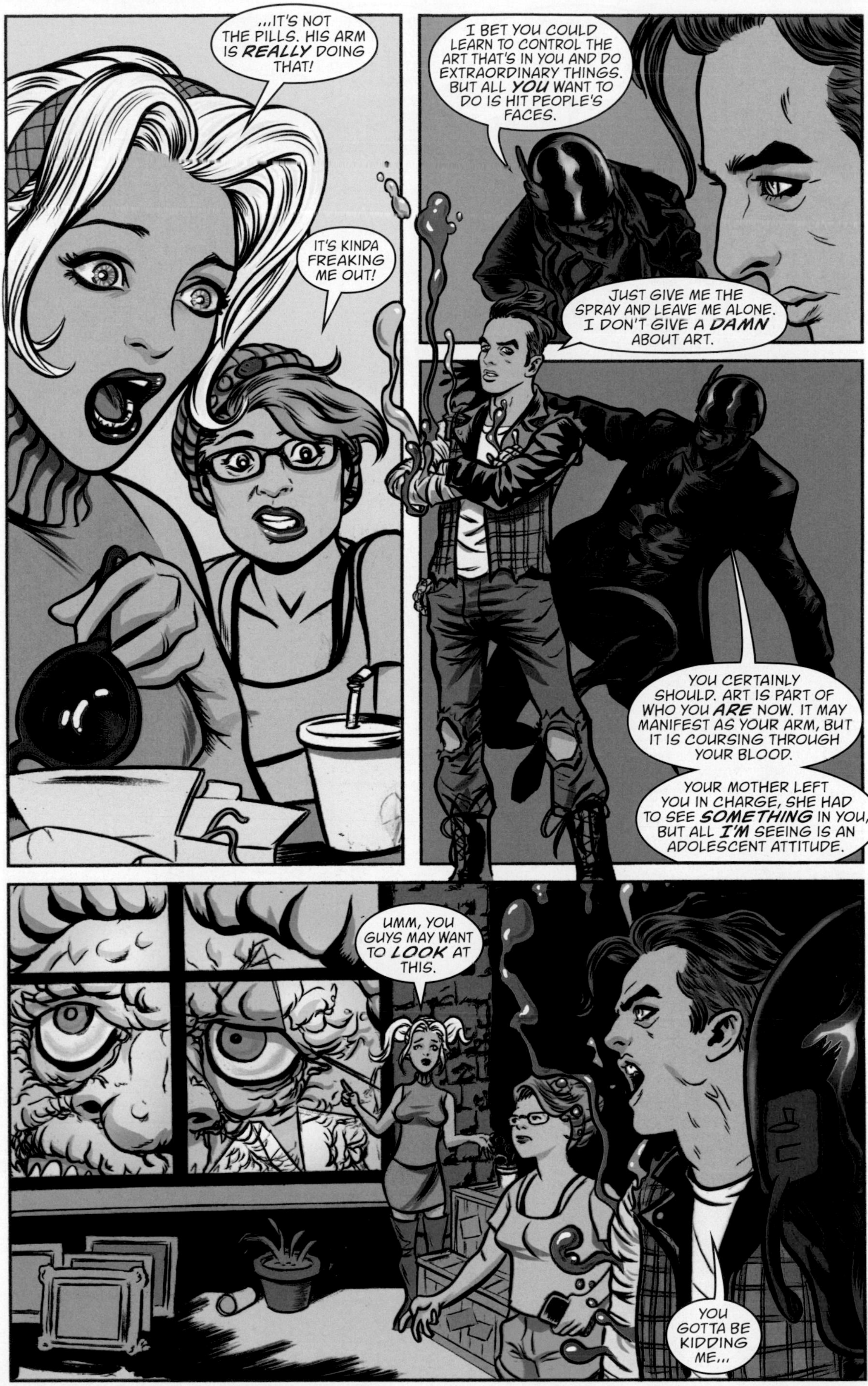
...IT'S NOT THE PILLS. HIS ARM IS REALLY DOING THAT!
IT'S KINDA FREAKING ME OUT!
I BET YOU COULD LEARN TO CONTROL THE ART THAT'S IN YOU AND DO EXTRAORDINARY THINGS. BUT ALL YOU WANT TO DO IS HIT PEOPLE'S FACES.
JUST GIVE ME THE SPRAY AND LEAVE ME ALONE. I DON'T GIVE A DAMN ABOUT ART.
YOU CERTAINLY SHOULD. ART IS PART OF WHO YOU ARE NOW. IT MAY MANIFEST AS YOUR ARM, BUT IT IS COURSING THROUGH YOUR BLOOD.
YOUR MOTHER LEFT YOU IN CHARGE, SHE HAD TO SEE SOMETHING IN YOU, BUT ALL I'M SEEING IS AN ADOLESCENT ATTITUDE.
UMM, YOU GUYS MAY WANT TO LOOK AT THIS.
YOU GOTTA BE KIDDING ME...

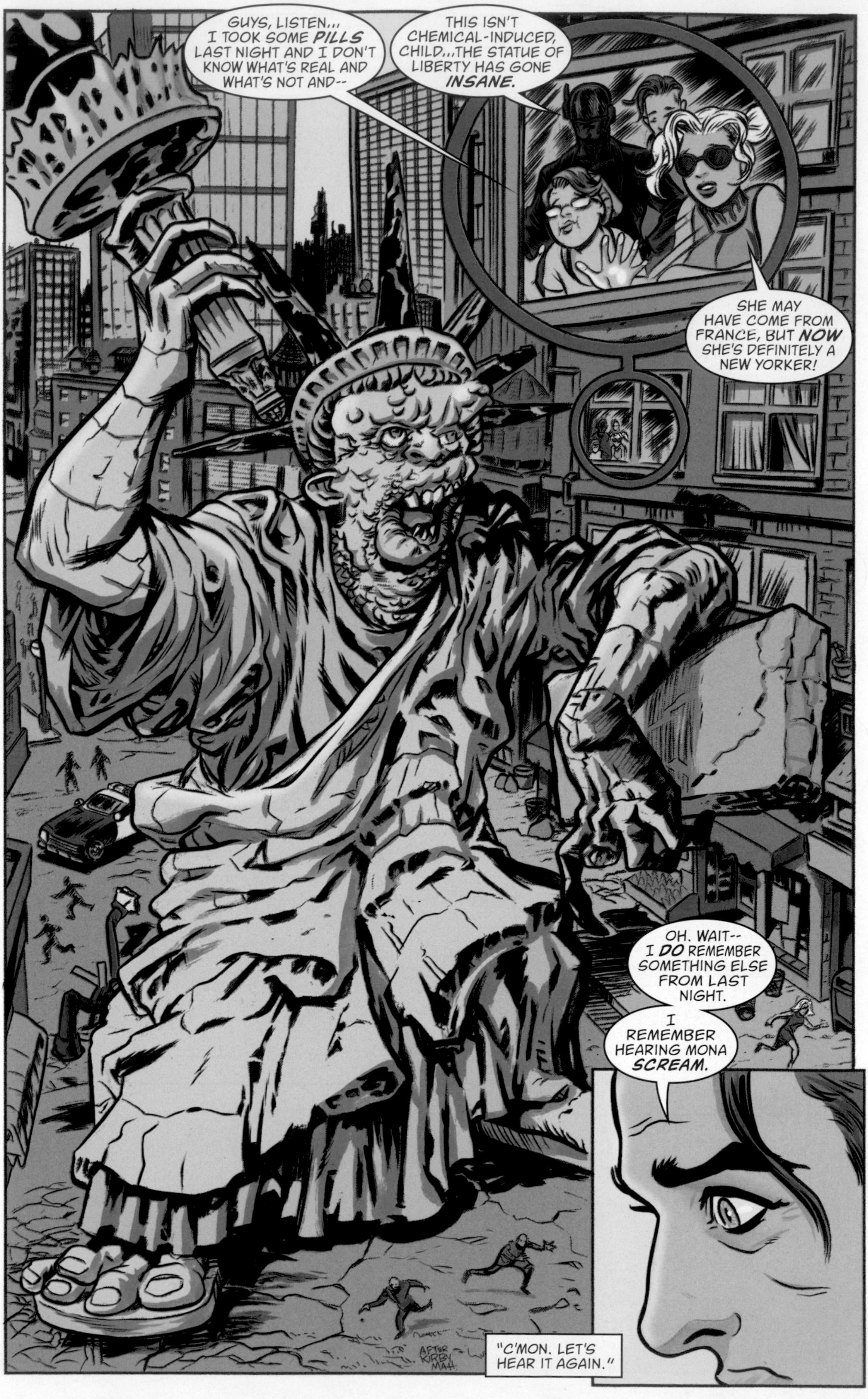
GUYS, LISTEN... I TOOK SOME ***PILLS*** LAST NIGHT AND I DON'T KNOW WHAT'S REAL AND WHAT'S NOT AND--
THIS ISN'T CHEMICAL-INDUCED, CHILD...THE STATUE OF LIBERTY HAS GONE ***INSANE.***
SHE MAY HAVE COME FROM FRANCE, BUT ***NOW*** SHE'S DEFINITELY A NEW YORKER!
"C'MON. LET'S HEAR IT AGAIN."
OH. WAIT-- I ***DO*** REMEMBER SOMETHING ELSE FROM LAST NIGHT.
I REMEMBER HEARING MONA ***SCREAM.***

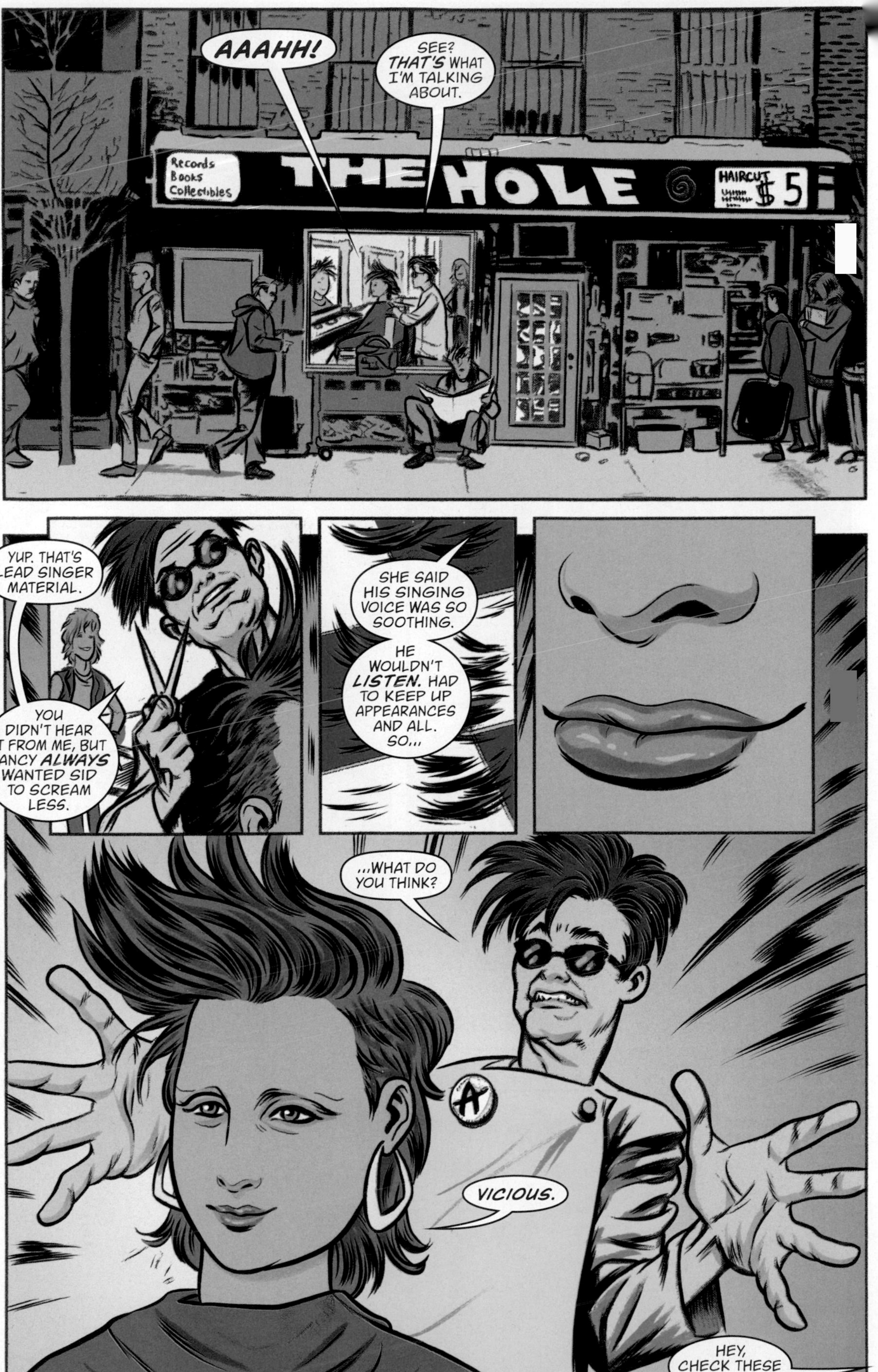
AAAHH!
SEE? THAT'S WHAT I'M TALKING ABOUT.
Records Books Collectibles
THE HOLE
HAIRCUT $5
YUP. THAT'S LEAD SINGER MATERIAL.
YOU DIDN'T HEAR IT FROM ME, BUT NANCY ALWAYS WANTED SID TO SCREAM LESS.
SHE SAID HIS SINGING VOICE WAS SO SOOTHING.
HE WOULDN'T LISTEN. HAD TO KEEP UP APPEARANCES AND ALL. SO...
...WHAT DO YOU THINK?
VICIOUS.
HEY, CHECK THESE OUT.

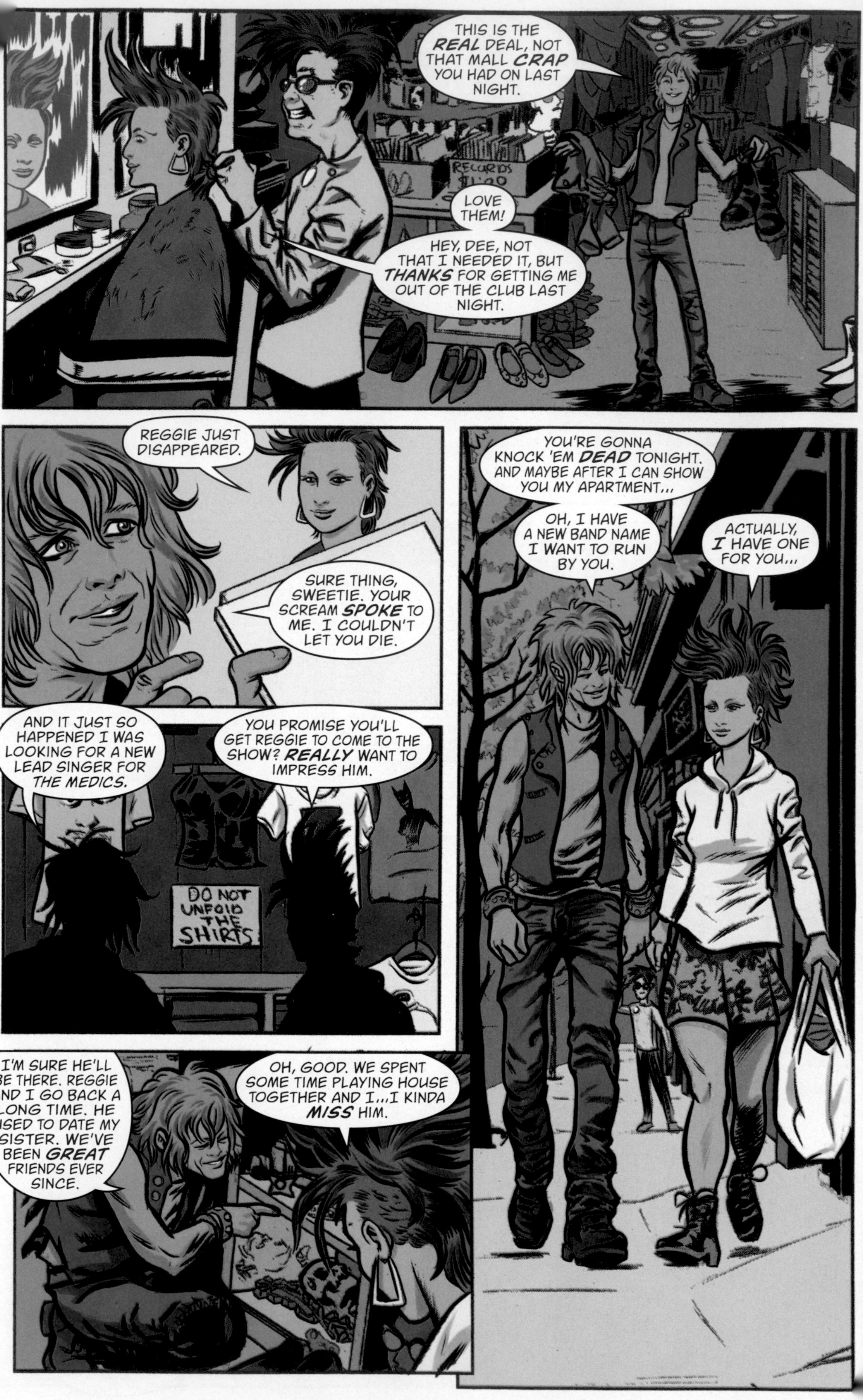
THIS IS THE REAL DEAL, NOT THAT MALL CRAP YOU HAD ON LAST NIGHT.
RECORDS $1.00
LOVE THEM!
HEY, DEE, NOT THAT I NEEDED IT, BUT THANKS FOR GETTING ME OUT OF THE CLUB LAST NIGHT.
REGGIE JUST DISAPPEARED.
SURE THING, SWEETIE. YOUR SCREAM SPOKE TO ME. I COULDN'T LET YOU DIE.
AND IT JUST SO HAPPENED I WAS LOOKING FOR A NEW LEAD SINGER FOR THE MEDICS.
YOU PROMISE YOU'LL GET REGGIE TO COME TO THE SHOW? REALLY WANT TO IMPRESS HIM.
DO NOT UNFOLD THE SHIRTS
I'M SURE HE'LL BE THERE. REGGIE AND I GO BACK A LONG TIME. HE USED TO DATE MY SISTER. WE'VE BEEN GREAT FRIENDS EVER SINCE.
OH, GOOD. WE SPENT SOME TIME PLAYING HOUSE TOGETHER AND I...I KINDA MISS HIM.
YOU'RE GONNA KNOCK 'EM DEAD TONIGHT. AND MAYBE AFTER I CAN SHOW YOU MY APARTMENT...
OH, I HAVE A NEW BAND NAME I WANT TO RUN BY YOU.
ACTUALLY, I HAVE ONE FOR YOU...

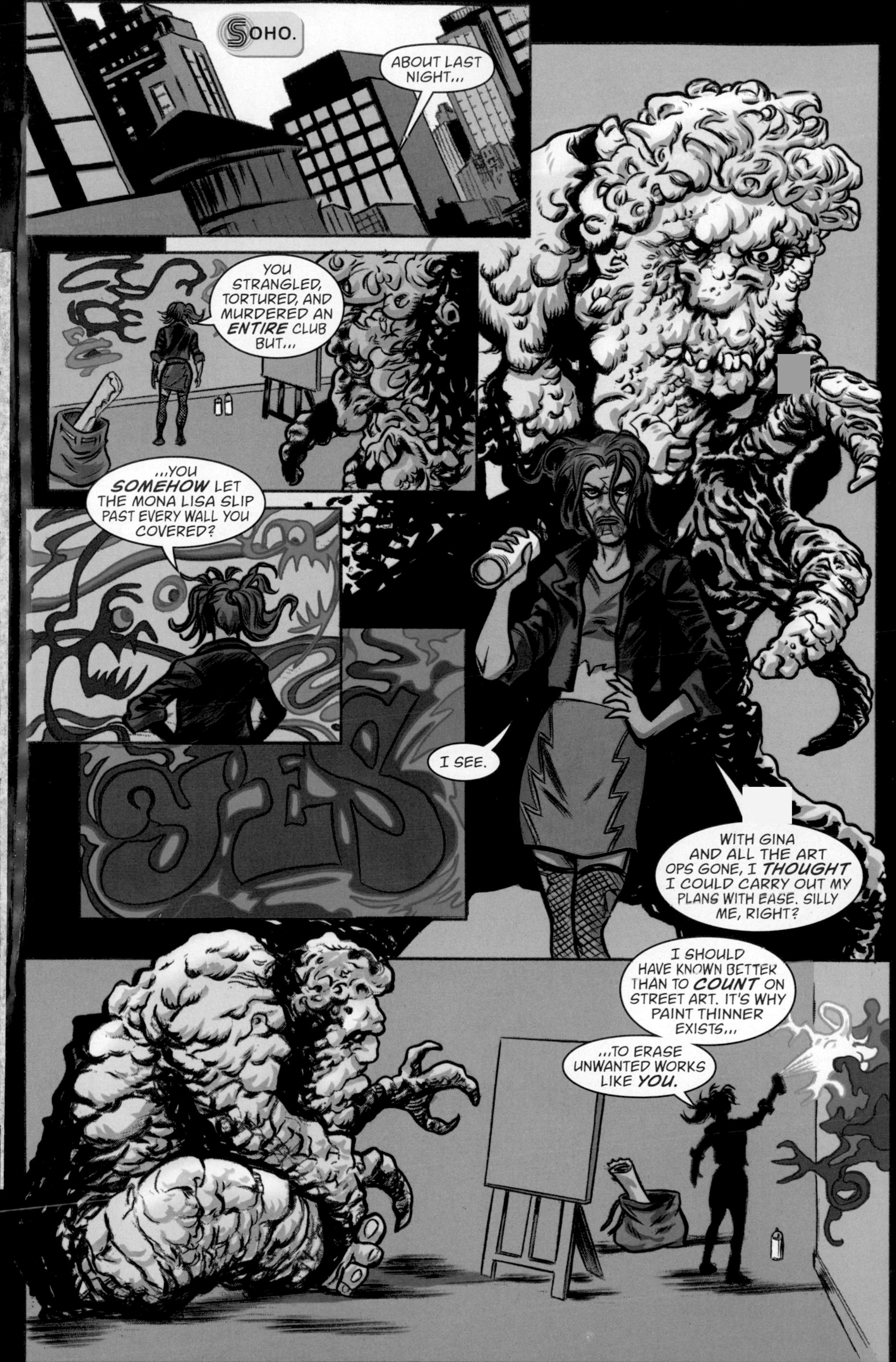

SOHO.
ABOUT LAST NIGHT...
YOU STRANGLED, TORTURED, AND MURDERED AN ENTIRE CLUB BUT...
...YOU SOMEHOW LET THE MONA LISA SLIP PAST EVERY WALL YOU COVERED?
I SEE.
WITH GINA AND ALL THE ART OPS GONE, I THOUGHT I COULD CARRY OUT MY PLANS WITH EASE. SILLY ME, RIGHT?
I SHOULD HAVE KNOWN BETTER THAN TO COUNT ON STREET ART. IT'S WHY PAINT THINNER EXISTS...
...TO ERASE UNWANTED WORKS LIKE YOU.

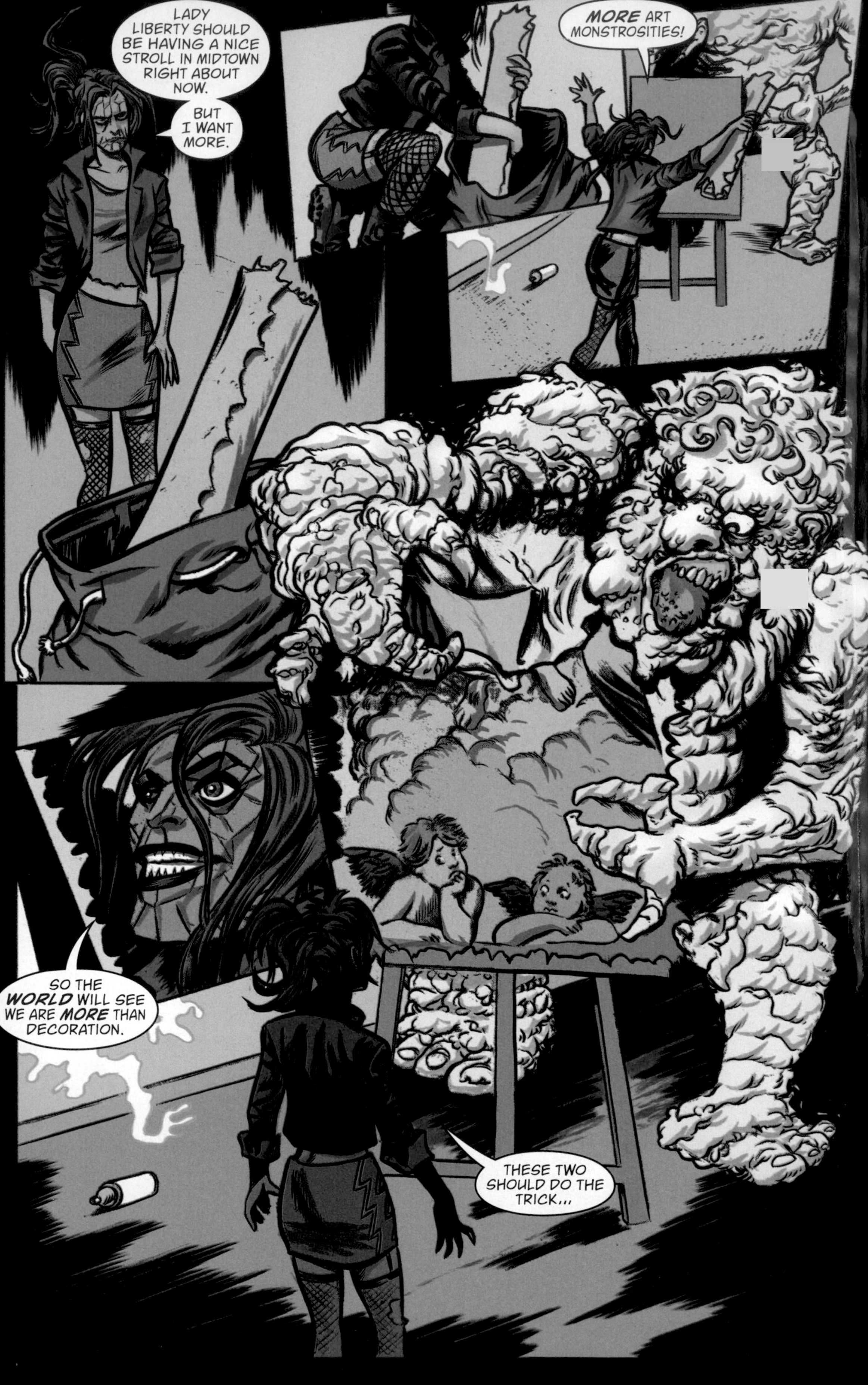
LADY LIBERTY SHOULD BE HAVING A NICE STROLL IN MIDTOWN RIGHT ABOUT NOW.
BUT I WANT MORE.
MORE ART MONSTROSITIES!
SO THE WORLD WILL SEE WE ARE MORE THAN DECORATION.
THESE TWO SHOULD DO THE TRICK...

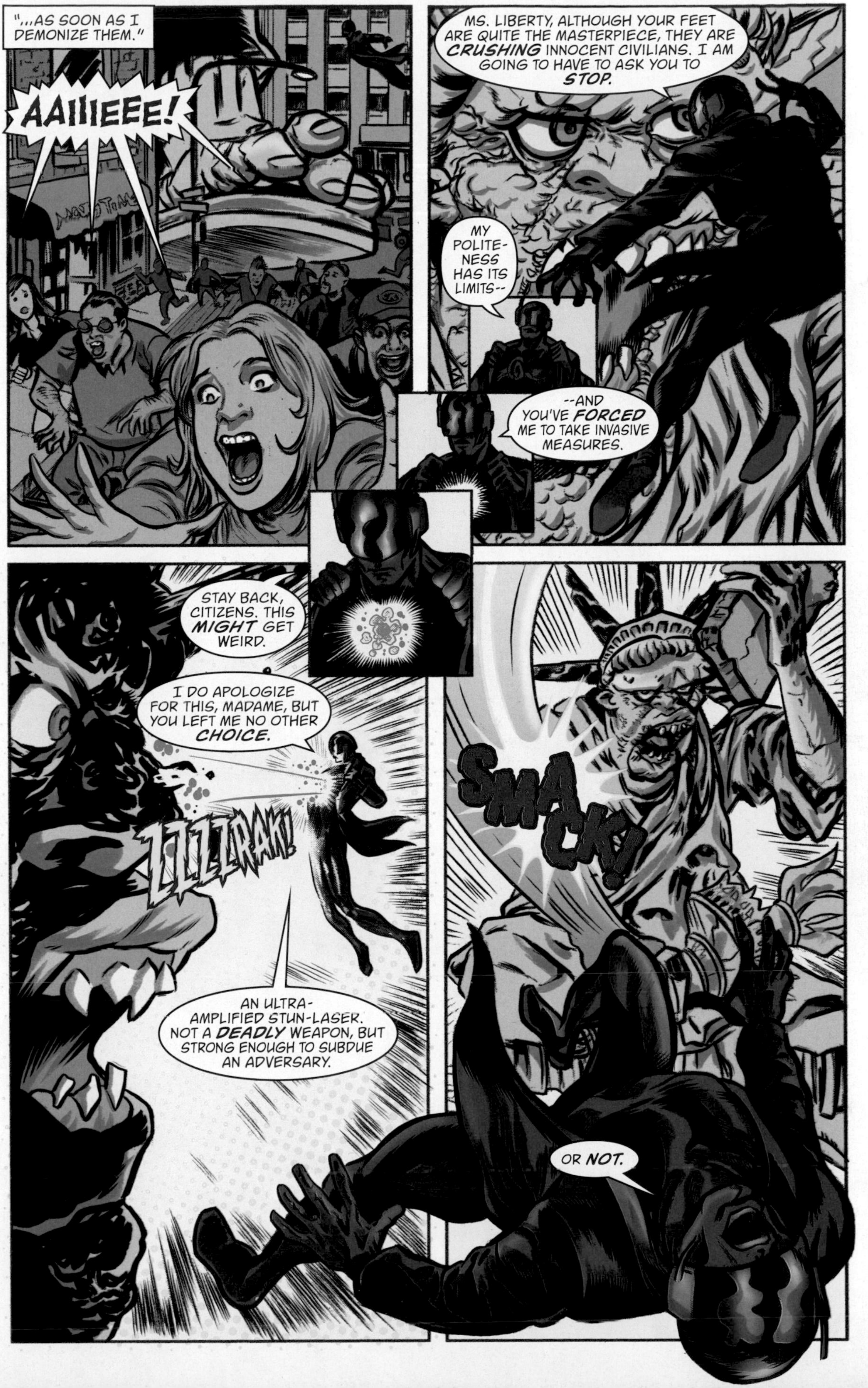
"...AS SOON AS I DEMONIZE THEM."
AAIIIEEE!
MS. LIBERTY, ALTHOUGH YOUR FEET ARE QUITE THE MASTERPIECE, THEY ARE **CRUSHING** INNOCENT CIVILIANS. I AM GOING TO HAVE TO ASK YOU TO **STOP.**
MY POLITENESS HAS ITS LIMITS--
--AND YOU'VE **FORCED** ME TO TAKE INVASIVE MEASURES.
STAY BACK, CITIZENS. THIS **MIGHT** GET WEIRD.
I DO APOLOGIZE FOR THIS, MADAME, BUT YOU LEFT ME NO OTHER **CHOICE.**
ZZZZRAK!
AN ULTRA-AMPLIFIED STUN-LASER. NOT A **DEADLY** WEAPON, BUT STRONG ENOUGH TO SUBDUE AN ADVERSARY.
SMACK!
OR **NOT.**

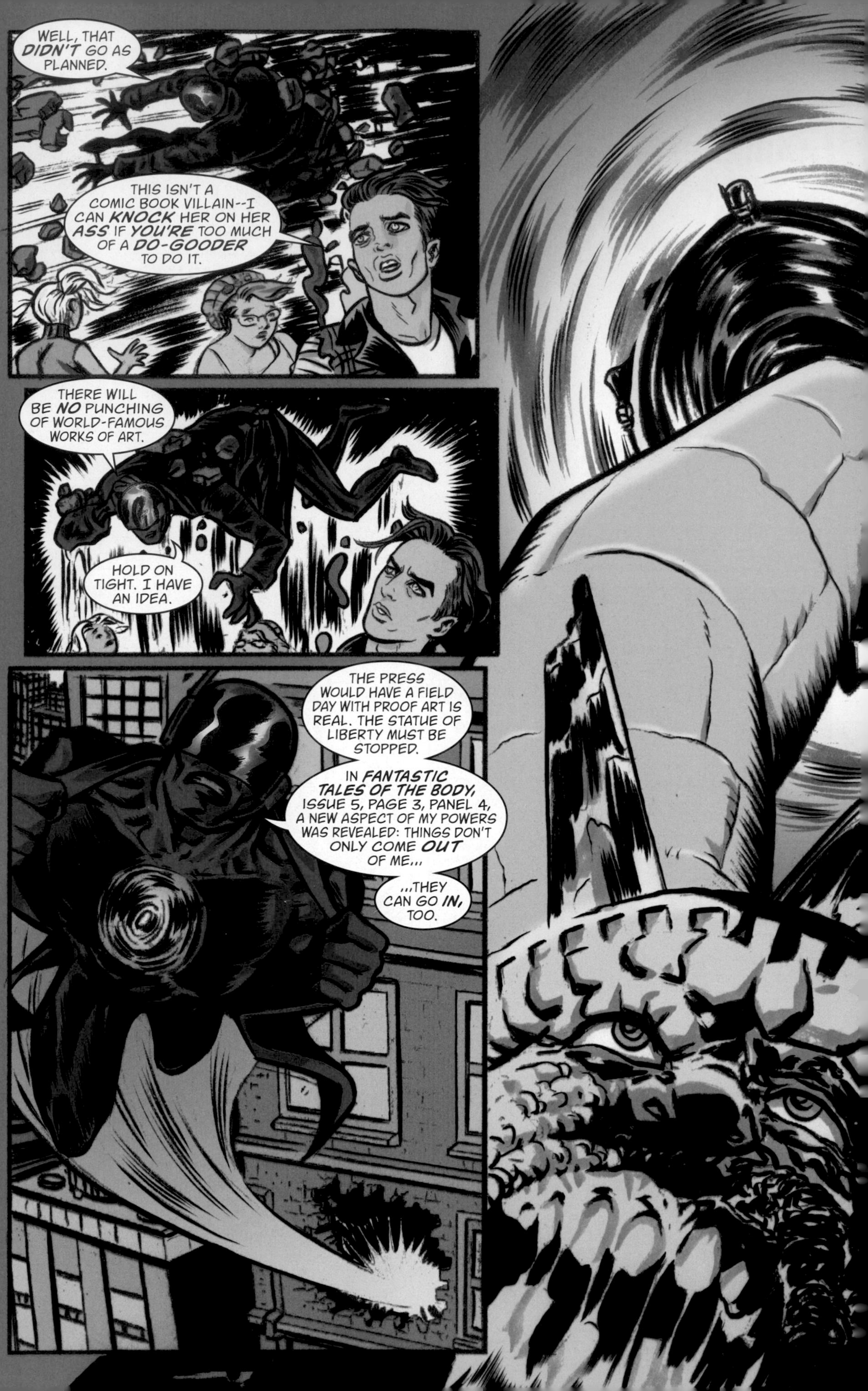
WELL, THAT DIDN'T GO AS PLANNED.
THIS ISN'T A COMIC BOOK VILLAIN--I CAN KNOCK HER ON HER ASS IF YOU'RE TOO MUCH OF A DO-GOODER TO DO IT.
THERE WILL BE NO PUNCHING OF WORLD-FAMOUS WORKS OF ART.
HOLD ON TIGHT. I HAVE AN IDEA.
THE PRESS WOULD HAVE A FIELD DAY WITH PROOF ART IS REAL. THE STATUE OF LIBERTY MUST BE STOPPED.
IN FANTASTIC TALES OF THE BODY, ISSUE 5, PAGE 3, PANEL 4, A NEW ASPECT OF MY POWERS WAS REVEALED: THINGS DON'T ONLY COME OUT OF ME...
...THEY CAN GO IN, TOO.

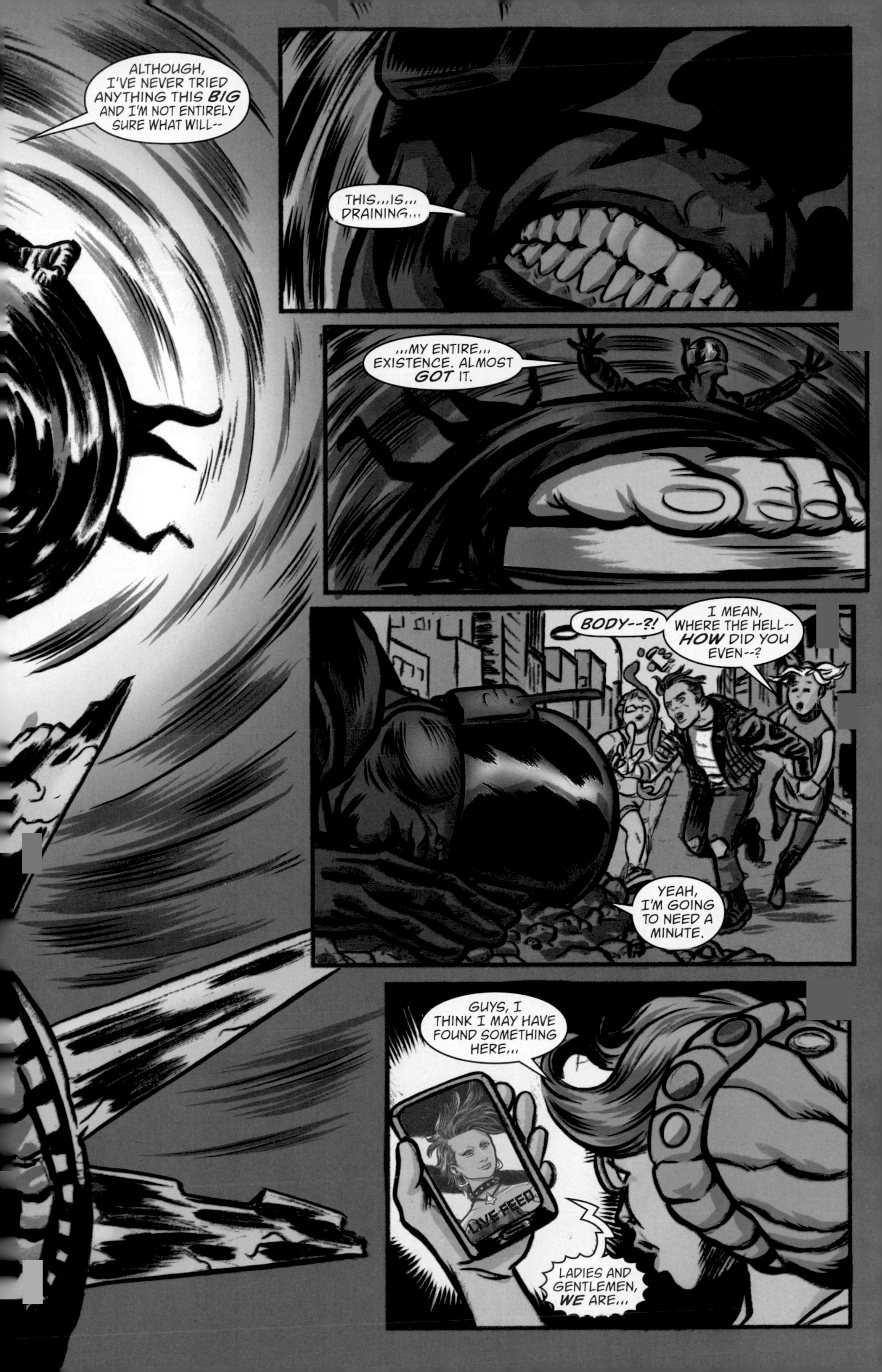
ALTHOUGH, I'VE NEVER TRIED ANYTHING THIS BIG AND I'M NOT ENTIRELY SURE WHAT WILL--
THIS...IS... DRAINING...
...MY ENTIRE... EXISTENCE. ALMOST GOT IT.
BODY--?!
I MEAN, WHERE THE HELL-- HOW DID YOU EVEN--?
YEAH, I'M GOING TO NEED A MINUTE.
GUYS, I THINK I MAY HAVE FOUND SOMETHING HERE...
LIVE FEED
LADIES AND GENTLEMEN, WE ARE...

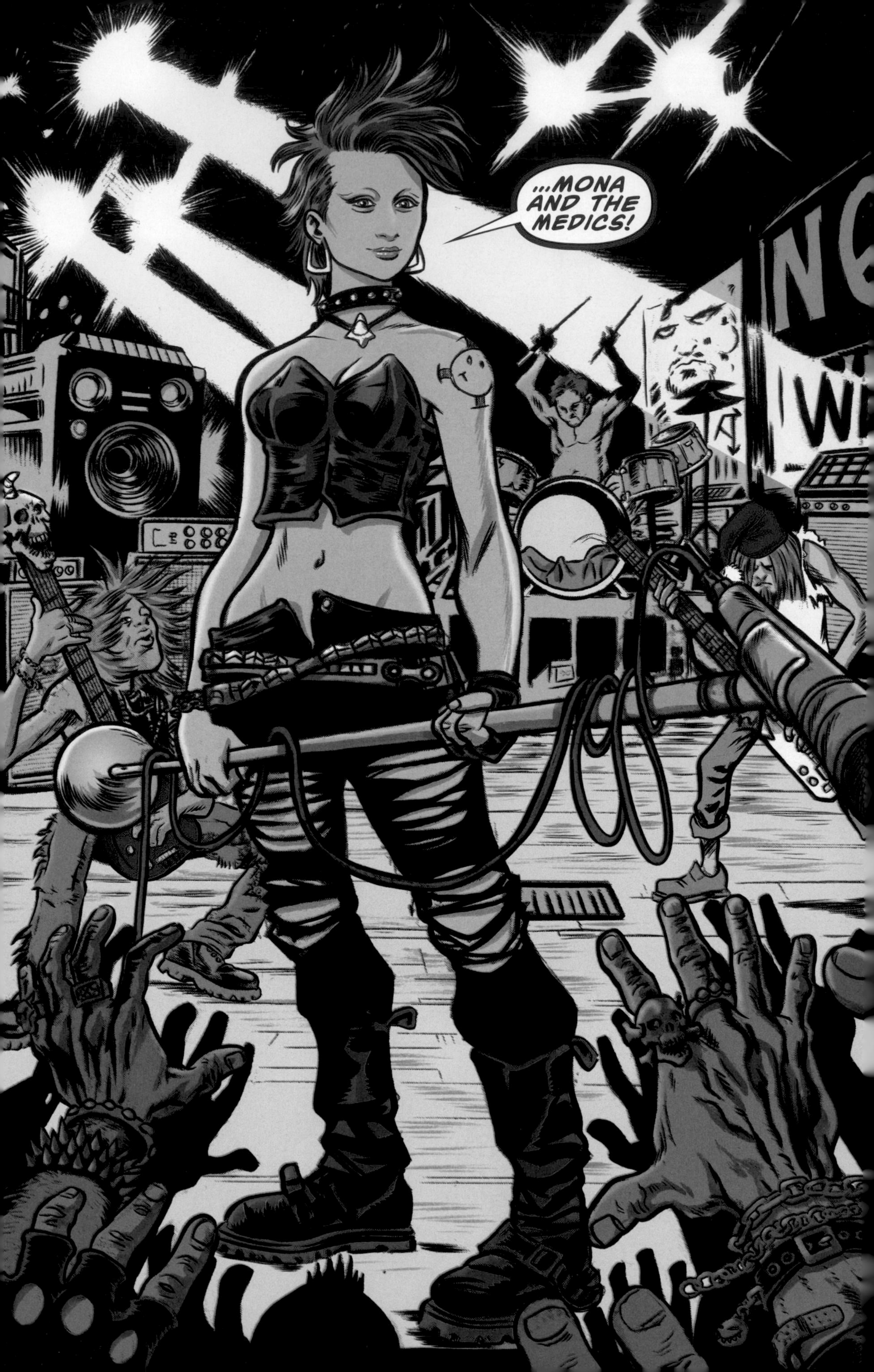
...MONA AND THE MEDICS!

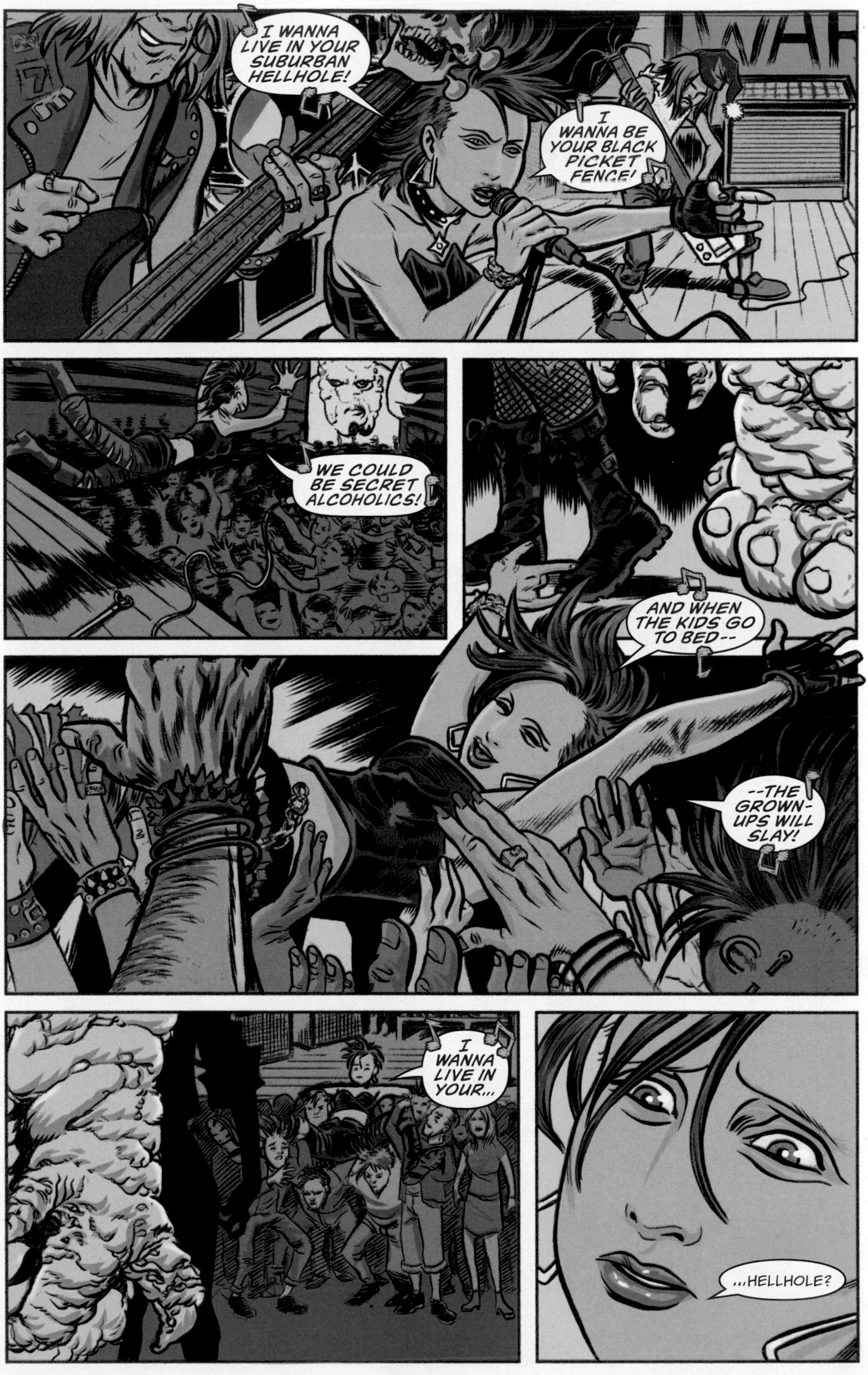

I WANNA LIVE IN YOUR SUBURBAN HELLHOLE!
I WANNA BE YOUR BLACK PICKET FENCE!
WE COULD BE SECRET ALCOHOLICS!
AND WHEN THE KIDS GO TO BED--
--THE GROWN-UPS WILL SLAY!
I WANNA LIVE IN YOUR...
...HELLHOLE?

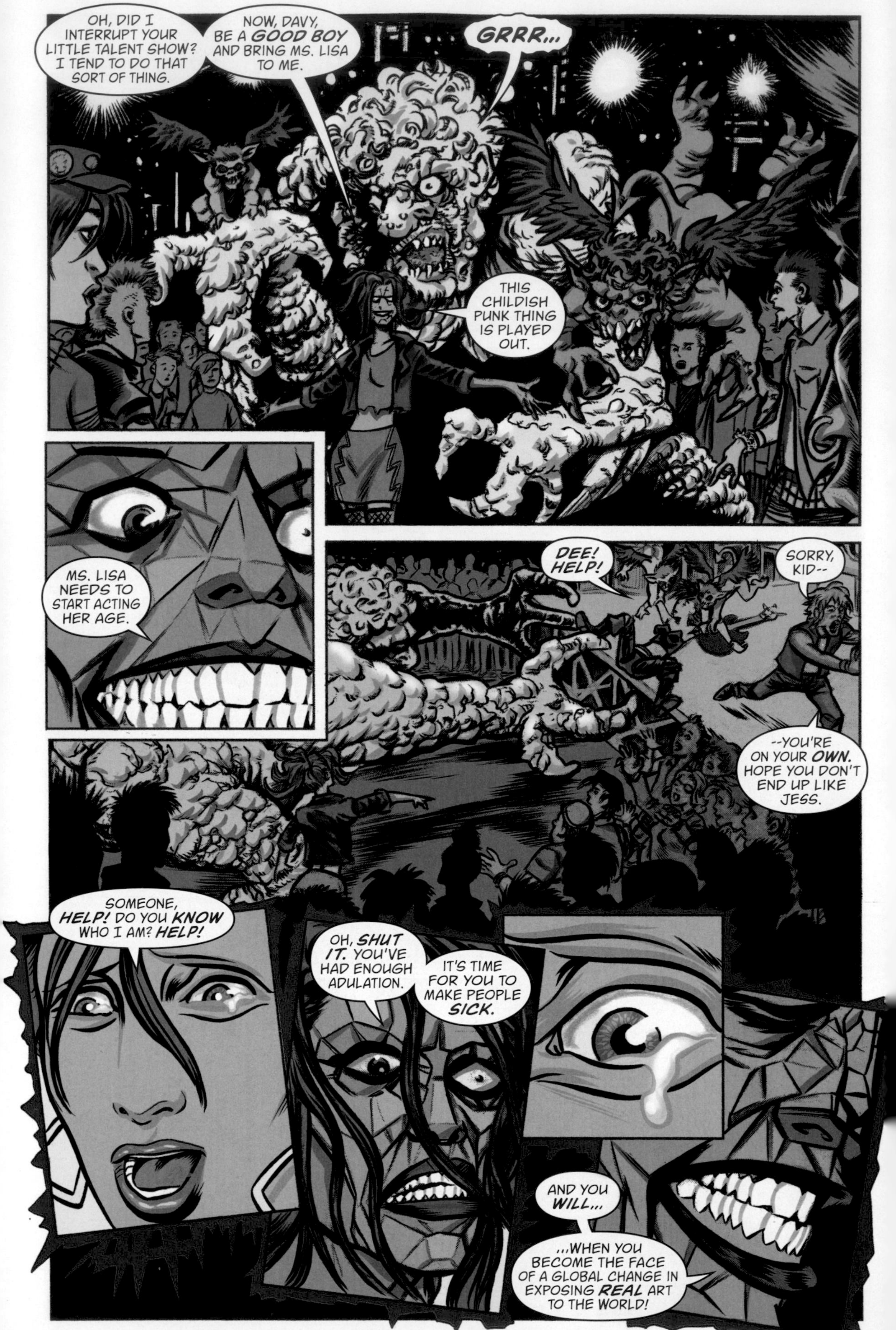
OH, DID I INTERRUPT YOUR LITTLE TALENT SHOW? I TEND TO DO THAT SORT OF THING.
NOW, DAVY, BE A GOOD BOY AND BRING MS. LISA TO ME.
GRRR...
THIS CHILDISH PUNK THING IS PLAYED OUT.
MS. LISA NEEDS TO START ACTING HER AGE.
DEE! HELP!
SORRY, KID--
--YOU'RE ON YOUR OWN. HOPE YOU DON'T END UP LIKE JESS.
SOMEONE, HELP! DO YOU KNOW WHO I AM? HELP!
OH, SHUT IT. YOU'VE HAD ENOUGH ADULATION.
IT'S TIME FOR YOU TO MAKE PEOPLE SICK.
AND YOU WILL...
...WHEN YOU BECOME THE FACE OF A GLOBAL CHANGE IN EXPOSING REAL ART TO THE WORLD!

CRISIS AVERTED. I HAVE **ERASED** THE DEBACLE FROM THE MINDS OF THE CIVILIANS. I SIMPLY LOOK LIKE A **BIRTHDAY** BALLOON TO THEM AND LADY LIBERTY IS SAFE INSIDE ME.

THE VENUE IS RIGHT AROUND HERE. NOT THAT PULLING A BLOATED "BODY" AROUND THE CITY ISN'T FUN AND ALL.

SORRY ABOUT THAT. I DO, HOWEVER, FEEL VERY **PATRIOTIC**-- AND WELCOMING. VERY WELCOMING.

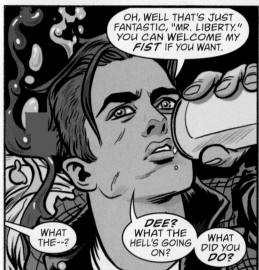

OH, WELL THAT'S JUST FANTASTIC, "MR. LIBERTY." YOU CAN WELCOME MY **FIST** IF YOU WANT.

WHAT THE--?

DEE? WHAT THE HELL'S GOING ON?

WHAT DID YOU **DO?**

THE SHOW...MY SINGER!

A MONSTER. MONSTERS! I--I GOTTA GO!

THERE'S BEEN A DISTURBANCE THREE BLOCKS AHEAD. I'M SENSING **DISEASE** MIXED WITH OIL-BASED PAINT.

IF I FIND OUT YOU HAD **ANYTHING** TO DO WITH MONA--

WHAT?

YOU'RE GOING TO **HELP** HER LIKE YOU HELPED **JESS?** YOU LET MY SISTER **DIE!**

YOU'RE A **JOKE,** REGGIE. YOU THINK YOU'RE GOING TO SAVE MONA?

"YOU CAN'T EVEN SAVE **YOURSELF!**"

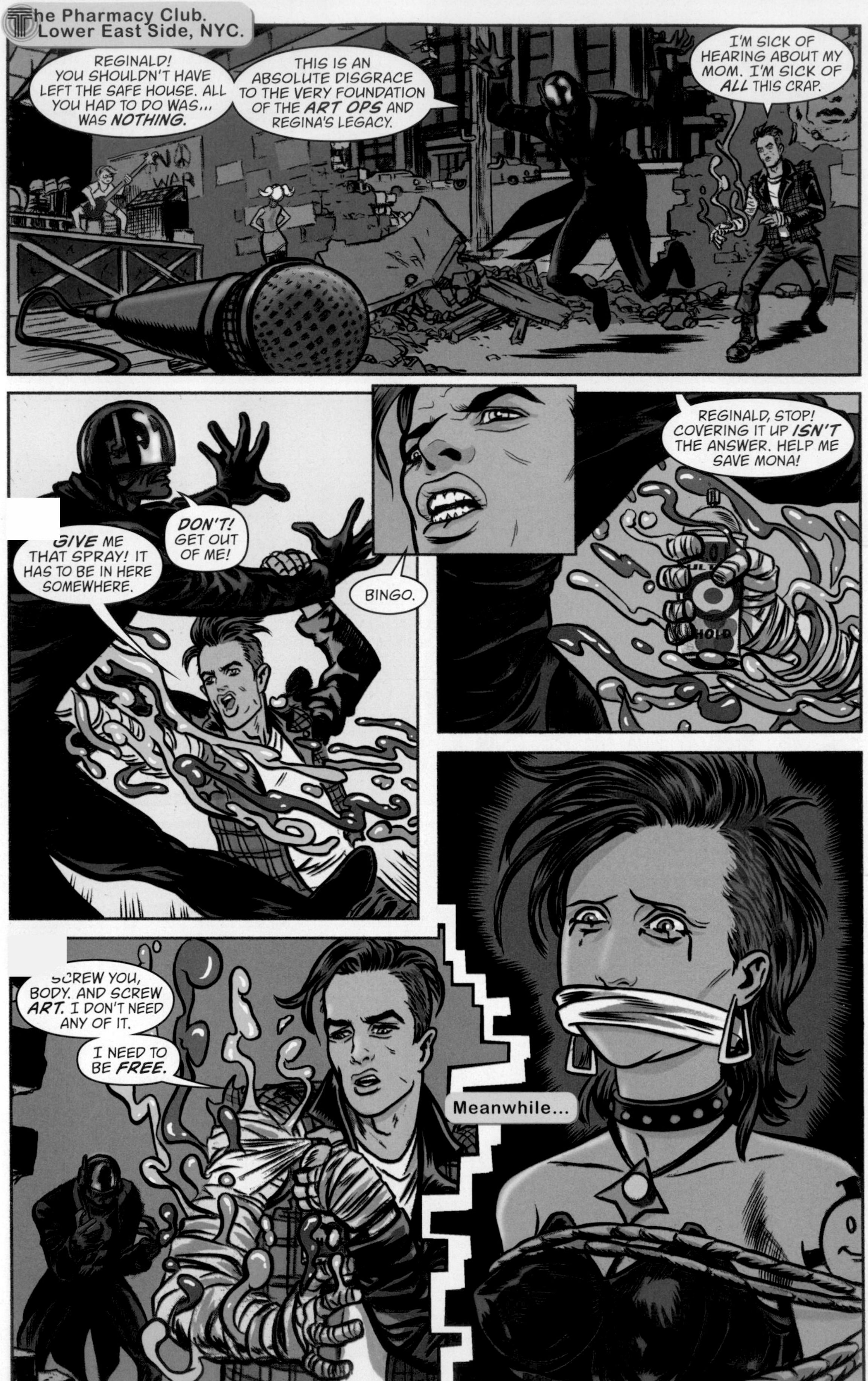
The Pharmacy Club.
Lower East Side, NYC.
REGINALD! YOU SHOULDN'T HAVE LEFT THE SAFE HOUSE. ALL YOU HAD TO DO WAS... WAS *NOTHING.*
THIS IS AN ABSOLUTE DISGRACE TO THE VERY FOUNDATION OF THE *ART OPS* AND REGINA'S LEGACY.
I'M SICK OF HEARING ABOUT MY MOM. I'M SICK OF *ALL* THIS CRAP.
GIVE ME THAT SPRAY! IT HAS TO BE IN HERE SOMEWHERE.
DON'T! GET OUT OF ME!
BINGO.
REGINALD, STOP! COVERING IT UP *ISN'T* THE ANSWER. HELP ME SAVE MONA!
SCREW YOU, BODY. AND SCREW *ART.* I DON'T NEED ANY OF IT.
I NEED TO BE *FREE.*
Meanwhile...

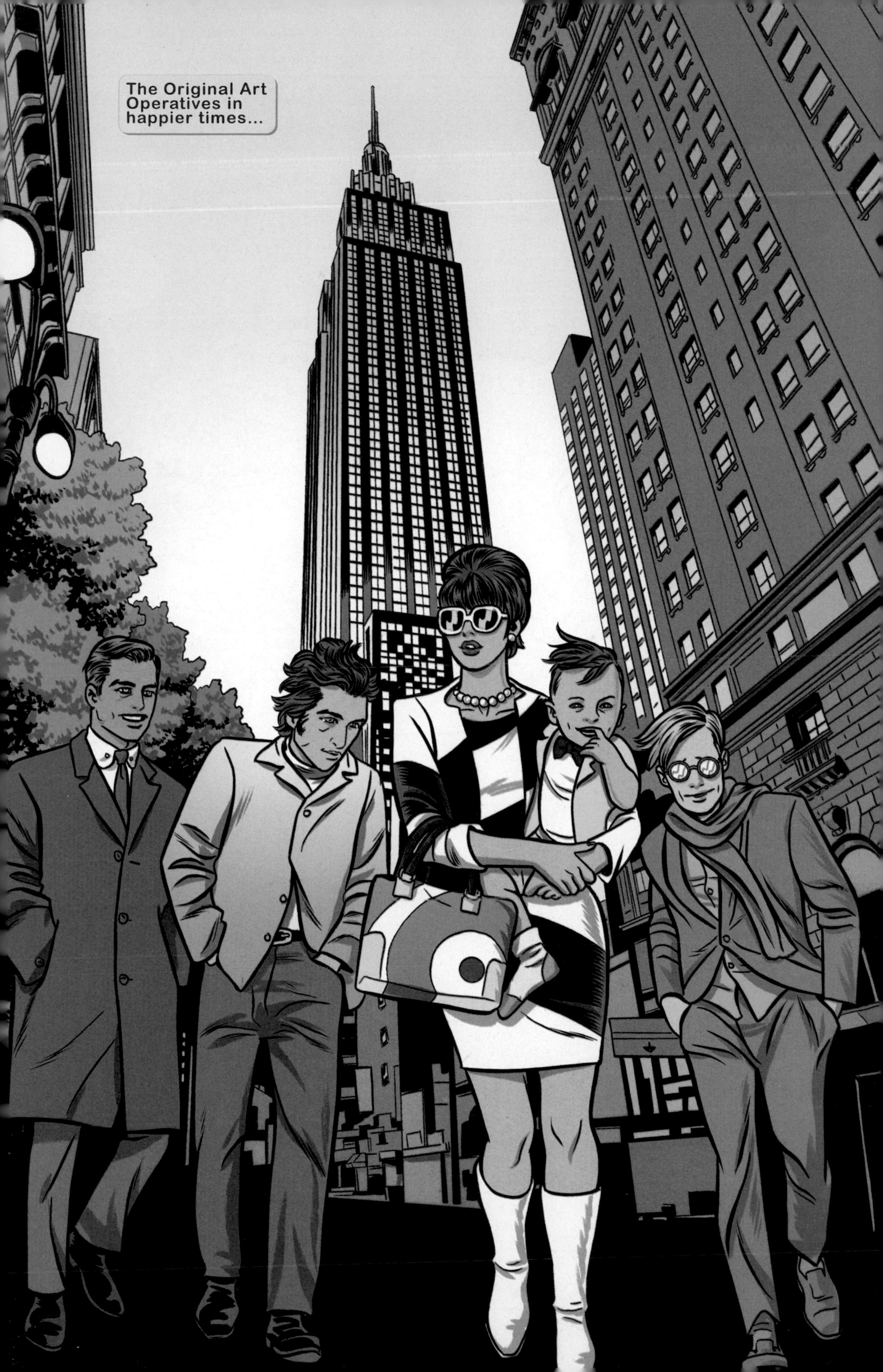
The Original Art Operatives in happier times...

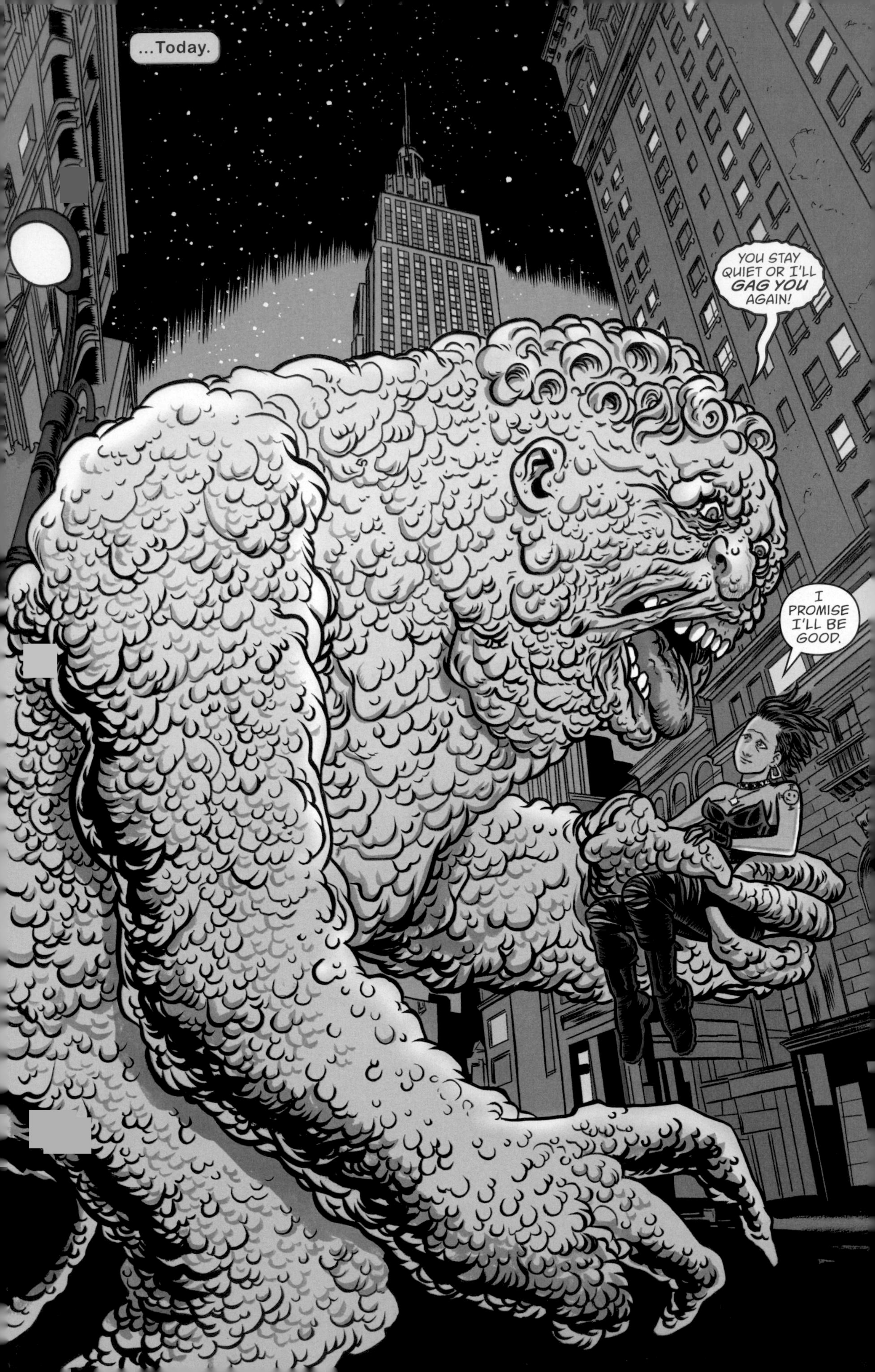
...Today.
YOU STAY QUIET OR I'LL GAG YOU AGAIN!
I PROMISE I'LL BE GOOD.

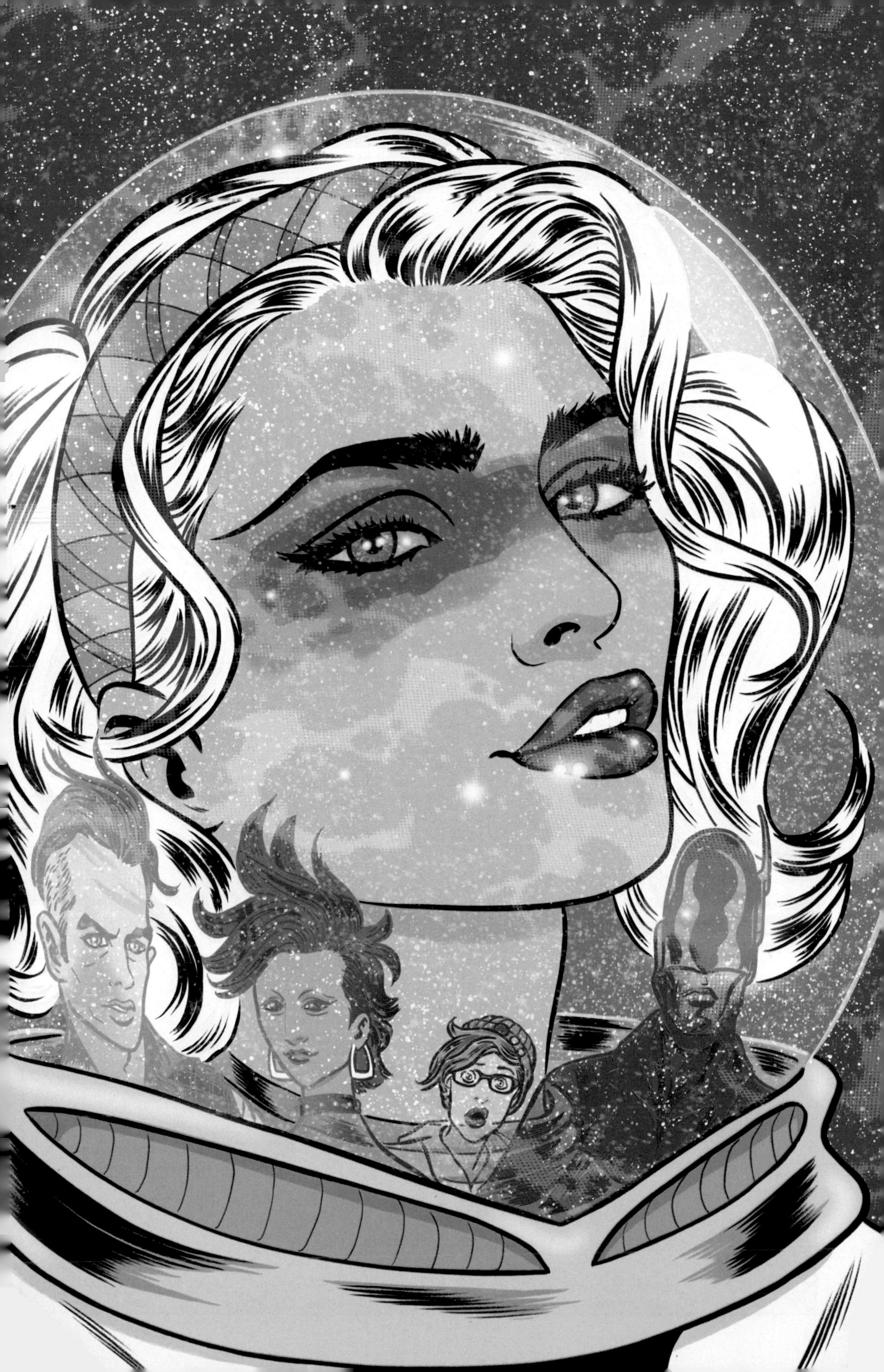

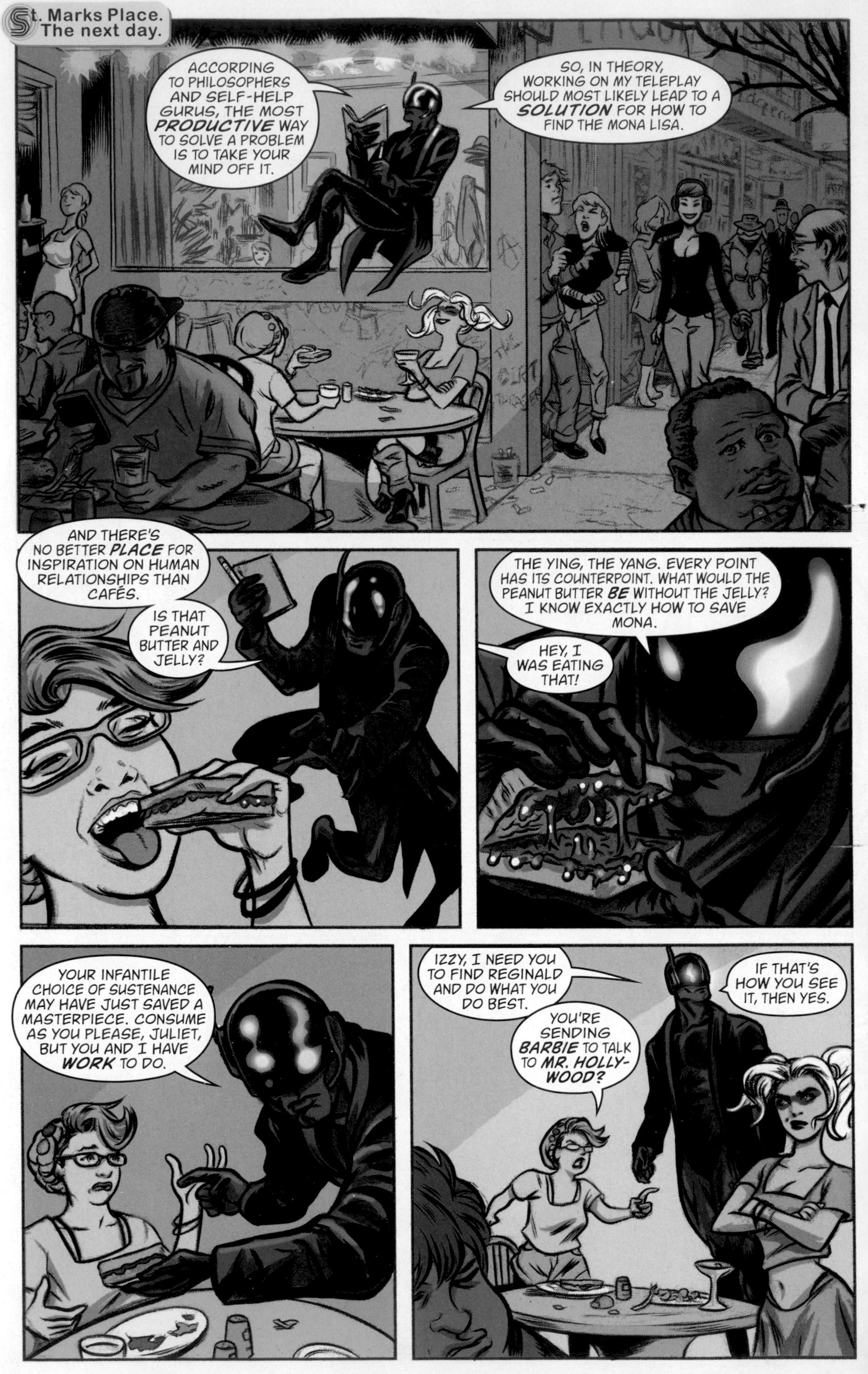
St. Marks Place. The next day.
ACCORDING TO PHILOSOPHERS AND SELF-HELP GURUS, THE MOST PRODUCTIVE WAY TO SOLVE A PROBLEM IS TO TAKE YOUR MIND OFF IT.
SO, IN THEORY, WORKING ON MY TELEPLAY SHOULD MOST LIKELY LEAD TO A SOLUTION FOR HOW TO FIND THE MONA LISA.
AND THERE'S NO BETTER PLACE FOR INSPIRATION ON HUMAN RELATIONSHIPS THAN CAFÉS.
IS THAT PEANUT BUTTER AND JELLY?
THE YING, THE YANG. EVERY POINT HAS ITS COUNTERPOINT. WHAT WOULD THE PEANUT BUTTER BE WITHOUT THE JELLY? I KNOW EXACTLY HOW TO SAVE MONA.
HEY, I WAS EATING THAT!
YOUR INFANTILE CHOICE OF SUSTENANCE MAY HAVE JUST SAVED A MASTERPIECE. CONSUME AS YOU PLEASE, JULIET, BUT YOU AND I HAVE WORK TO DO.
IZZY, I NEED YOU TO FIND REGINALD AND DO WHAT YOU DO BEST.
YOU'RE SENDING BARBIE TO TALK TO MR. HOLLY-WOOD?
IF THAT'S HOW YOU SEE IT, THEN YES.

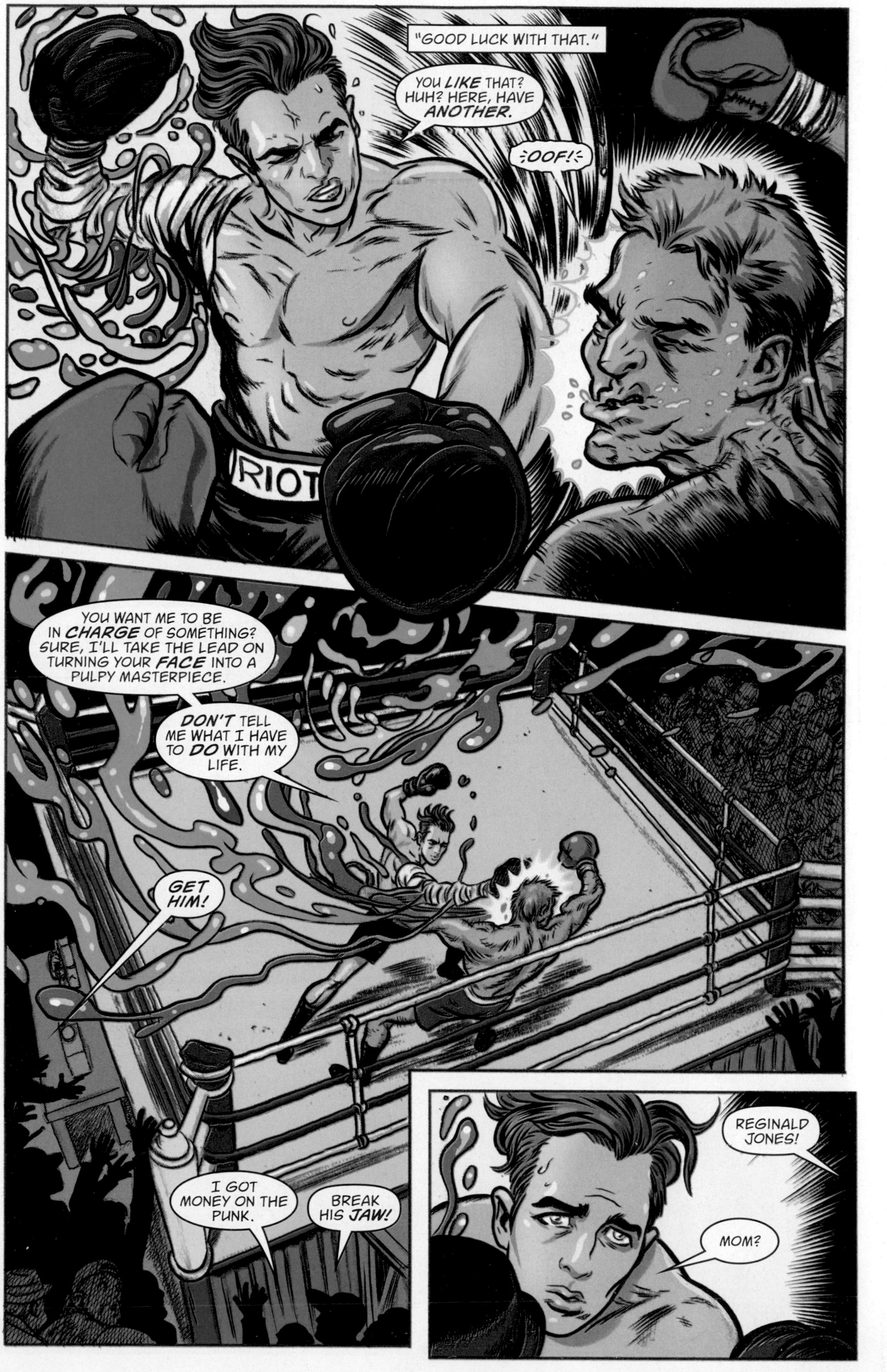
"GOOD LUCK WITH THAT."
YOU LIKE THAT? HUH? HERE, HAVE ANOTHER.
OOF!
RIOT
YOU WANT ME TO BE IN CHARGE OF SOMETHING? SURE, I'LL TAKE THE LEAD ON TURNING YOUR FACE INTO A PULPY MASTERPIECE.
DON'T TELL ME WHAT I HAVE TO DO WITH MY LIFE.
GET HIM!
I GOT MONEY ON THE PUNK.
BREAK HIS JAW!
REGINALD JONES!
MOM?

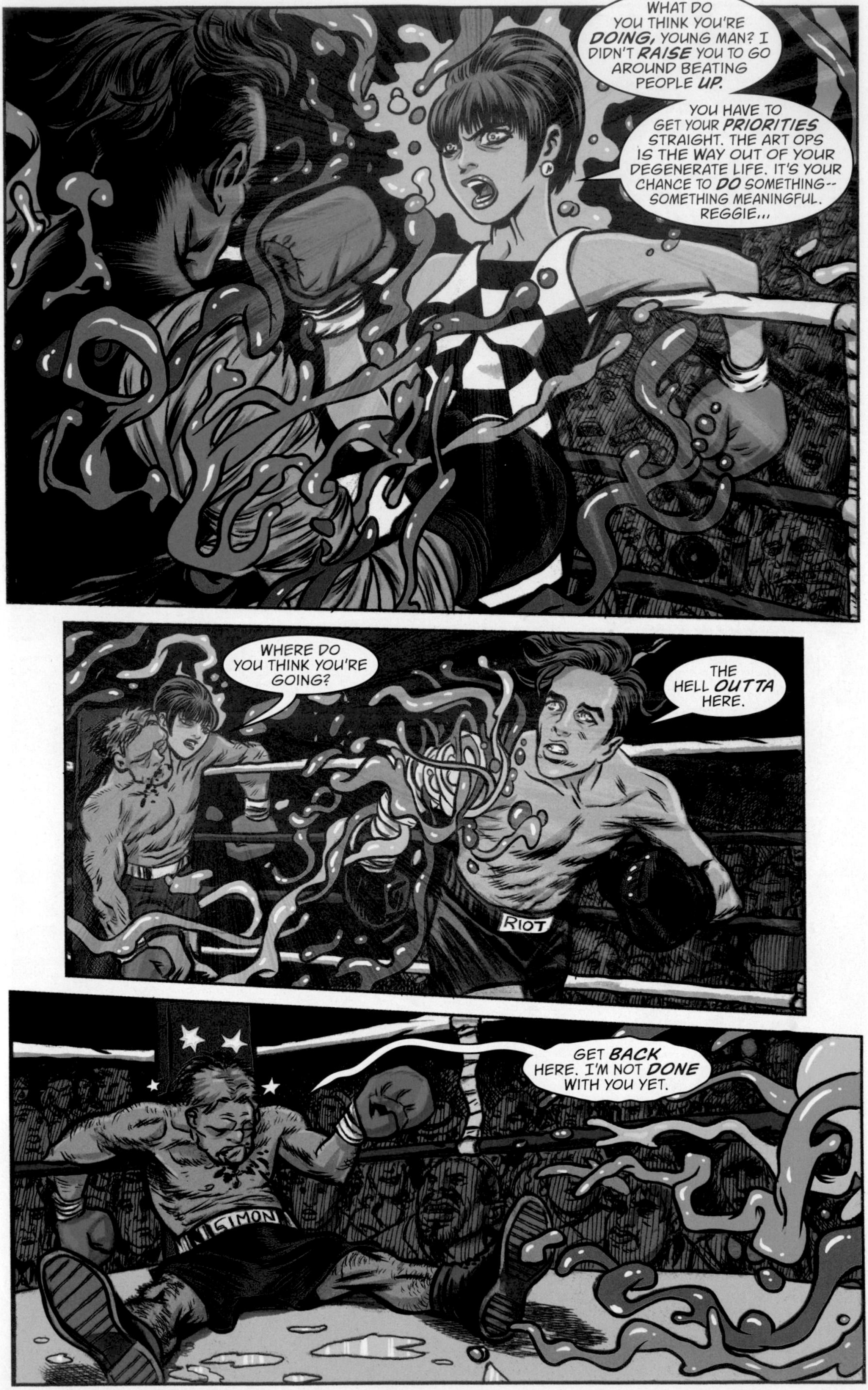
WHAT DO YOU THINK YOU'RE DOING, YOUNG MAN? I DIDN'T RAISE YOU TO GO AROUND BEATING PEOPLE UP.
YOU HAVE TO GET YOUR PRIORITIES STRAIGHT. THE ART OPS IS THE WAY OUT OF YOUR DEGENERATE LIFE. IT'S YOUR CHANCE TO DO SOMETHING-- SOMETHING MEANINGFUL. REGGIE...
WHERE DO YOU THINK YOU'RE GOING?
THE HELL OUTTA HERE.
RIOT
GET BACK HERE. I'M NOT DONE WITH YOU YET.
SIMON

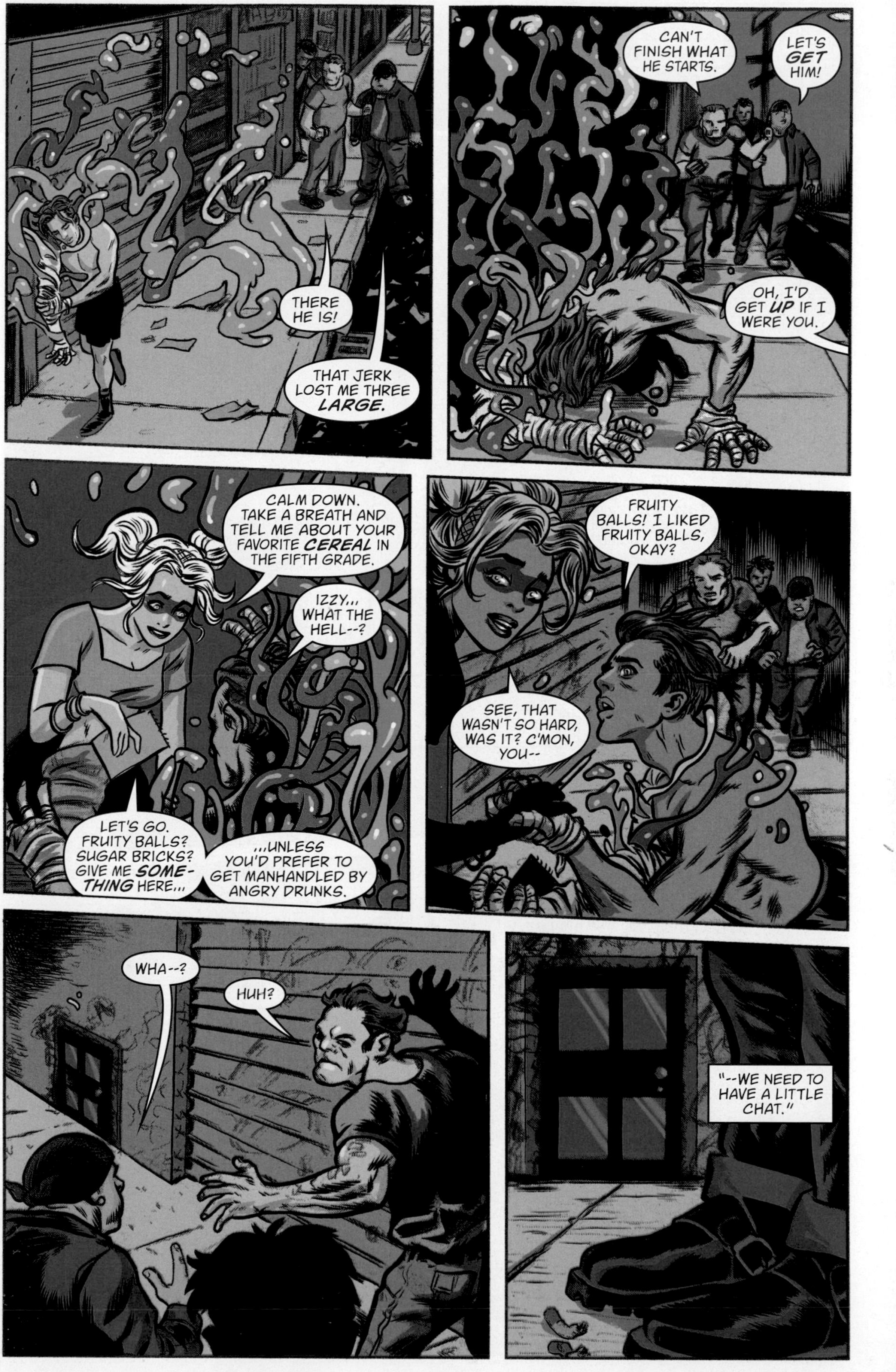
THERE HE IS!
THAT JERK LOST ME THREE LARGE.
CAN'T FINISH WHAT HE STARTS.
LET'S GET HIM!
OH, I'D GET UP IF I WERE YOU.
CALM DOWN. TAKE A BREATH AND TELL ME ABOUT YOUR FAVORITE CEREAL IN THE FIFTH GRADE.
IZZY... WHAT THE HELL--?
LET'S GO. FRUITY BALLS? SUGAR BRICKS? GIVE ME SOME-THING HERE...
...UNLESS YOU'D PREFER TO GET MANHANDLED BY ANGRY DRUNKS.
FRUITY BALLS! I LIKED FRUITY BALLS, OKAY?
SEE, THAT WASN'T SO HARD, WAS IT? C'MON, YOU--
WHA--?
HUH?
"--WE NEED TO HAVE A LITTLE CHAT."

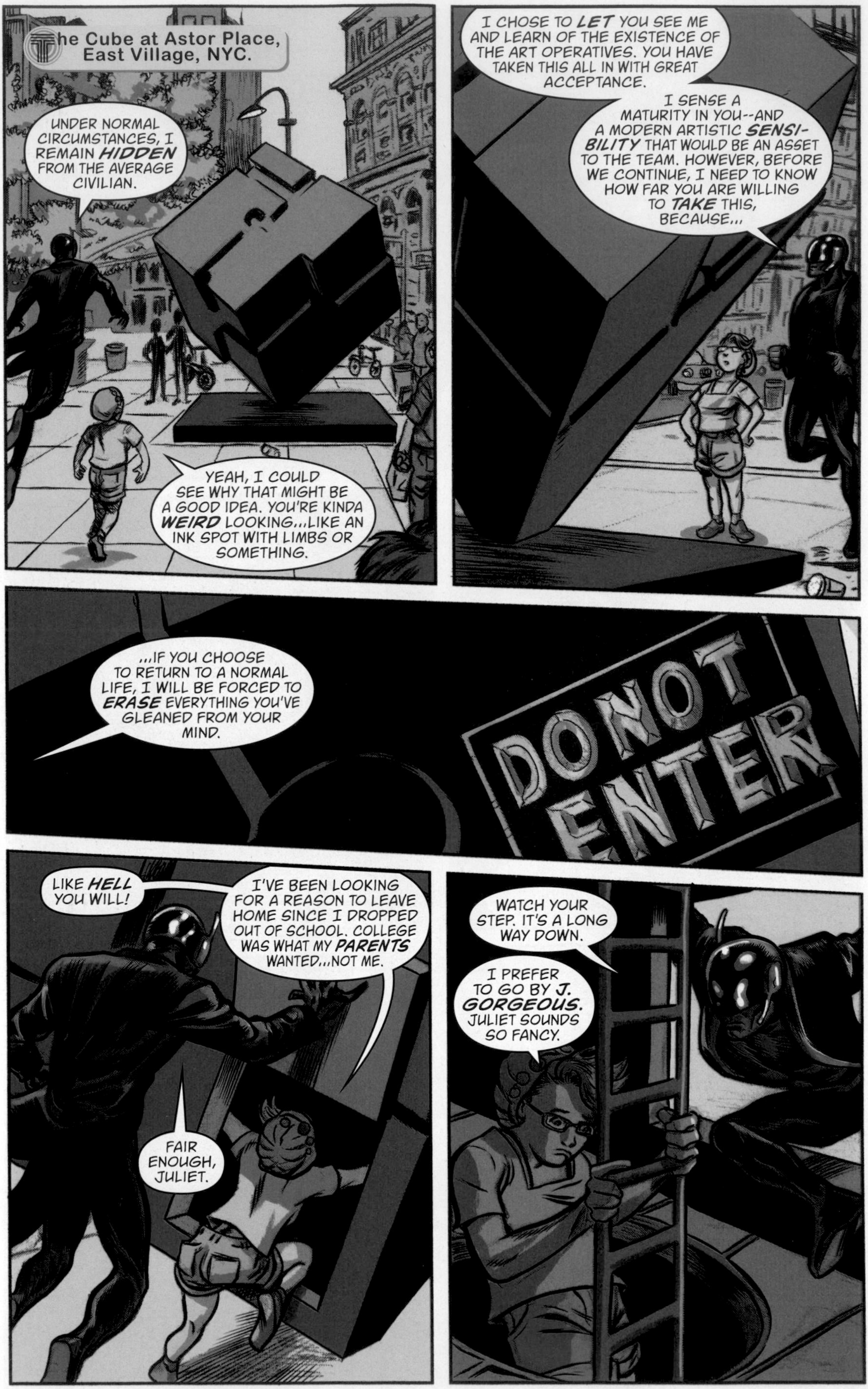
The Cube at Astor Place, East Village, NYC.
UNDER NORMAL CIRCUMSTANCES, I REMAIN HIDDEN FROM THE AVERAGE CIVILIAN.
YEAH, I COULD SEE WHY THAT MIGHT BE A GOOD IDEA. YOU'RE KINDA WEIRD LOOKING...LIKE AN INK SPOT WITH LIMBS OR SOMETHING.
I CHOSE TO LET YOU SEE ME AND LEARN OF THE EXISTENCE OF THE ART OPERATIVES. YOU HAVE TAKEN THIS ALL IN WITH GREAT ACCEPTANCE.
I SENSE A MATURITY IN YOU--AND A MODERN ARTISTIC SENSIBILITY THAT WOULD BE AN ASSET TO THE TEAM. HOWEVER, BEFORE WE CONTINUE, I NEED TO KNOW HOW FAR YOU ARE WILLING TO TAKE THIS, BECAUSE...
...IF YOU CHOOSE TO RETURN TO A NORMAL LIFE, I WILL BE FORCED TO ERASE EVERYTHING YOU'VE GLEANED FROM YOUR MIND.
DO NOT ENTER
LIKE HELL YOU WILL!
I'VE BEEN LOOKING FOR A REASON TO LEAVE HOME SINCE I DROPPED OUT OF SCHOOL. COLLEGE WAS WHAT MY PARENTS WANTED...NOT ME.
FAIR ENOUGH, JULIET.
WATCH YOUR STEP. IT'S A LONG WAY DOWN.
I PREFER TO GO BY J. GORGEOUS. JULIET SOUNDS SO FANCY.

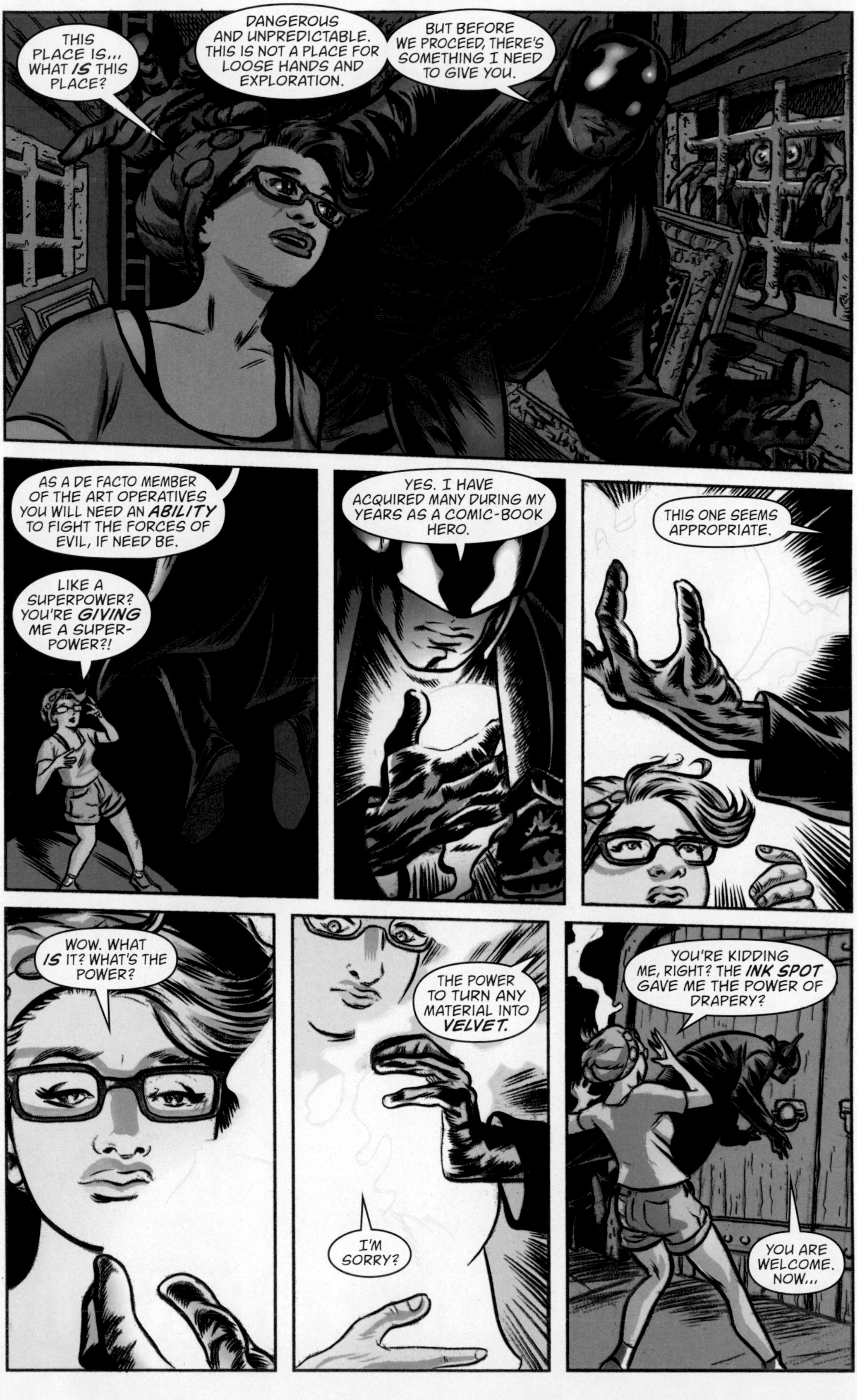
THIS PLACE IS... WHAT *IS* THIS PLACE?
DANGEROUS AND UNPREDICTABLE. THIS IS NOT A PLACE FOR LOOSE HANDS AND EXPLORATION.
BUT BEFORE WE PROCEED, THERE'S SOMETHING I NEED TO GIVE YOU.
AS A DE FACTO MEMBER OF THE ART OPERATIVES YOU WILL NEED AN *ABILITY* TO FIGHT THE FORCES OF EVIL, IF NEED BE.
LIKE A SUPERPOWER? YOU'RE *GIVING* ME A SUPER-POWER?!
YES. I HAVE ACQUIRED MANY DURING MY YEARS AS A COMIC-BOOK HERO.
THIS ONE SEEMS APPROPRIATE.
WOW. WHAT *IS* IT? WHAT'S THE POWER?
THE POWER TO TURN ANY MATERIAL INTO *VELVET.*
I'M SORRY?
YOU'RE KIDDING ME, RIGHT? THE *INK SPOT* GAVE ME THE POWER OF DRAPERY?
YOU ARE WELCOME. NOW...

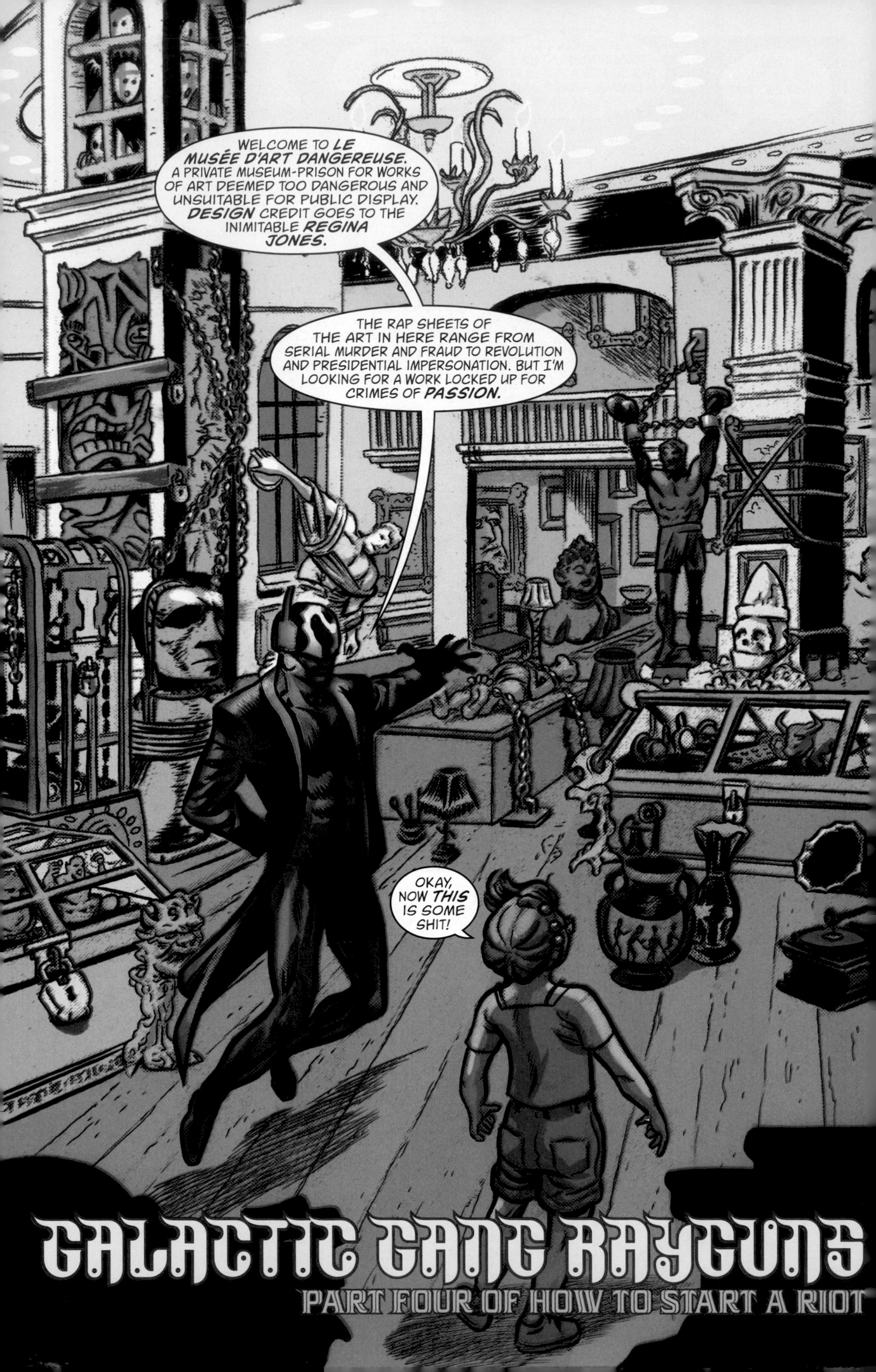

WELCOME TO LE MUSÉE D'ART DANGEREUSE. A PRIVATE MUSEUM-PRISON FOR WORKS OF ART DEEMED TOO DANGEROUS AND UNSUITABLE FOR PUBLIC DISPLAY. DESIGN CREDIT GOES TO THE INIMITABLE REGINA JONES.
THE RAP SHEETS OF THE ART IN HERE RANGE FROM SERIAL MURDER AND FRAUD TO REVOLUTION AND PRESIDENTIAL IMPERSONATION. BUT I'M LOOKING FOR A WORK LOCKED UP FOR CRIMES OF PASSION.
OKAY, NOW THIS IS SOME SHIT!
GALACTIC GANG RAYGUNS
PART FOUR OF HOW TO START A RIOT

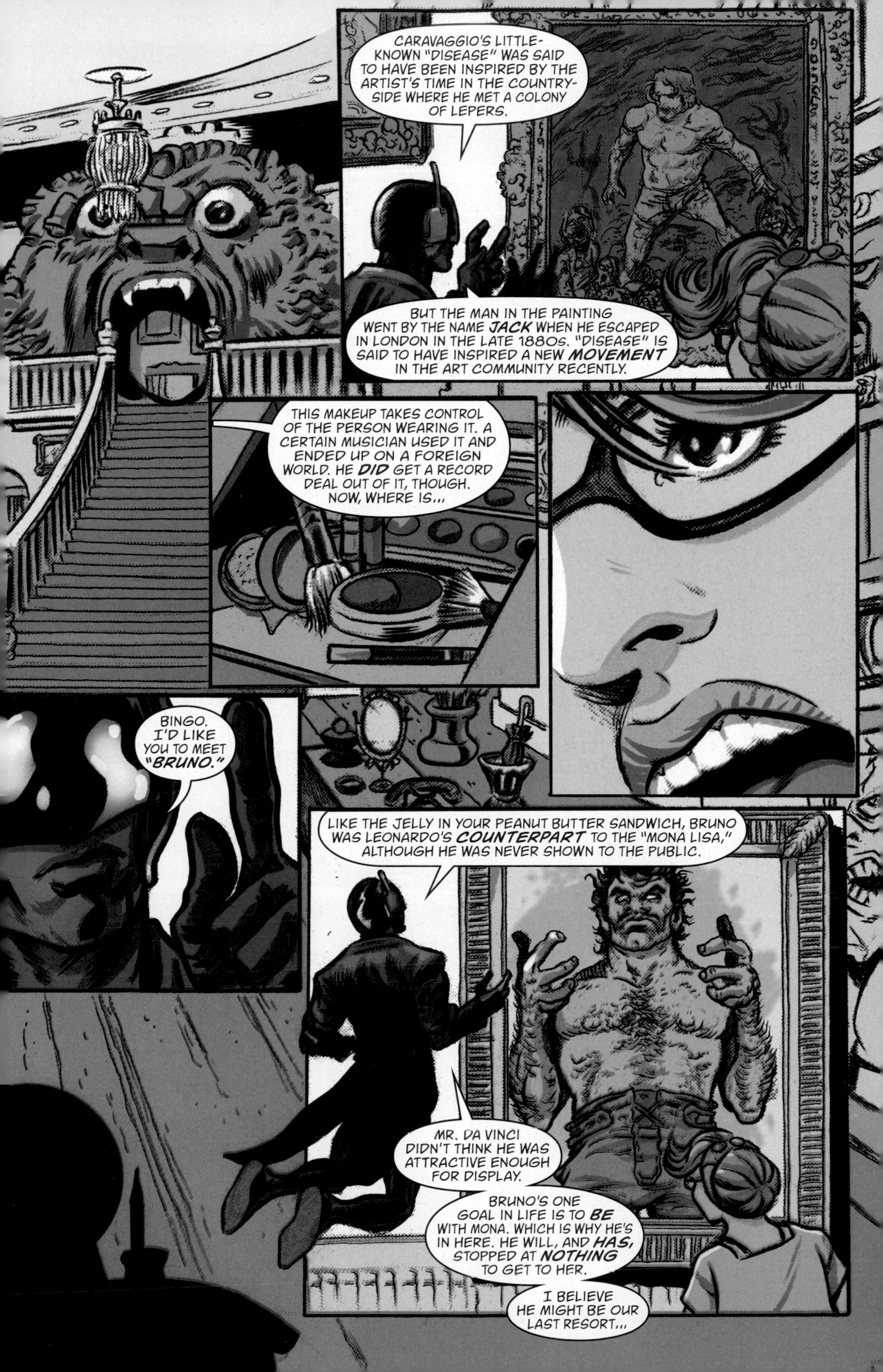
CARAVAGGIO'S LITTLE-KNOWN "DISEASE" WAS SAID TO HAVE BEEN INSPIRED BY THE ARTIST'S TIME IN THE COUNTRYSIDE WHERE HE MET A COLONY OF LEPERS.
BUT THE MAN IN THE PAINTING WENT BY THE NAME ***JACK*** WHEN HE ESCAPED IN LONDON IN THE LATE 1880s. "DISEASE" IS SAID TO HAVE INSPIRED A NEW ***MOVEMENT*** IN THE ART COMMUNITY RECENTLY.
THIS MAKEUP TAKES CONTROL OF THE PERSON WEARING IT. A CERTAIN MUSICIAN USED IT AND ENDED UP ON A FOREIGN WORLD. HE ***DID*** GET A RECORD DEAL OUT OF IT, THOUGH. NOW, WHERE IS...
BINGO. I'D LIKE YOU TO MEET ***"BRUNO."***
LIKE THE JELLY IN YOUR PEANUT BUTTER SANDWICH, BRUNO WAS LEONARDO'S ***COUNTERPART*** TO THE "MONA LISA," ALTHOUGH HE WAS NEVER SHOWN TO THE PUBLIC.
MR. DA VINCI DIDN'T THINK HE WAS ATTRACTIVE ENOUGH FOR DISPLAY.
BRUNO'S ONE GOAL IN LIFE IS TO ***BE*** WITH MONA. WHICH IS WHY HE'S IN HERE. HE WILL, AND ***HAS,*** STOPPED AT ***NOTHING*** TO GET TO HER.
I BELIEVE HE MIGHT BE OUR LAST RESORT...

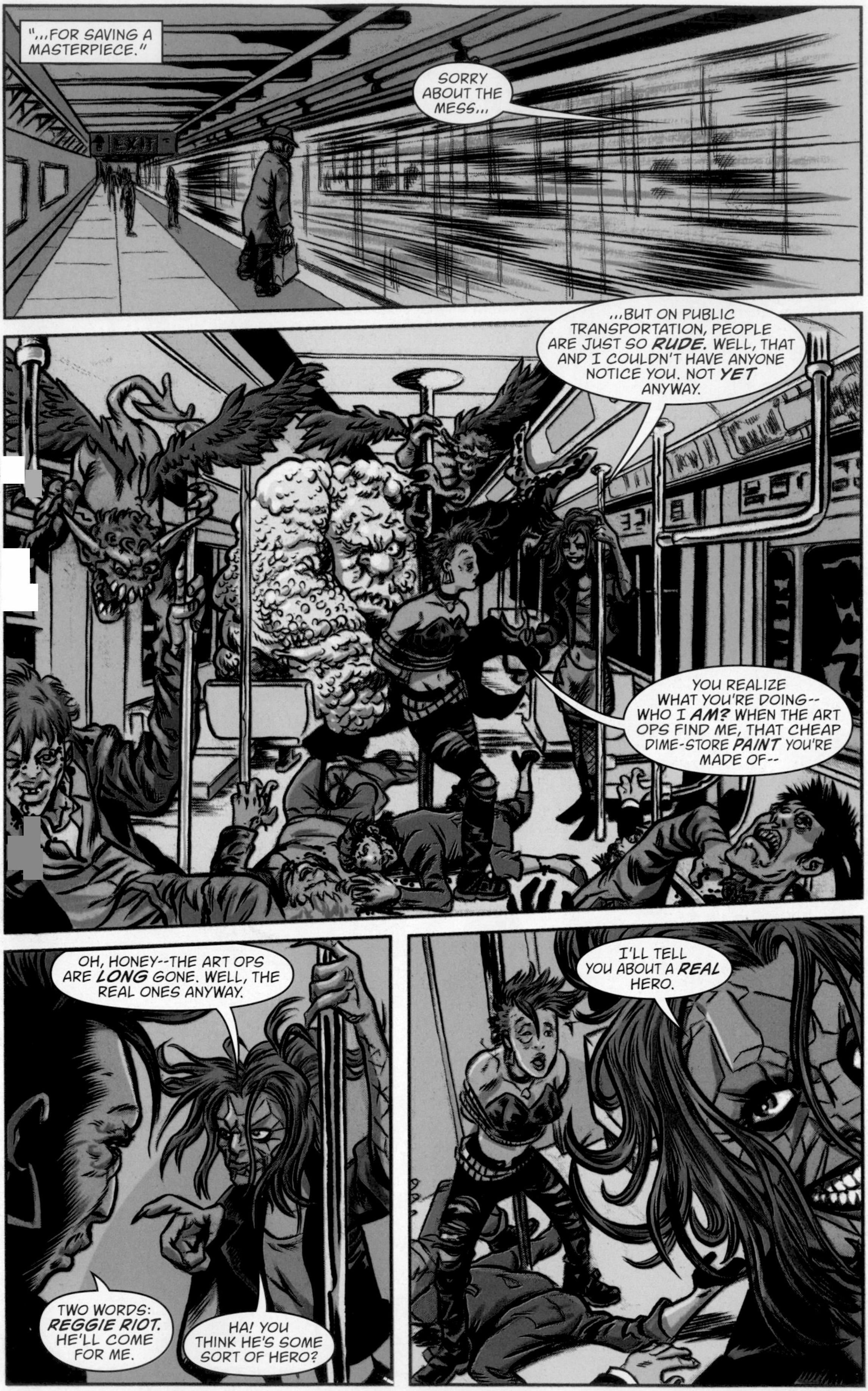
"...FOR SAVING A MASTERPIECE."
SORRY ABOUT THE MESS...
...BUT ON PUBLIC TRANSPORTATION, PEOPLE ARE JUST SO RUDE. WELL, THAT AND I COULDN'T HAVE ANYONE NOTICE YOU. NOT YET ANYWAY.
YOU REALIZE WHAT YOU'RE DOING-- WHO I AM? WHEN THE ART OPS FIND ME, THAT CHEAP DIME-STORE PAINT YOU'RE MADE OF--
OH, HONEY--THE ART OPS ARE LONG GONE. WELL, THE REAL ONES ANYWAY.
TWO WORDS: REGGIE RIOT. HE'LL COME FOR ME.
HA! YOU THINK HE'S SOME SORT OF HERO?
I'LL TELL YOU ABOUT A REAL HERO.
EXIT

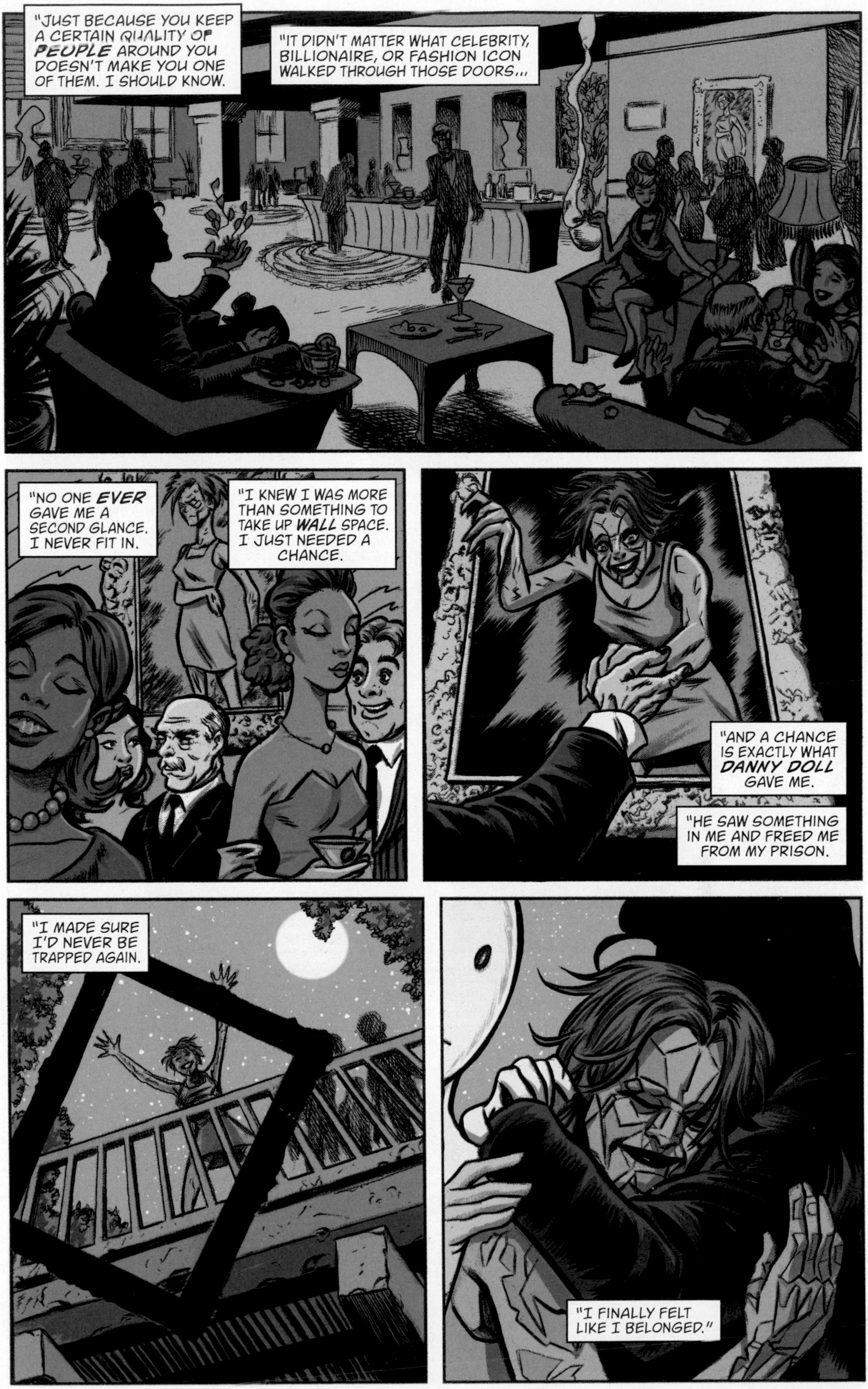
"JUST BECAUSE YOU KEEP A CERTAIN QUALITY OF *PEOPLE* AROUND YOU DOESN'T MAKE YOU ONE OF THEM. I SHOULD KNOW.
"IT DIDN'T MATTER WHAT CELEBRITY, BILLIONAIRE, OR FASHION ICON WALKED THROUGH THOSE DOORS...
"NO ONE *EVER* GAVE ME A SECOND GLANCE. I NEVER FIT IN.
"I KNEW I WAS MORE THAN SOMETHING TO TAKE UP *WALL* SPACE. I JUST NEEDED A CHANCE.
"AND A CHANCE IS EXACTLY WHAT *DANNY DOLL* GAVE ME.
"HE SAW SOMETHING IN ME AND FREED ME FROM MY PRISON.
"I MADE SURE I'D NEVER BE TRAPPED AGAIN.
"I FINALLY FELT LIKE I BELONGED."

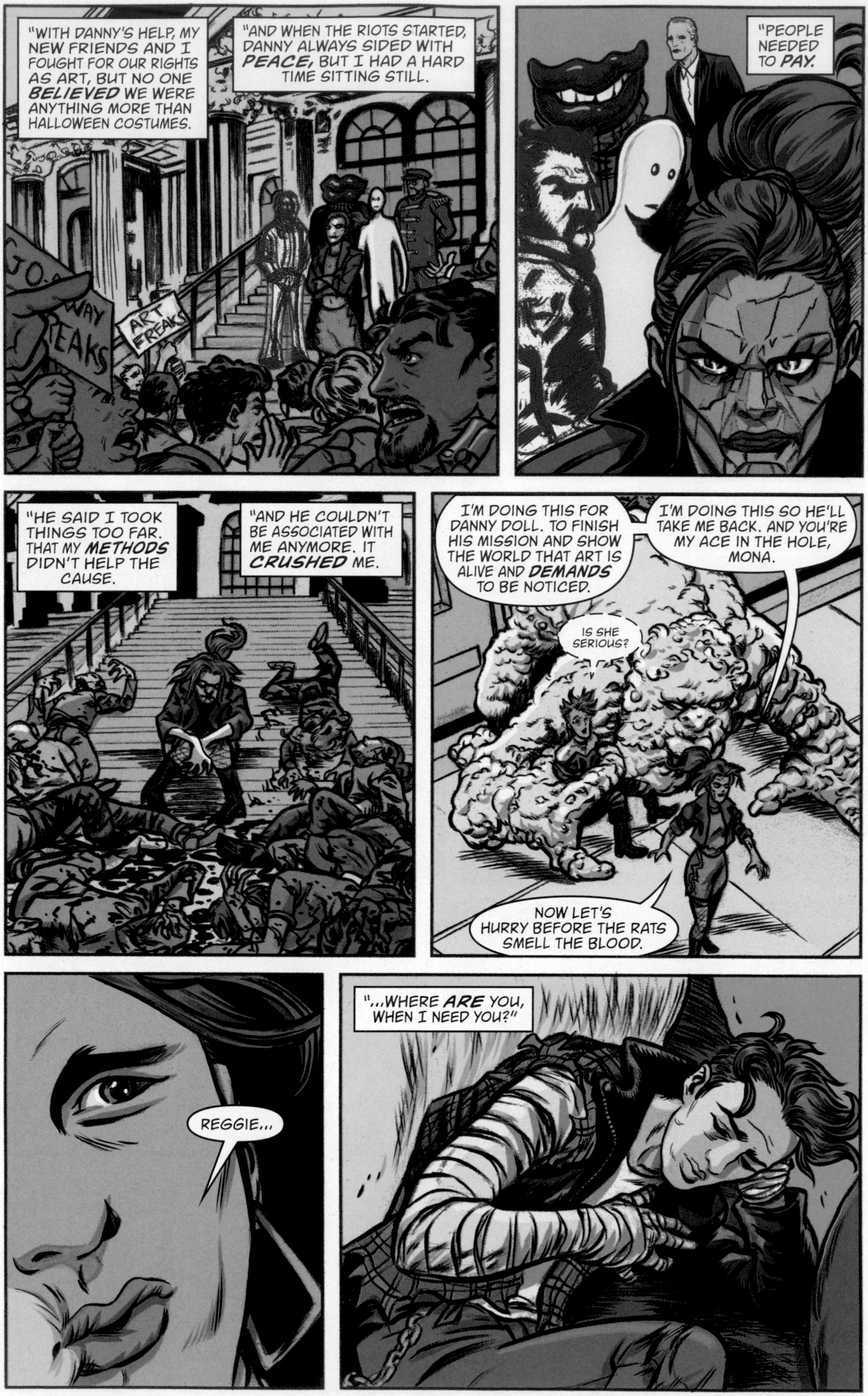
"WITH DANNY'S HELP, MY NEW FRIENDS AND I FOUGHT FOR OUR RIGHTS AS ART, BUT NO ONE BELIEVED WE WERE ANYTHING MORE THAN HALLOWEEN COSTUMES.
ART FREAKS
"AND WHEN THE RIOTS STARTED, DANNY ALWAYS SIDED WITH PEACE, BUT I HAD A HARD TIME SITTING STILL.
"PEOPLE NEEDED TO PAY.
"HE SAID I TOOK THINGS TOO FAR. THAT MY METHODS DIDN'T HELP THE CAUSE.
"AND HE COULDN'T BE ASSOCIATED WITH ME ANYMORE. IT CRUSHED ME.
I'M DOING THIS FOR DANNY DOLL. TO FINISH HIS MISSION AND SHOW THE WORLD THAT ART IS ALIVE AND DEMANDS TO BE NOTICED.
I'M DOING THIS SO HE'LL TAKE ME BACK. AND YOU'RE MY ACE IN THE HOLE, MONA.
IS SHE SERIOUS?
NOW LET'S HURRY BEFORE THE RATS SMELL THE BLOOD.
REGGIE...
"...WHERE ARE YOU, WHEN I NEED YOU?"

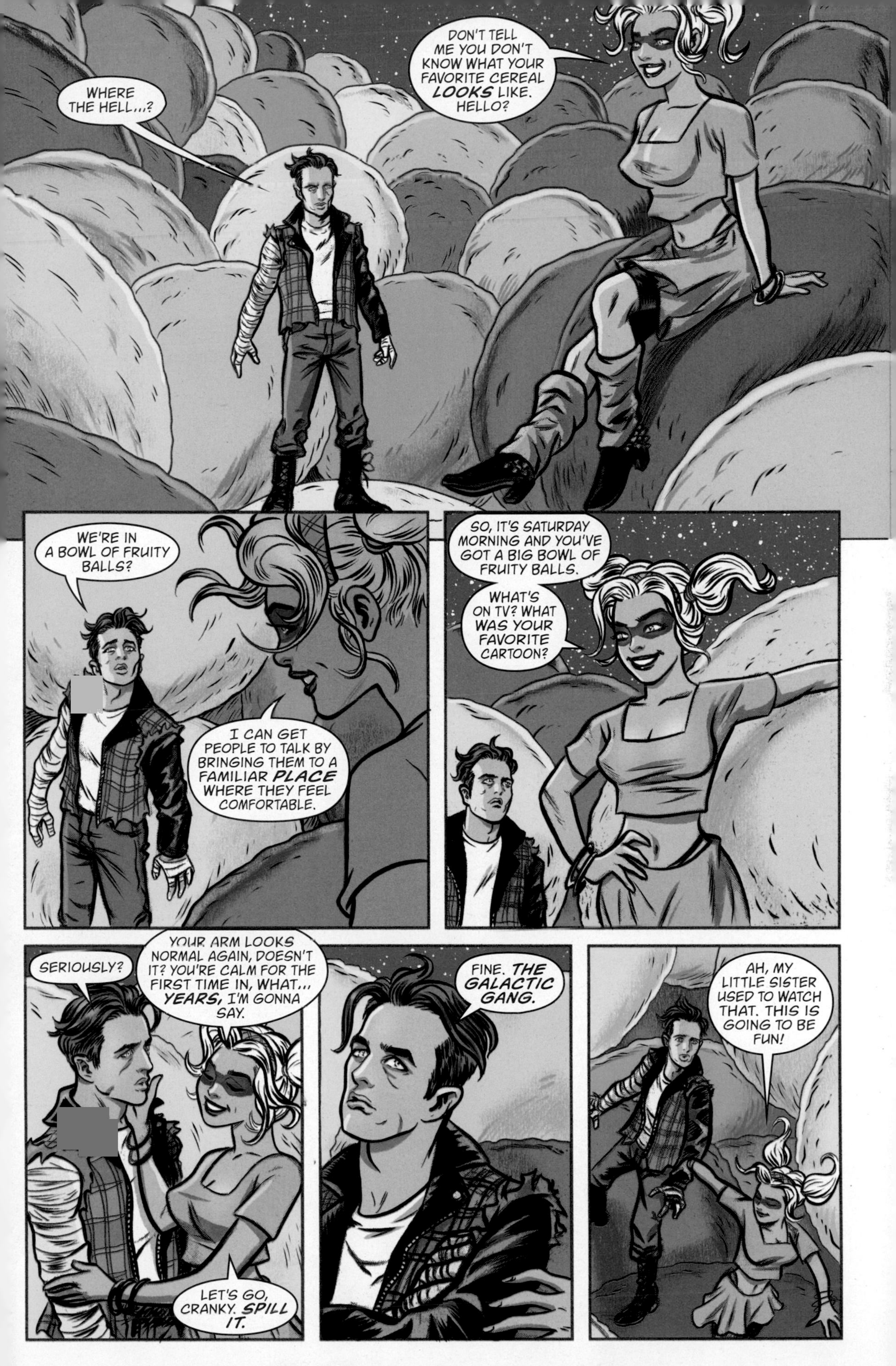
WHERE THE HELL...?
DON'T TELL ME YOU DON'T KNOW WHAT YOUR FAVORITE CEREAL LOOKS LIKE. HELLO?
WE'RE IN A BOWL OF FRUITY BALLS?
I CAN GET PEOPLE TO TALK BY BRINGING THEM TO A FAMILIAR PLACE WHERE THEY FEEL COMFORTABLE.
SO, IT'S SATURDAY MORNING AND YOU'VE GOT A BIG BOWL OF FRUITY BALLS.
WHAT'S ON TV? WHAT WAS YOUR FAVORITE CARTOON?
SERIOUSLY?
YOUR ARM LOOKS NORMAL AGAIN, DOESN'T IT? YOU'RE CALM FOR THE FIRST TIME IN, WHAT... YEARS, I'M GONNA SAY.
LET'S GO, CRANKY. SPILL IT.
FINE. THE GALACTIC GANG.
AH, MY LITTLE SISTER USED TO WATCH THAT. THIS IS GOING TO BE FUN!

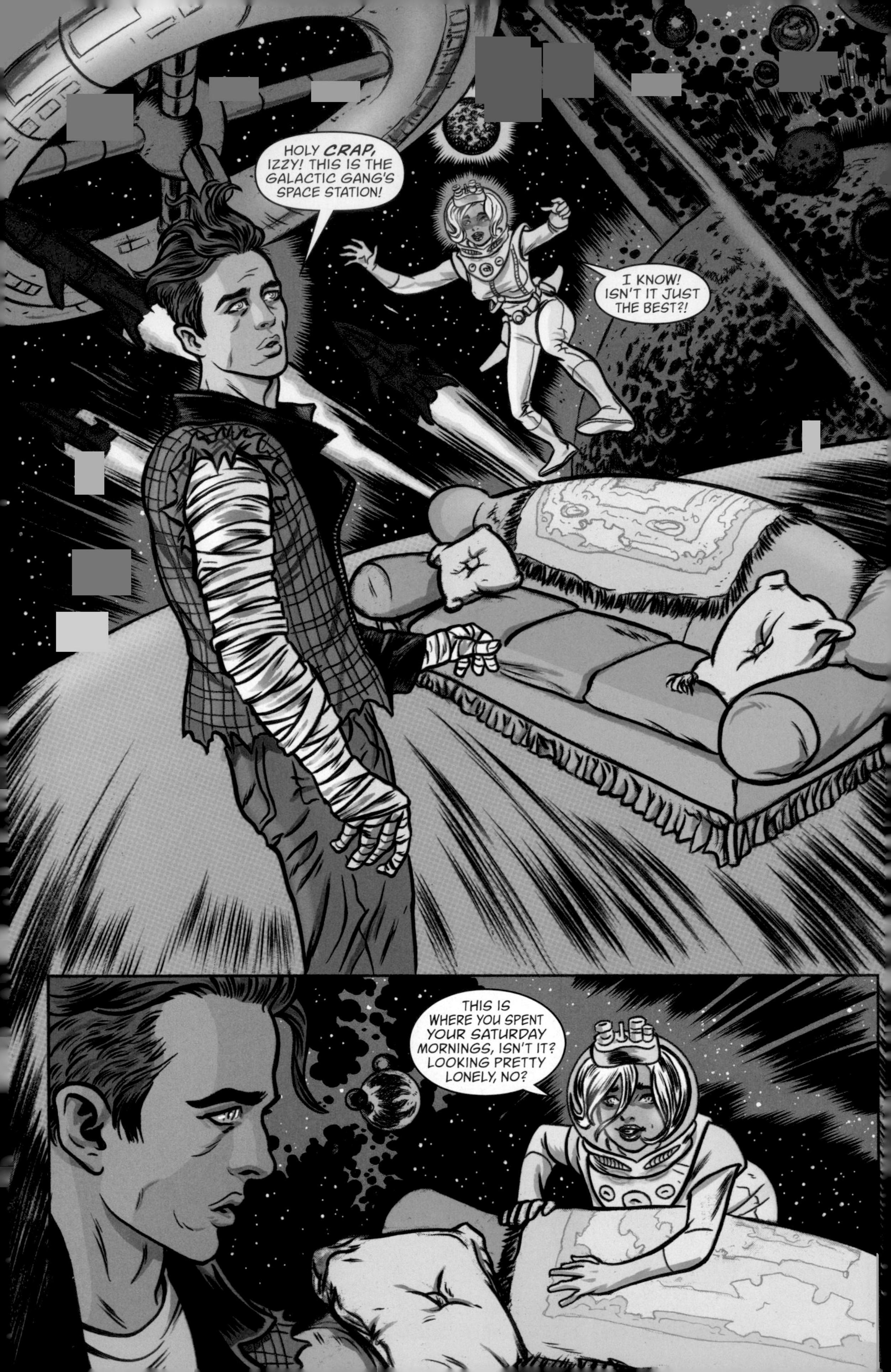
HOLY CRAP, IZZY! THIS IS THE GALACTIC GANG'S SPACE STATION!
I KNOW! ISN'T IT JUST THE BEST?!
THIS IS WHERE YOU SPENT YOUR SATURDAY MORNINGS, ISN'T IT? LOOKING PRETTY LONELY, NO?

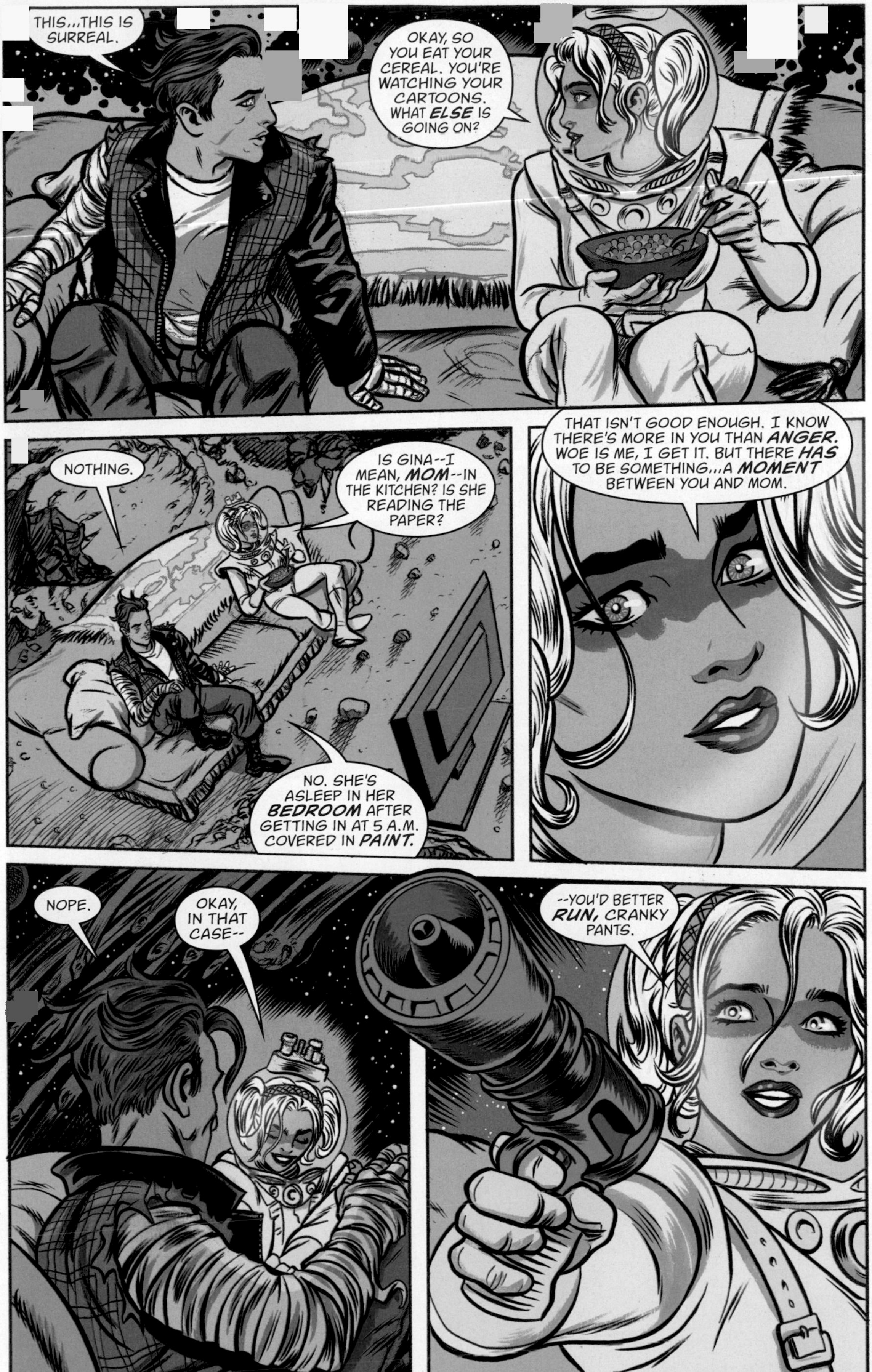

THIS...THIS IS SURREAL.
OKAY, SO YOU EAT YOUR CEREAL. YOU'RE WATCHING YOUR CARTOONS. WHAT ELSE IS GOING ON?
NOTHING.
IS GINA--I MEAN, MOM--IN THE KITCHEN? IS SHE READING THE PAPER?
NO. SHE'S ASLEEP IN HER BEDROOM AFTER GETTING IN AT 5 A.M. COVERED IN PAINT.
THAT ISN'T GOOD ENOUGH. I KNOW THERE'S MORE IN YOU THAN ANGER. WOE IS ME, I GET IT. BUT THERE HAS TO BE SOMETHING...A MOMENT BETWEEN YOU AND MOM.
NOPE.
OKAY, IN THAT CASE--
--YOU'D BETTER RUN, CRANKY PANTS.

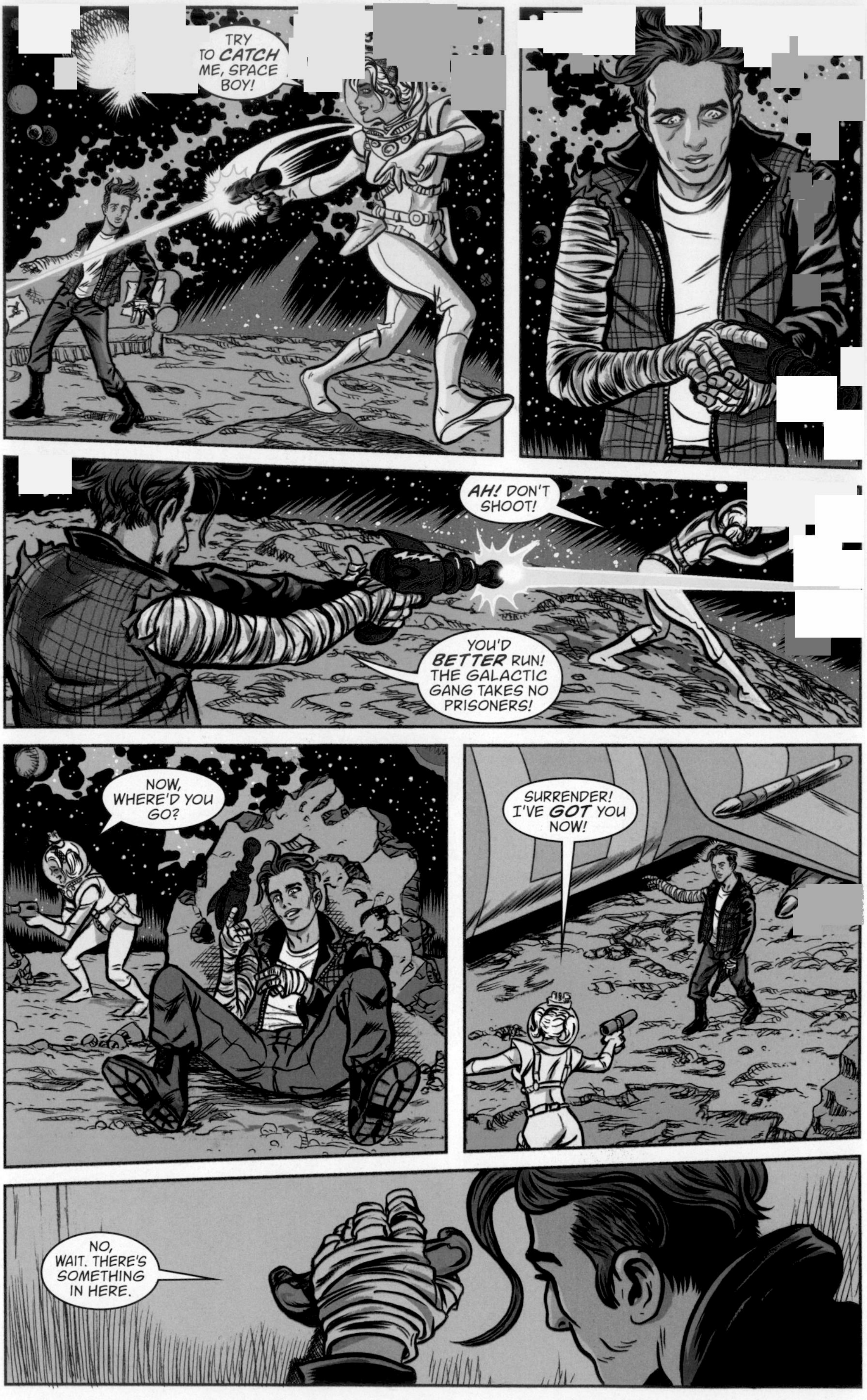
TRY TO CATCH ME, SPACE BOY!
AH! DON'T SHOOT!
YOU'D BETTER RUN! THE GALACTIC GANG TAKES NO PRISONERS!
NOW, WHERE'D YOU GO?
SURRENDER! I'VE GOT YOU NOW!
NO, WAIT. THERE'S SOMETHING IN HERE.

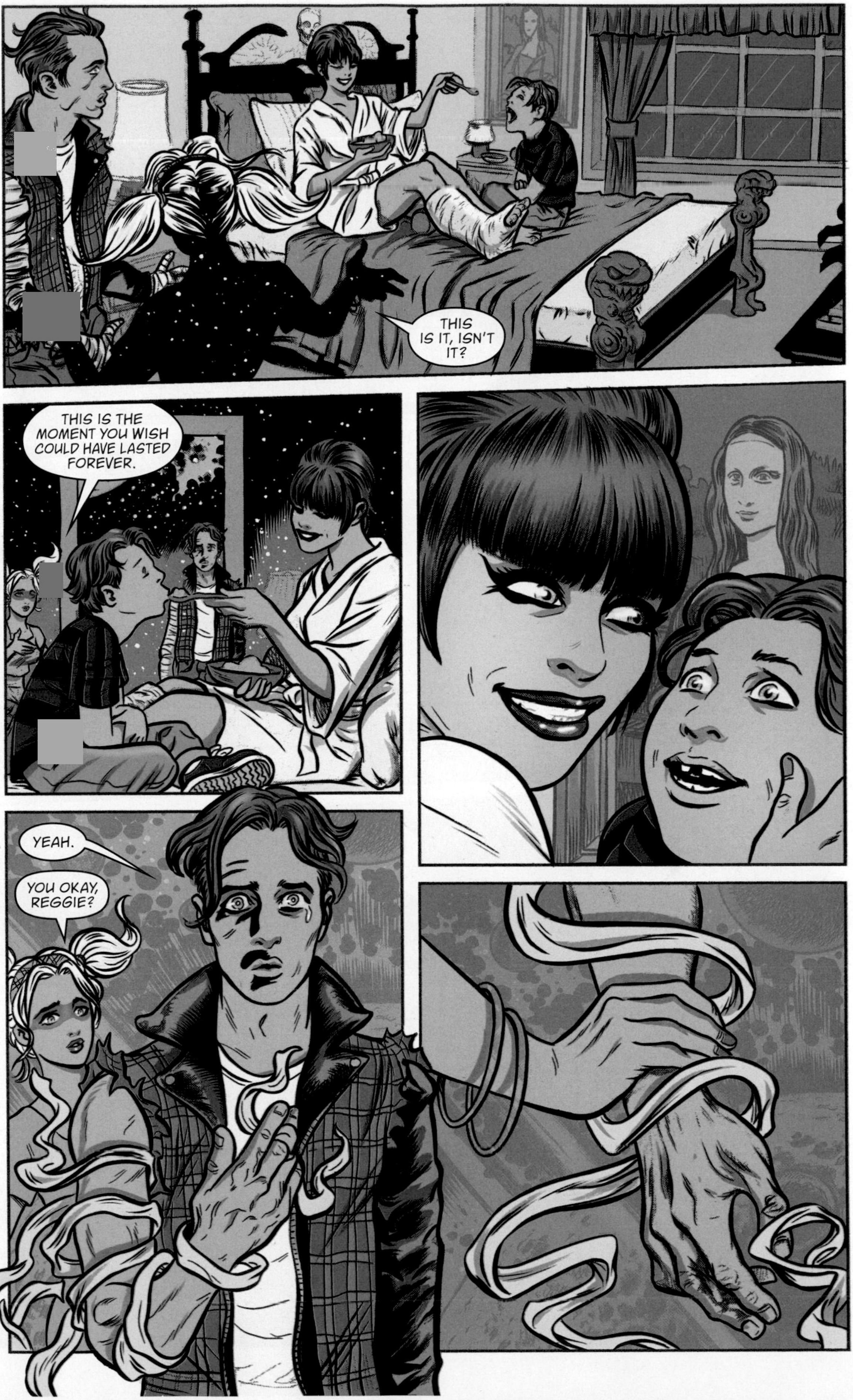
THIS IS IT, ISN'T IT?
THIS IS THE MOMENT YOU WISH COULD HAVE LASTED FOREVER.
YEAH.
YOU OKAY, REGGIE?

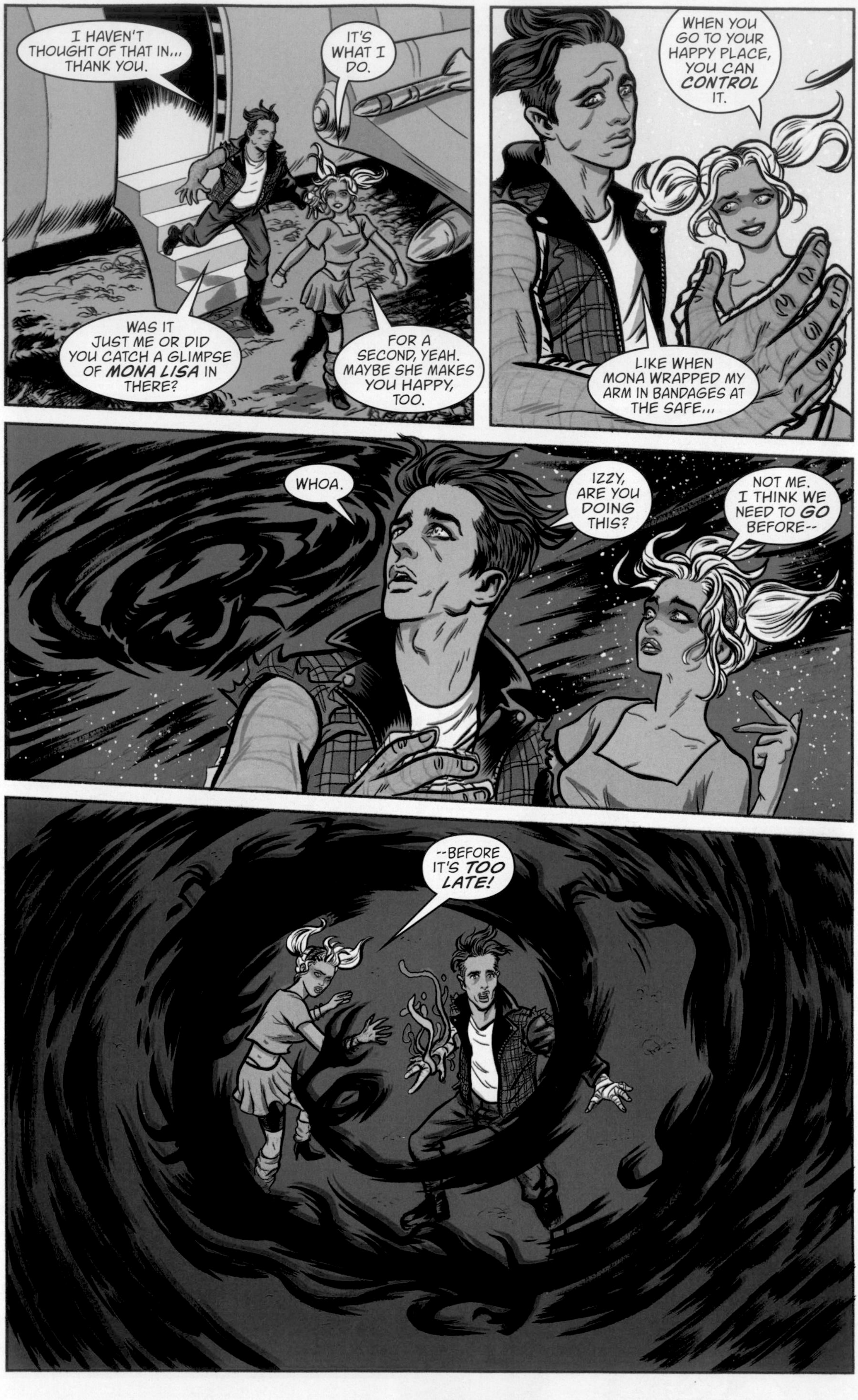

I HAVEN'T THOUGHT OF THAT IN... THANK YOU.
IT'S WHAT I DO.
WAS IT JUST ME OR DID YOU CATCH A GLIMPSE OF *MONA LISA* IN THERE?
FOR A SECOND, YEAH. MAYBE SHE MAKES YOU HAPPY, TOO.
WHEN YOU GO TO YOUR HAPPY PLACE, YOU CAN *CONTROL* IT.
LIKE WHEN MONA WRAPPED MY ARM IN BANDAGES AT THE SAFE...
WHOA.
IZZY, ARE YOU DOING THIS?
NOT ME. I THINK WE NEED TO *GO* BEFORE--
--BEFORE IT'S *TOO LATE!*

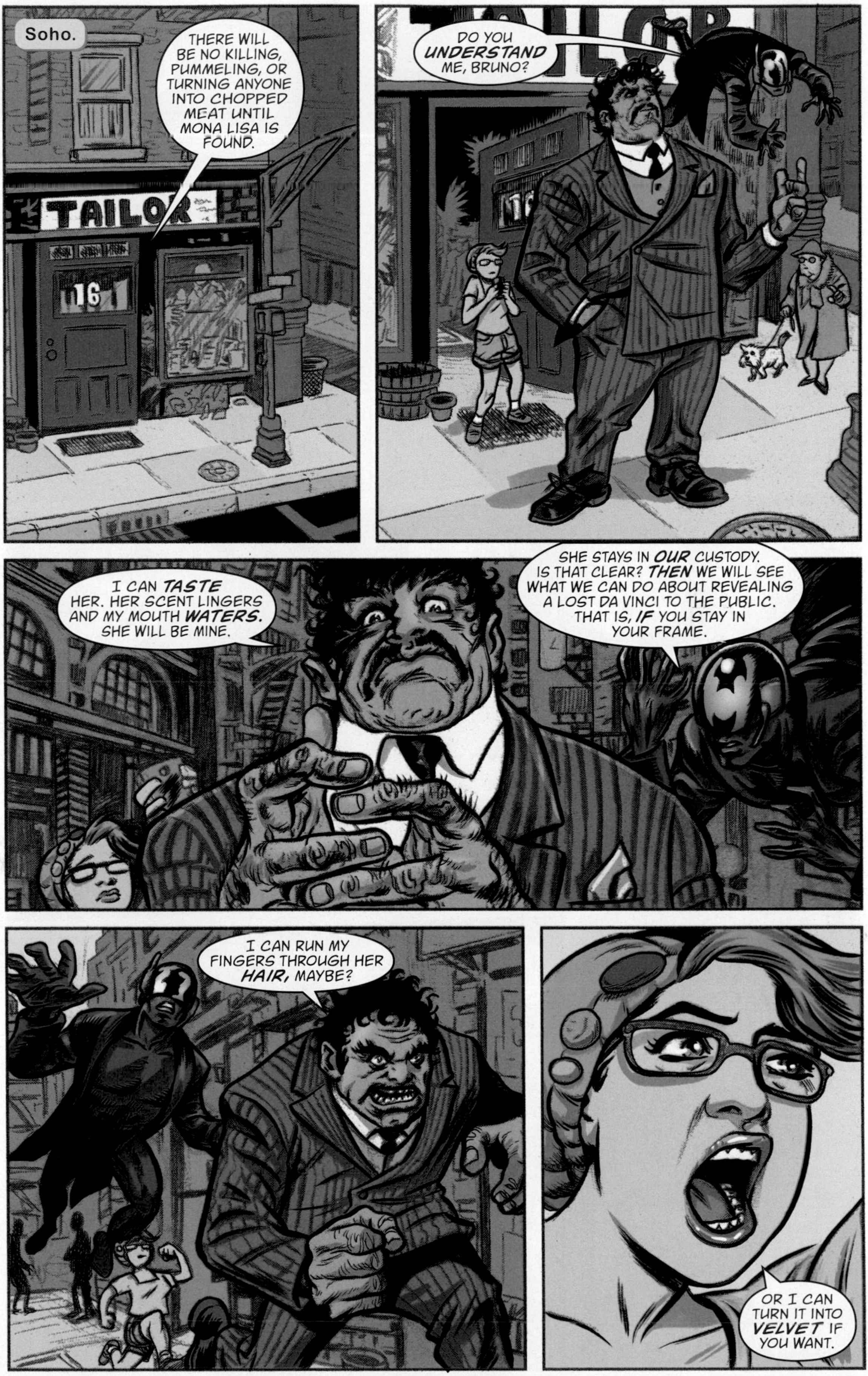
Soho.
THERE WILL BE NO KILLING, PUMMELING, OR TURNING ANYONE INTO CHOPPED MEAT UNTIL MONA LISA IS FOUND.
TAILOR
16
DO YOU UNDERSTAND ME, BRUNO?
I CAN TASTE HER. HER SCENT LINGERS AND MY MOUTH WATERS. SHE WILL BE MINE.
SHE STAYS IN OUR CUSTODY. IS THAT CLEAR? THEN WE WILL SEE WHAT WE CAN DO ABOUT REVEALING A LOST DA VINCI TO THE PUBLIC. THAT IS, IF YOU STAY IN YOUR FRAME.
I CAN RUN MY FINGERS THROUGH HER HAIR, MAYBE?
OR I CAN TURN IT INTO VELVET IF YOU WANT.

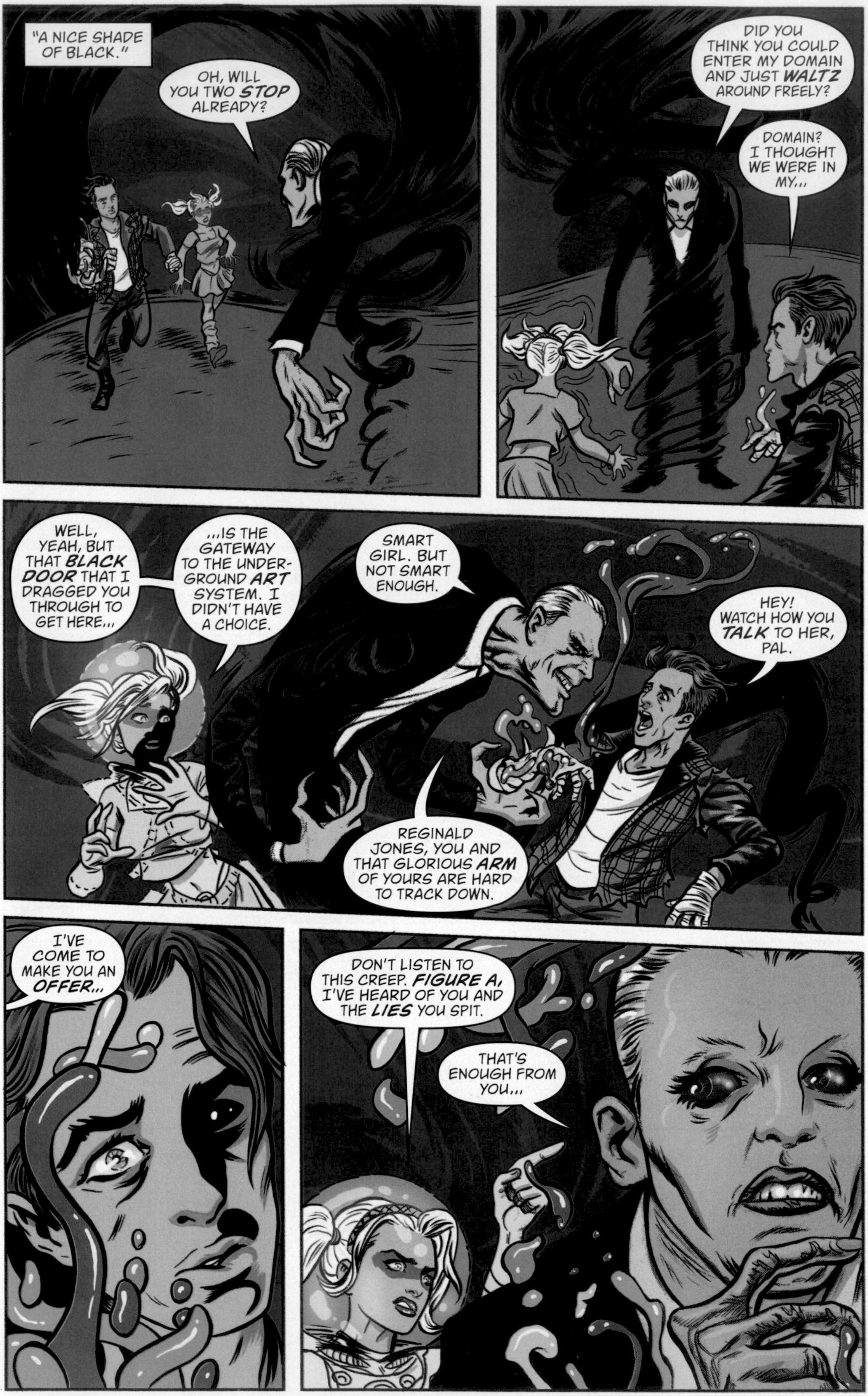
"A NICE SHADE OF BLACK."
OH, WILL YOU TWO *STOP* ALREADY?
DID YOU THINK YOU COULD ENTER MY DOMAIN AND JUST *WALTZ* AROUND FREELY?
DOMAIN? I THOUGHT WE WERE IN MY...
WELL, YEAH, BUT THAT *BLACK DOOR* THAT I DRAGGED YOU THROUGH TO GET HERE...
...IS THE GATEWAY TO THE UNDERGROUND *ART* SYSTEM. I DIDN'T HAVE A CHOICE.
SMART GIRL. BUT NOT SMART ENOUGH.
HEY! WATCH HOW YOU *TALK* TO HER, PAL.
REGINALD JONES, YOU AND THAT GLORIOUS *ARM* OF YOURS ARE HARD TO TRACK DOWN.
I'VE COME TO MAKE YOU AN *OFFER*...
DON'T LISTEN TO THIS CREEP. *FIGURE A*, I'VE HEARD OF YOU AND THE *LIES* YOU SPIT.
THAT'S ENOUGH FROM YOU...

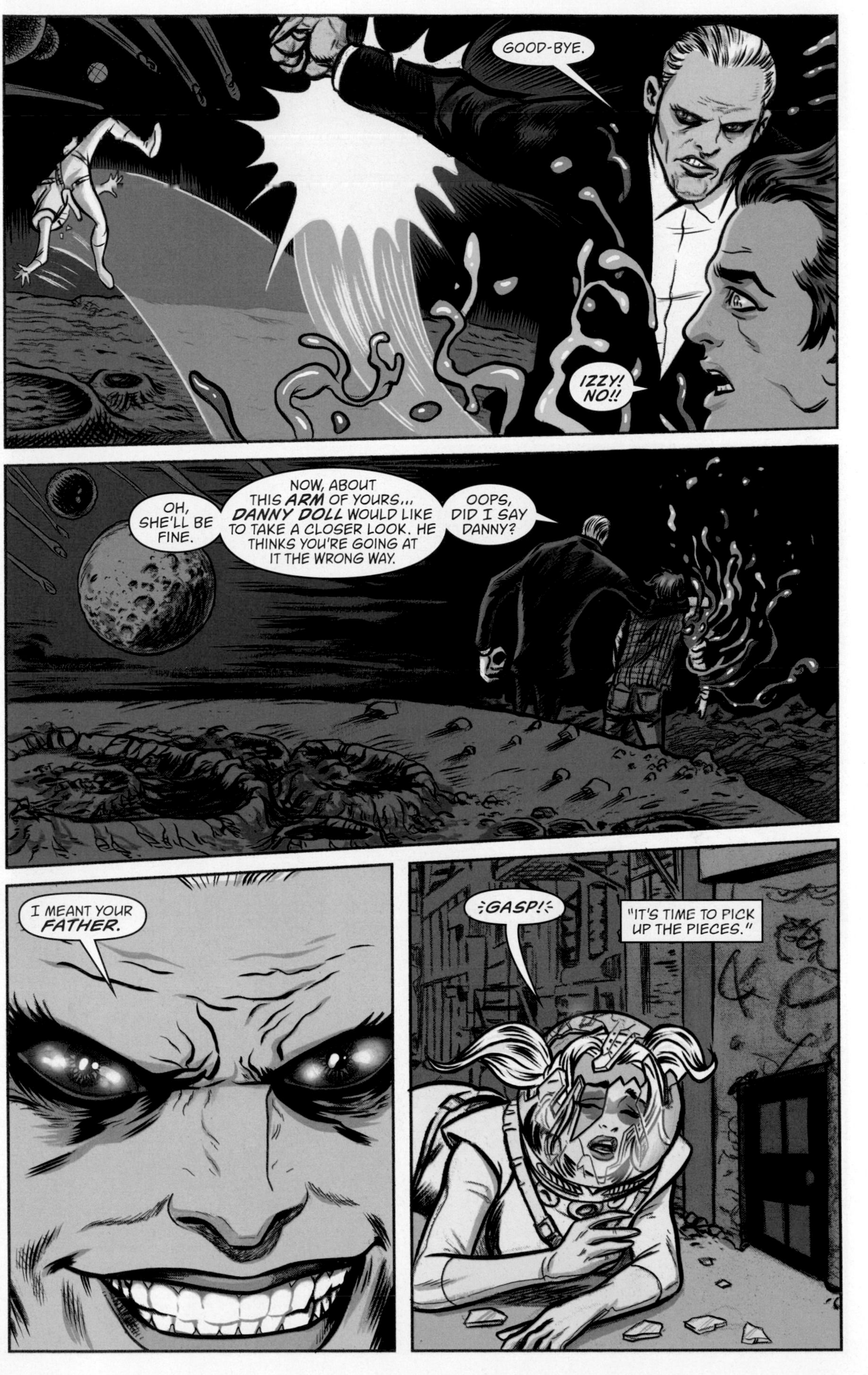
GOOD-BYE.
IZZY! NO!!
OH, SHE'LL BE FINE.
NOW, ABOUT THIS ARM OF YOURS... DANNY DOLL WOULD LIKE TO TAKE A CLOSER LOOK. HE THINKS YOU'RE GOING AT IT THE WRONG WAY.
OOPS, DID I SAY DANNY?
I MEANT YOUR FATHER.
GASP!
"IT'S TIME TO PICK UP THE PIECES."

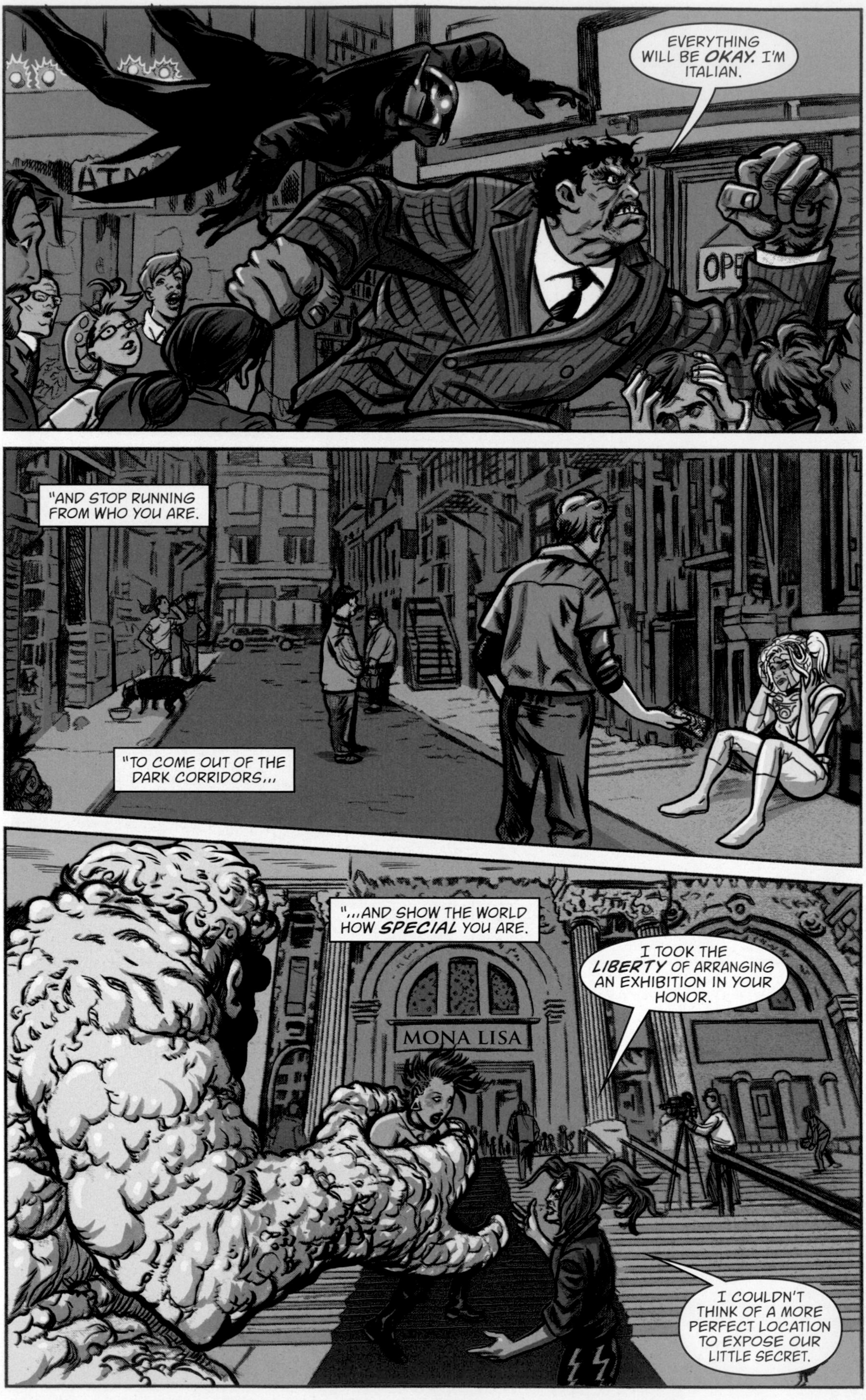
EVERYTHING WILL BE OKAY. I'M ITALIAN.
ATM
OPE
"AND STOP RUNNING FROM WHO YOU ARE.
"TO COME OUT OF THE DARK CORRIDORS...
"...AND SHOW THE WORLD HOW SPECIAL YOU ARE.
MONA LISA
I TOOK THE LIBERTY OF ARRANGING AN EXHIBITION IN YOUR HONOR.
I COULDN'T THINK OF A MORE PERFECT LOCATION TO EXPOSE OUR LITTLE SECRET.

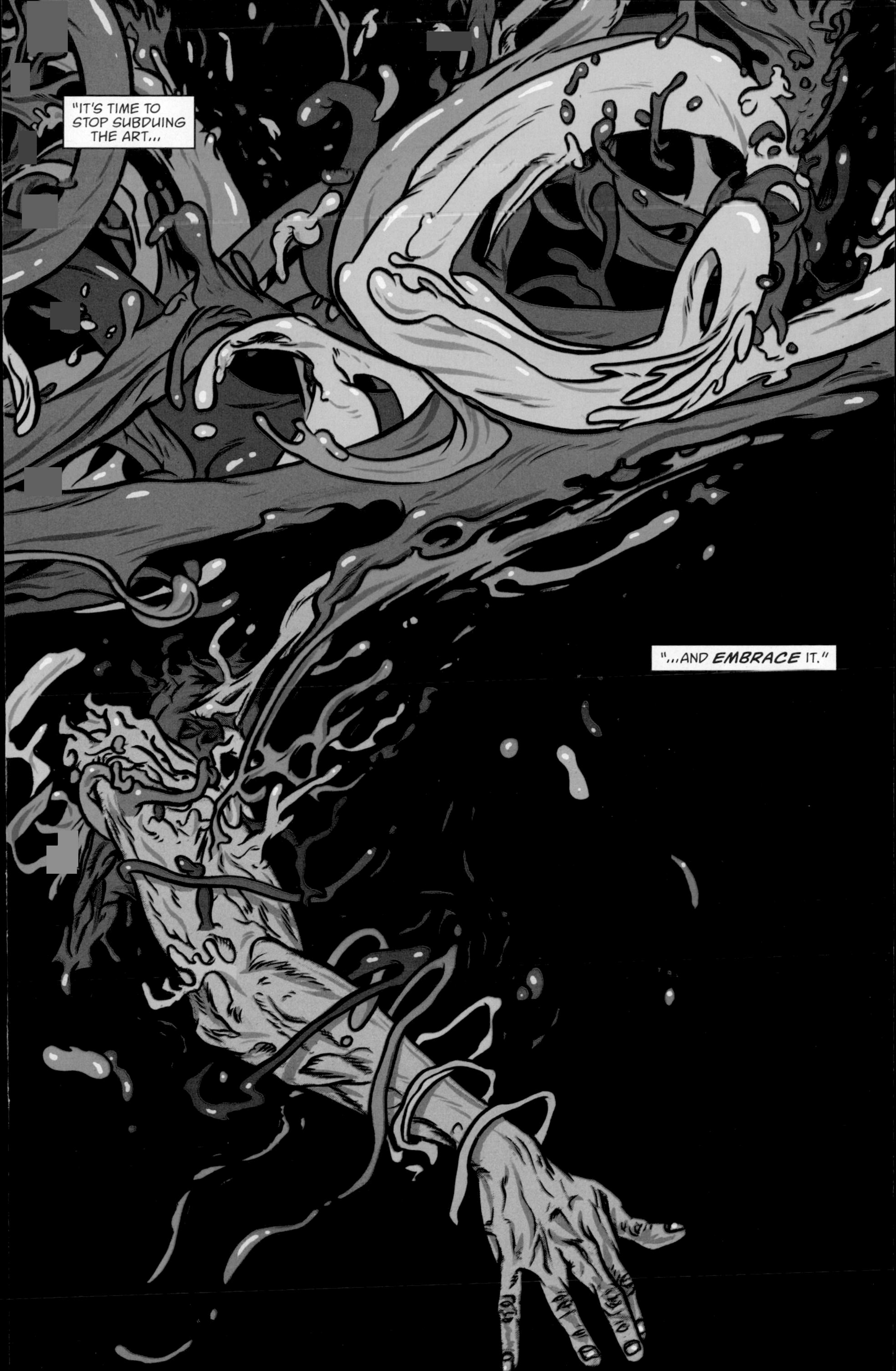
"IT'S TIME TO STOP SUBDUING THE ART...
"...AND EMBRACE IT."

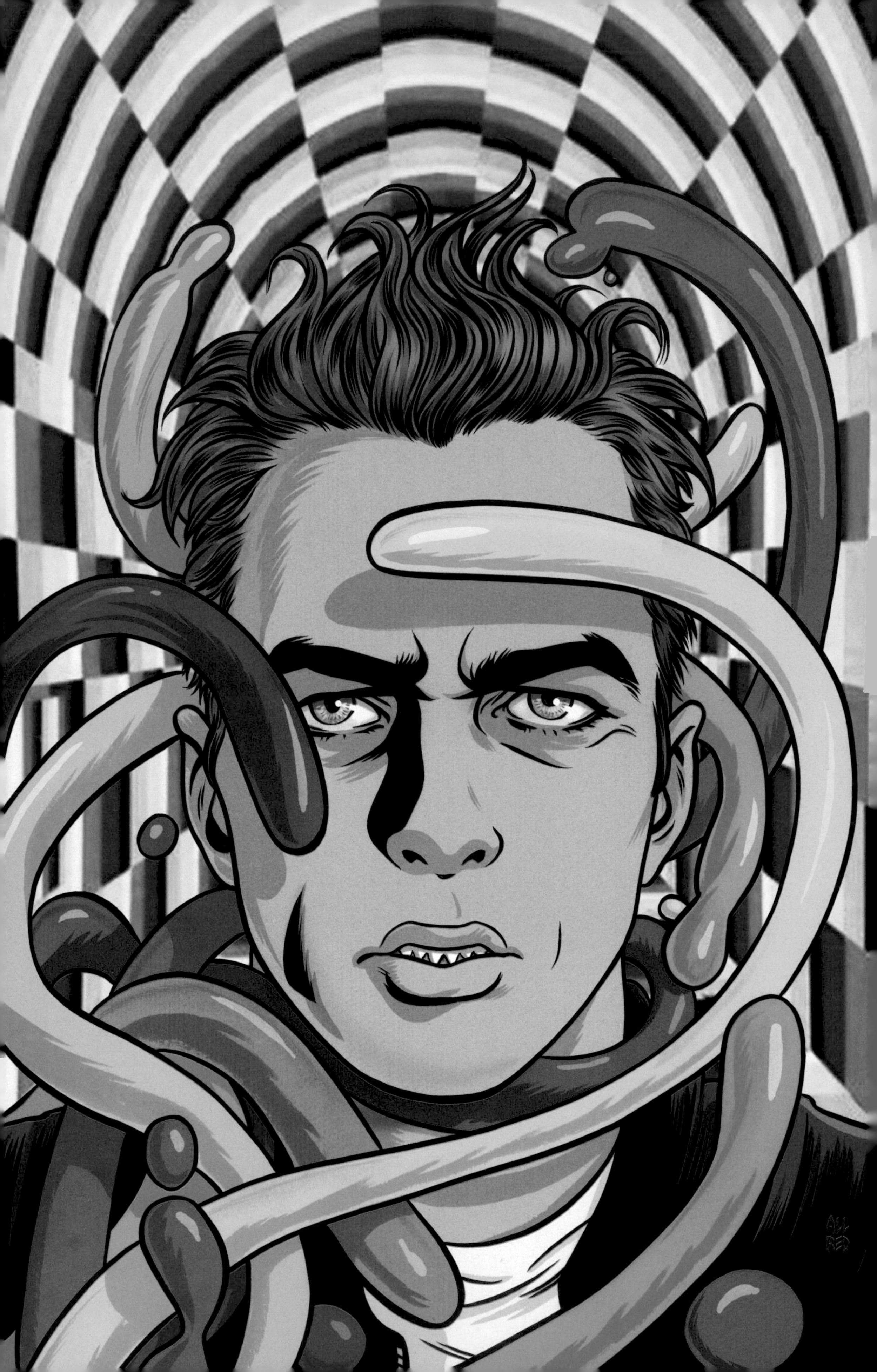
ALL
RED

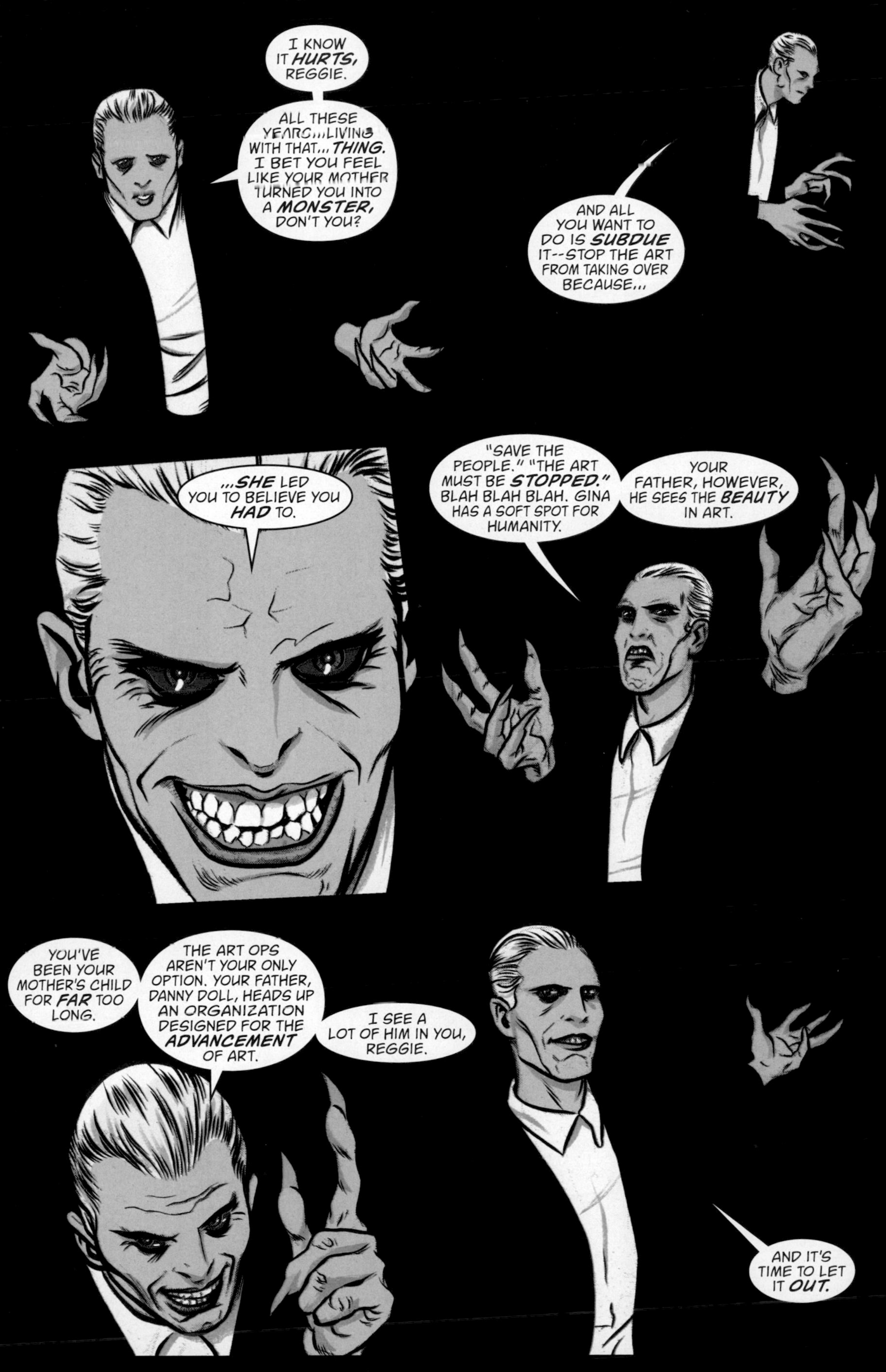
I KNOW IT HURTS, REGGIE.
ALL THESE YEARS...LIVING WITH THAT...THING. I BET YOU FEEL LIKE YOUR MOTHER TURNED YOU INTO A MONSTER, DON'T YOU?
AND ALL YOU WANT TO DO IS SUBDUE IT--STOP THE ART FROM TAKING OVER BECAUSE...
...SHE LED YOU TO BELIEVE YOU HAD TO.
"SAVE THE PEOPLE." "THE ART MUST BE STOPPED." BLAH BLAH BLAH. GINA HAS A SOFT SPOT FOR HUMANITY.
YOUR FATHER, HOWEVER, HE SEES THE BEAUTY IN ART.
YOU'VE BEEN YOUR MOTHER'S CHILD FOR FAR TOO LONG.
THE ART OPS AREN'T YOUR ONLY OPTION. YOUR FATHER, DANNY DOLL, HEADS UP AN ORGANIZATION DESIGNED FOR THE ADVANCEMENT OF ART.
I SEE A LOT OF HIM IN YOU, REGGIE.
AND IT'S TIME TO LET IT OUT.

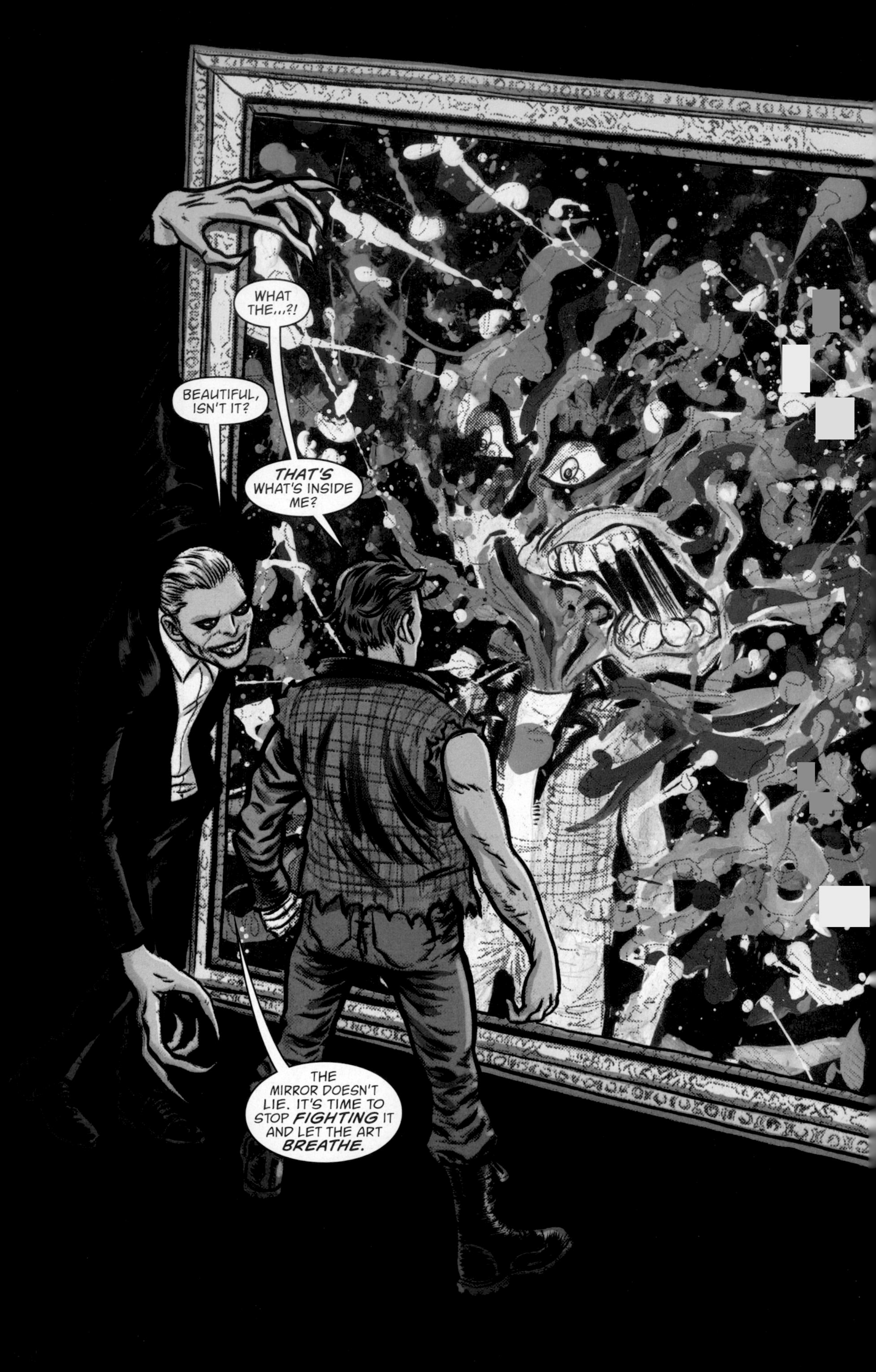
WHAT THE...?!
BEAUTIFUL, ISN'T IT?
THAT'S WHAT'S INSIDE ME?
THE MIRROR DOESN'T LIE. IT'S TIME TO STOP *FIGHTING* IT AND LET THE ART *BREATHE.*

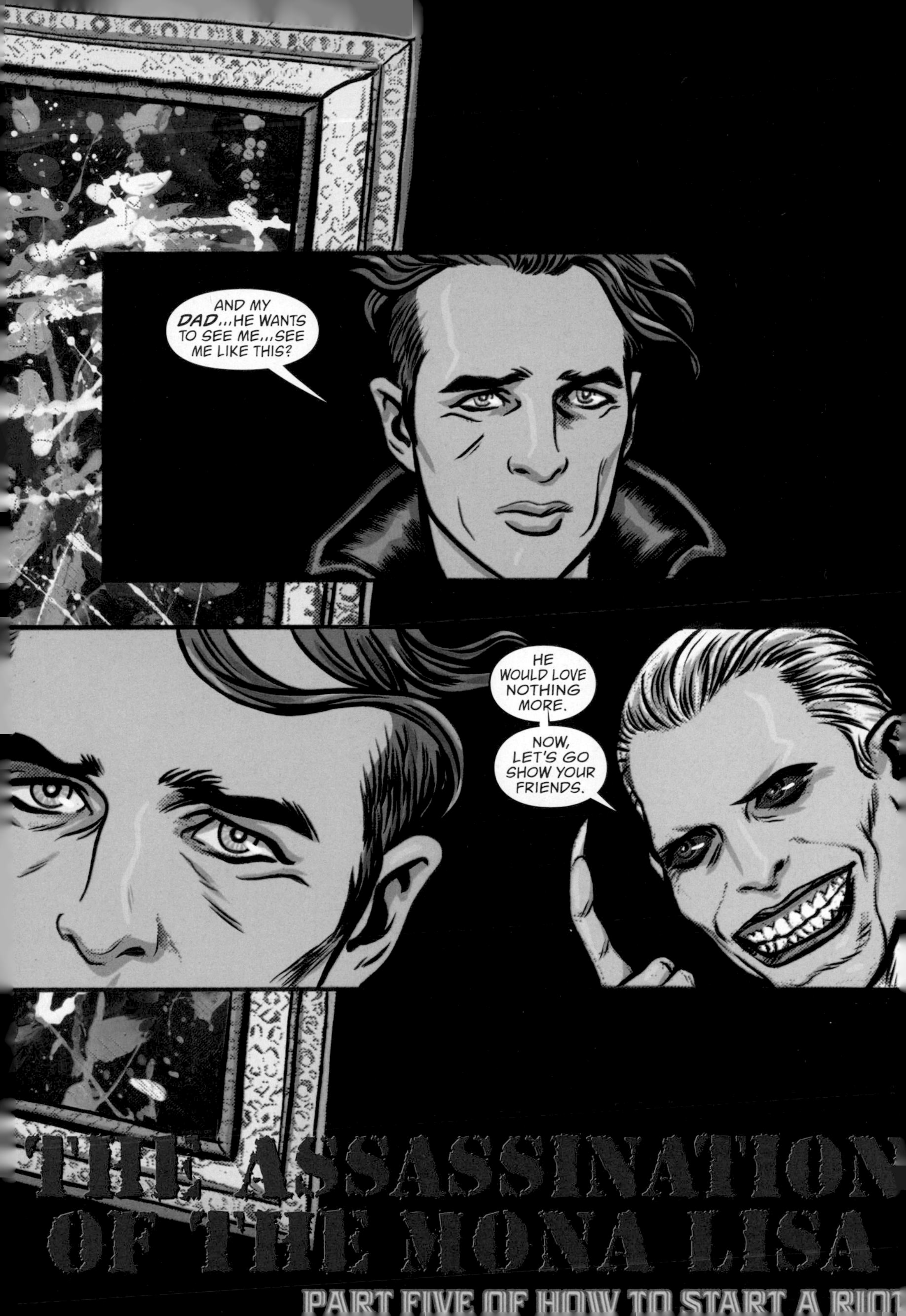
AND MY DAD...HE WANTS TO SEE ME...SEE ME LIKE THIS?
HE WOULD LOVE NOTHING MORE.
NOW, LET'S GO SHOW YOUR FRIENDS.
THE ASSASSINATION OF THE MONA LISA
PART FIVE OF HOW TO START A RIOT

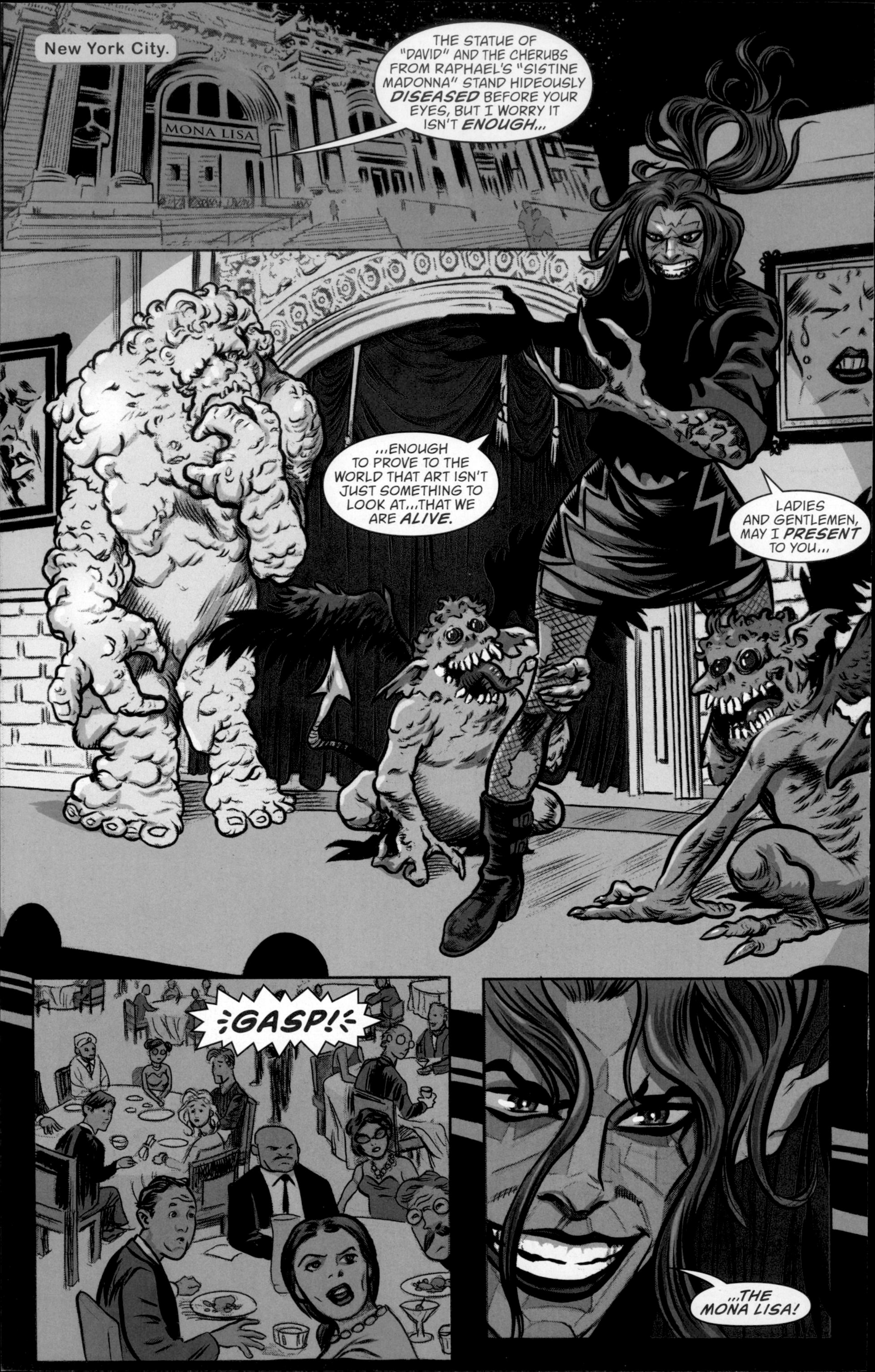
New York City.
MONA LISA
THE STATUE OF "DAVID" AND THE CHERUBS FROM RAPHAEL'S "SISTINE MADONNA" STAND HIDEOUSLY DISEASED BEFORE YOUR EYES, BUT I WORRY IT ISN'T ENOUGH...
...ENOUGH TO PROVE TO THE WORLD THAT ART ISN'T JUST SOMETHING TO LOOK AT...THAT WE ARE ALIVE.
LADIES AND GENTLEMEN, MAY I PRESENT TO YOU...
GASP!
...THE MONA LISA!

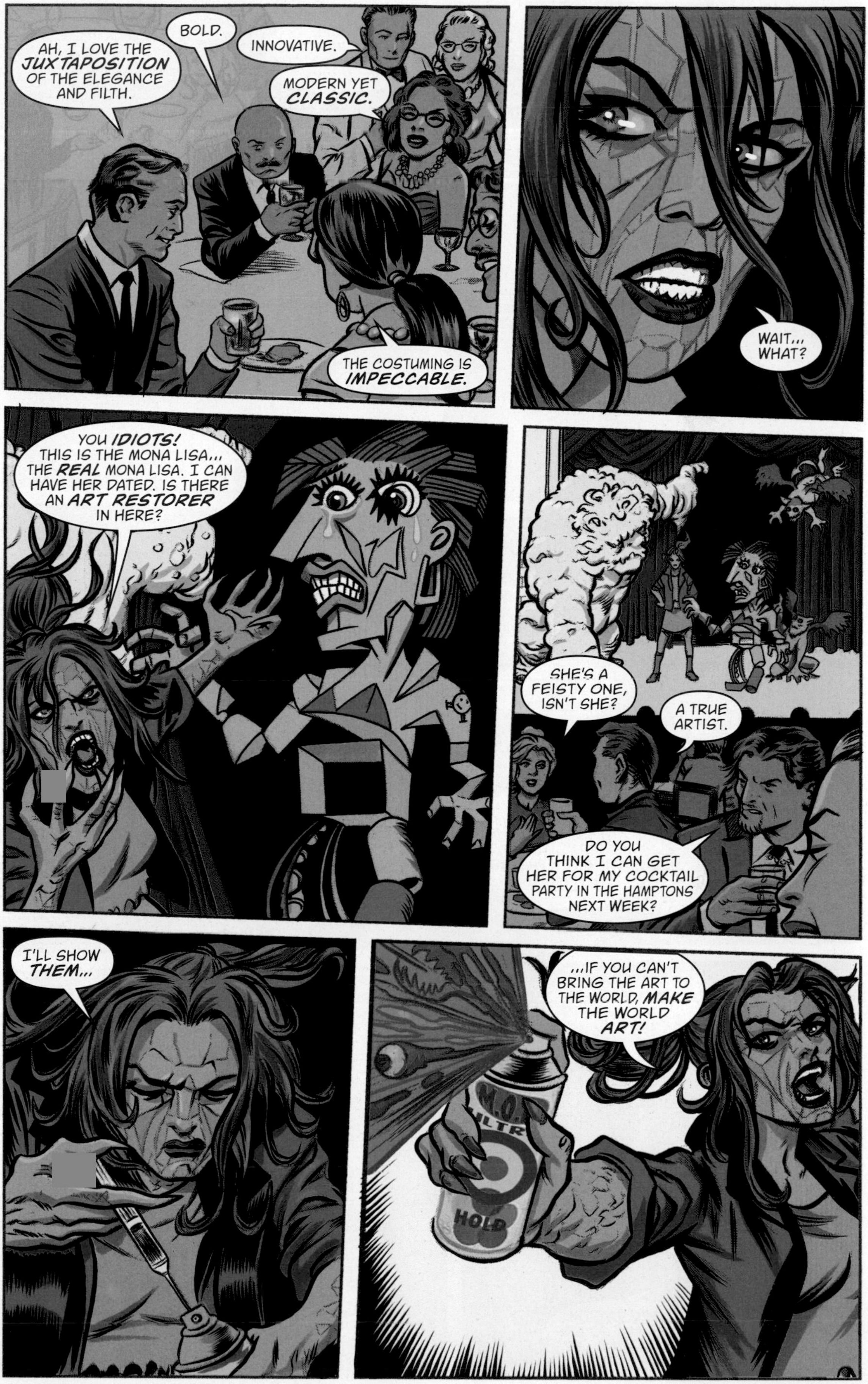
AH, I LOVE THE *JUXTAPOSITION* OF THE ELEGANCE AND FILTH.
BOLD.
INNOVATIVE.
MODERN YET *CLASSIC.*
THE COSTUMING IS *IMPECCABLE.*
WAIT... WHAT?
YOU *IDIOTS!* THIS IS THE MONA LISA... THE *REAL* MONA LISA. I CAN HAVE HER DATED. IS THERE AN *ART RESTORER* IN HERE?
SHE'S A FEISTY ONE, ISN'T SHE?
A TRUE ARTIST.
DO YOU THINK I CAN GET HER FOR MY COCKTAIL PARTY IN THE HAMPTONS NEXT WEEK?
I'LL SHOW *THEM...*
...IF YOU CAN'T BRING THE ART TO THE WORLD, *MAKE* THE WORLD *ART!*
HOLD

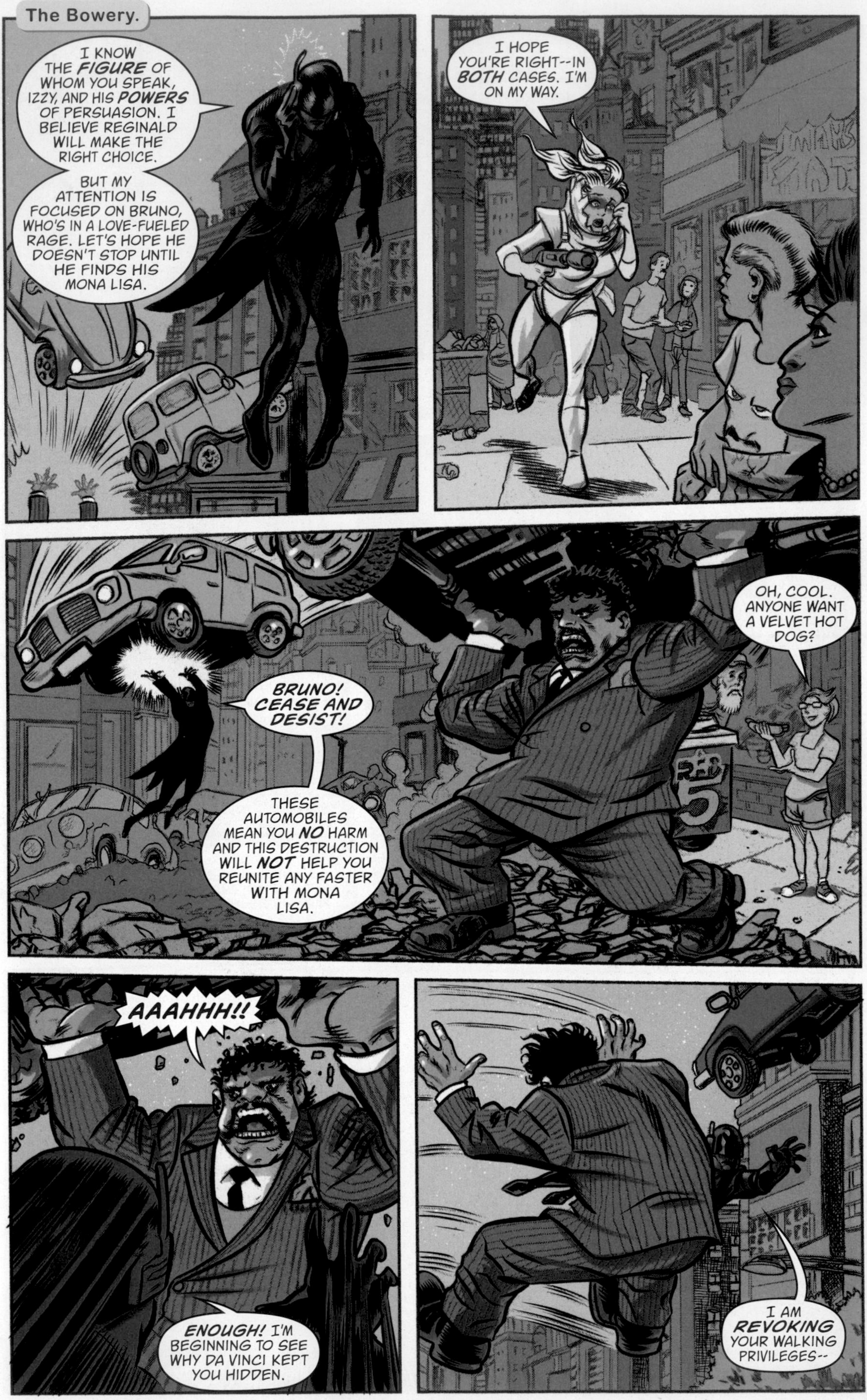

The Bowery.
I KNOW THE FIGURE OF WHOM YOU SPEAK, IZZY, AND HIS POWERS OF PERSUASION. I BELIEVE REGINALD WILL MAKE THE RIGHT CHOICE.
BUT MY ATTENTION IS FOCUSED ON BRUNO, WHO'S IN A LOVE-FUELED RAGE. LET'S HOPE HE DOESN'T STOP UNTIL HE FINDS HIS MONA LISA.
I HOPE YOU'RE RIGHT--IN BOTH CASES. I'M ON MY WAY.
BRUNO! CEASE AND DESIST!
THESE AUTOMOBILES MEAN YOU NO HARM AND THIS DESTRUCTION WILL NOT HELP YOU REUNITE ANY FASTER WITH MONA LISA.
OH, COOL. ANYONE WANT A VELVET HOT DOG?
RED 5
AAAHHH!!
ENOUGH! I'M BEGINNING TO SEE WHY DA VINCI KEPT YOU HIDDEN.
I AM REVOKING YOUR WALKING PRIVILEGES--

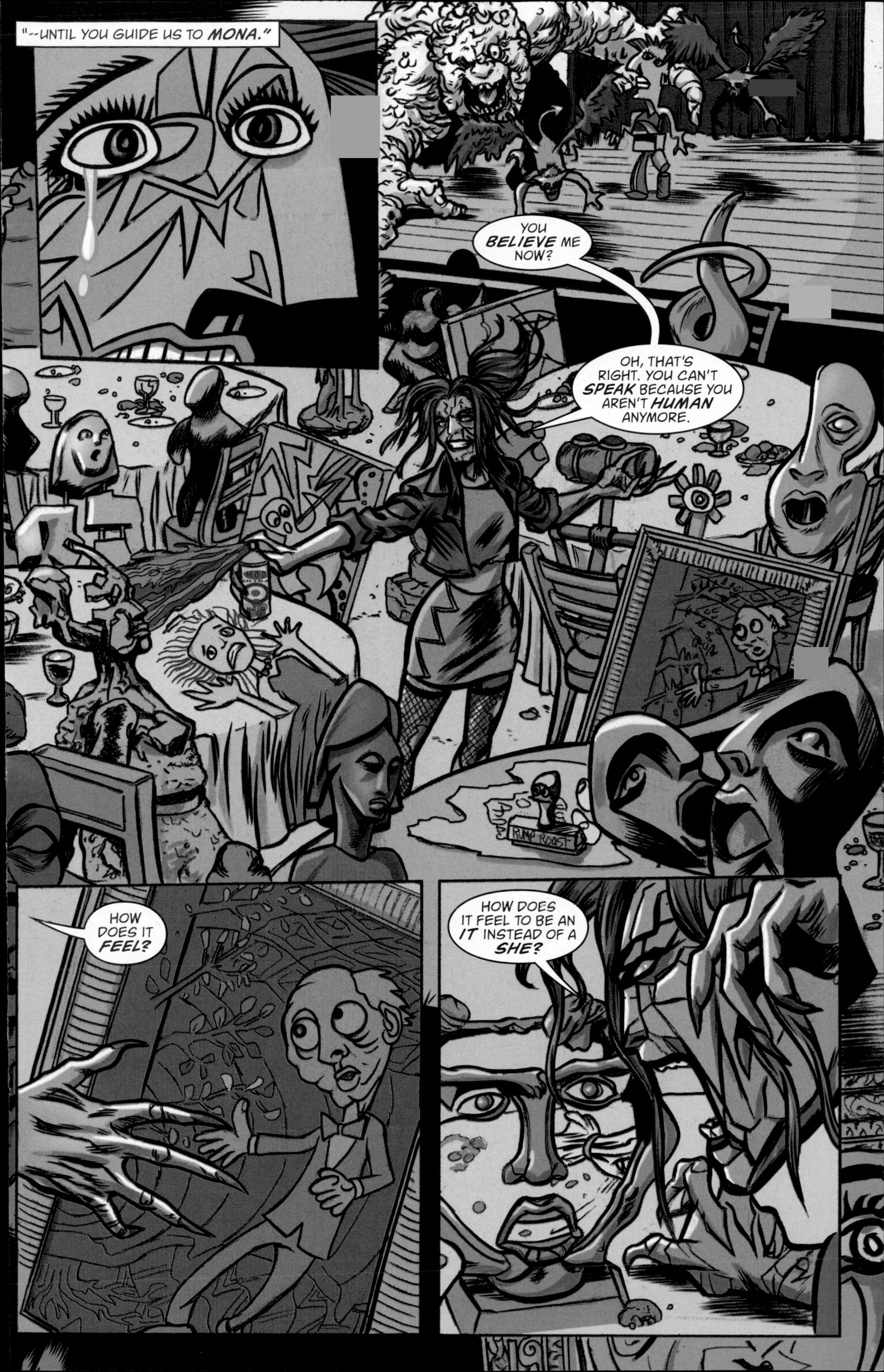

"--UNTIL YOU GUIDE US TO **MONA.**"
YOU **BELIEVE** ME NOW?
OH, THAT'S RIGHT. YOU CAN'T **SPEAK** BECAUSE YOU AREN'T **HUMAN** ANYMORE.
HOW DOES IT **FEEL?**
HOW DOES IT FEEL TO BE AN ***IT*** INSTEAD OF A **SHE?**

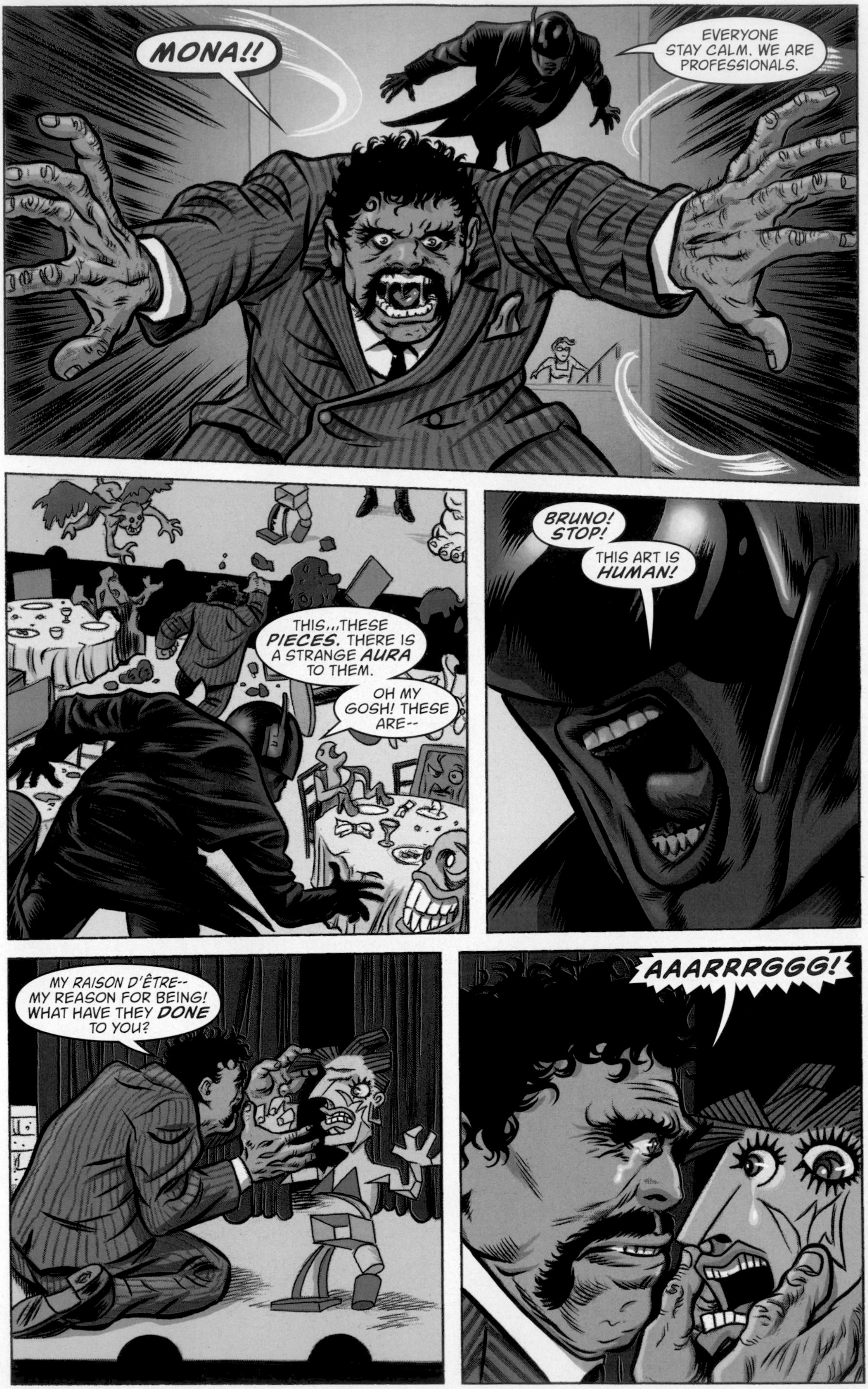
MONA!!
EVERYONE STAY CALM. WE ARE PROFESSIONALS.
THIS...THESE PIECES. THERE IS A STRANGE AURA TO THEM.
OH MY GOSH! THESE ARE--
BRUNO! STOP!
THIS ART IS HUMAN!
MY RAISON D'ÊTRE-- MY REASON FOR BEING! WHAT HAVE THEY DONE TO YOU?
AAARRRGGG!

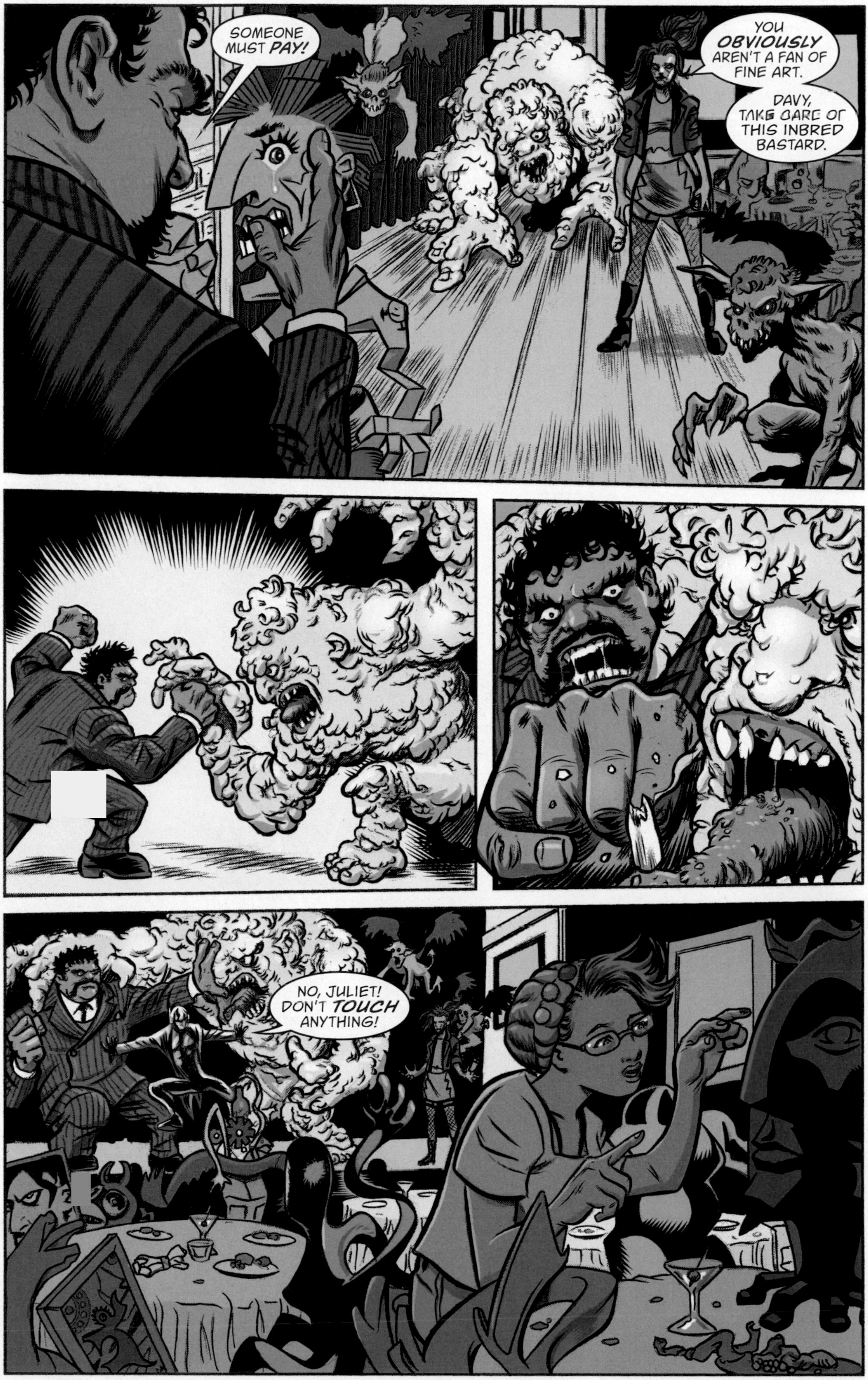
SOMEONE MUST PAY!
YOU OBVIOUSLY AREN'T A FAN OF FINE ART.
DAVY, TAKE CARE OF THIS INBRED BASTARD.
NO, JULIET! DON'T TOUCH ANYTHING!

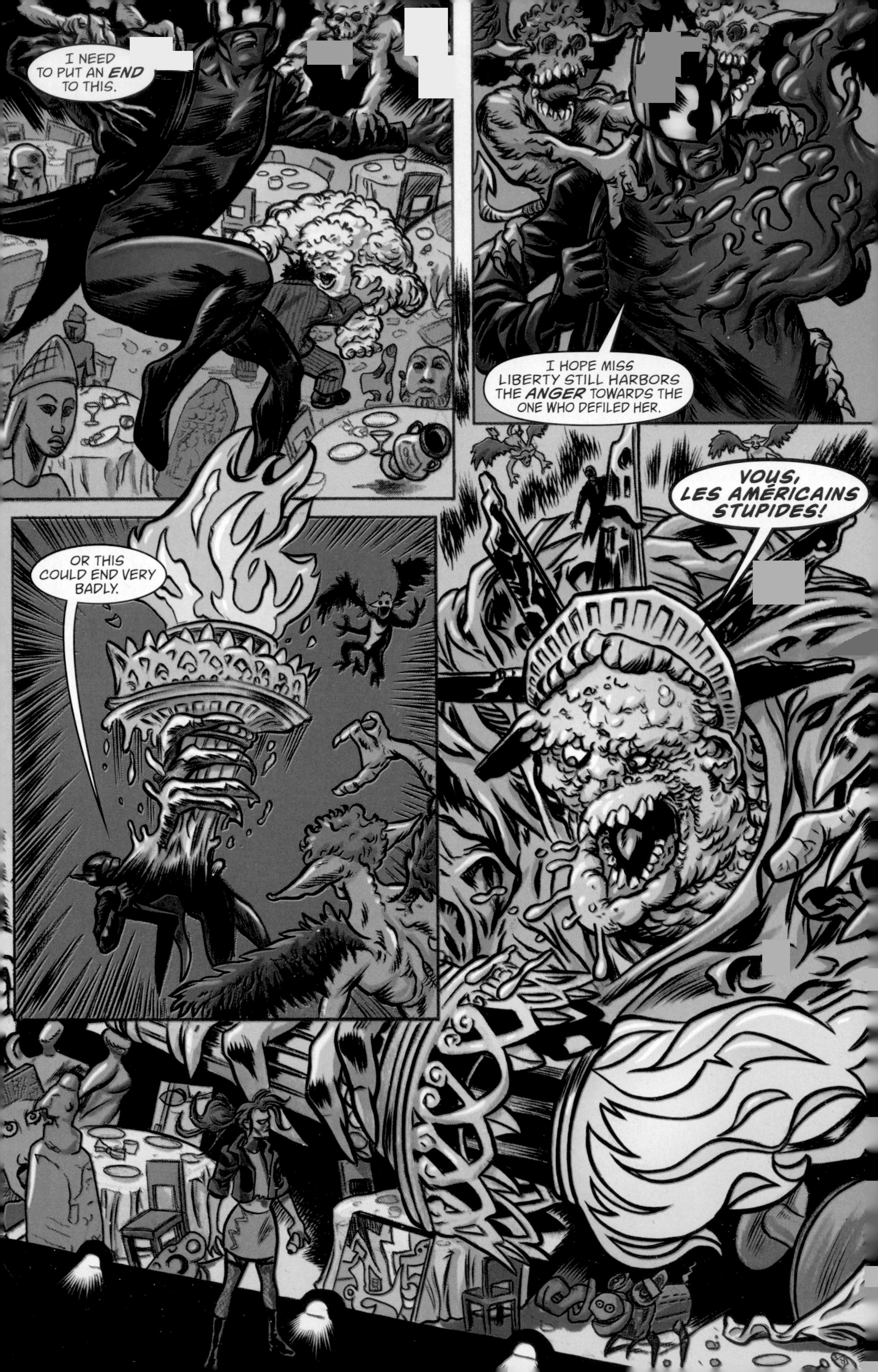
I NEED TO PUT AN ***END*** TO THIS.
I HOPE MISS LIBERTY STILL HARBORS THE ***ANGER*** TOWARDS THE ONE WHO DEFILED HER.
OR THIS COULD END VERY BADLY.
VOUS, LES AMÉRICAINS STUPIDES!

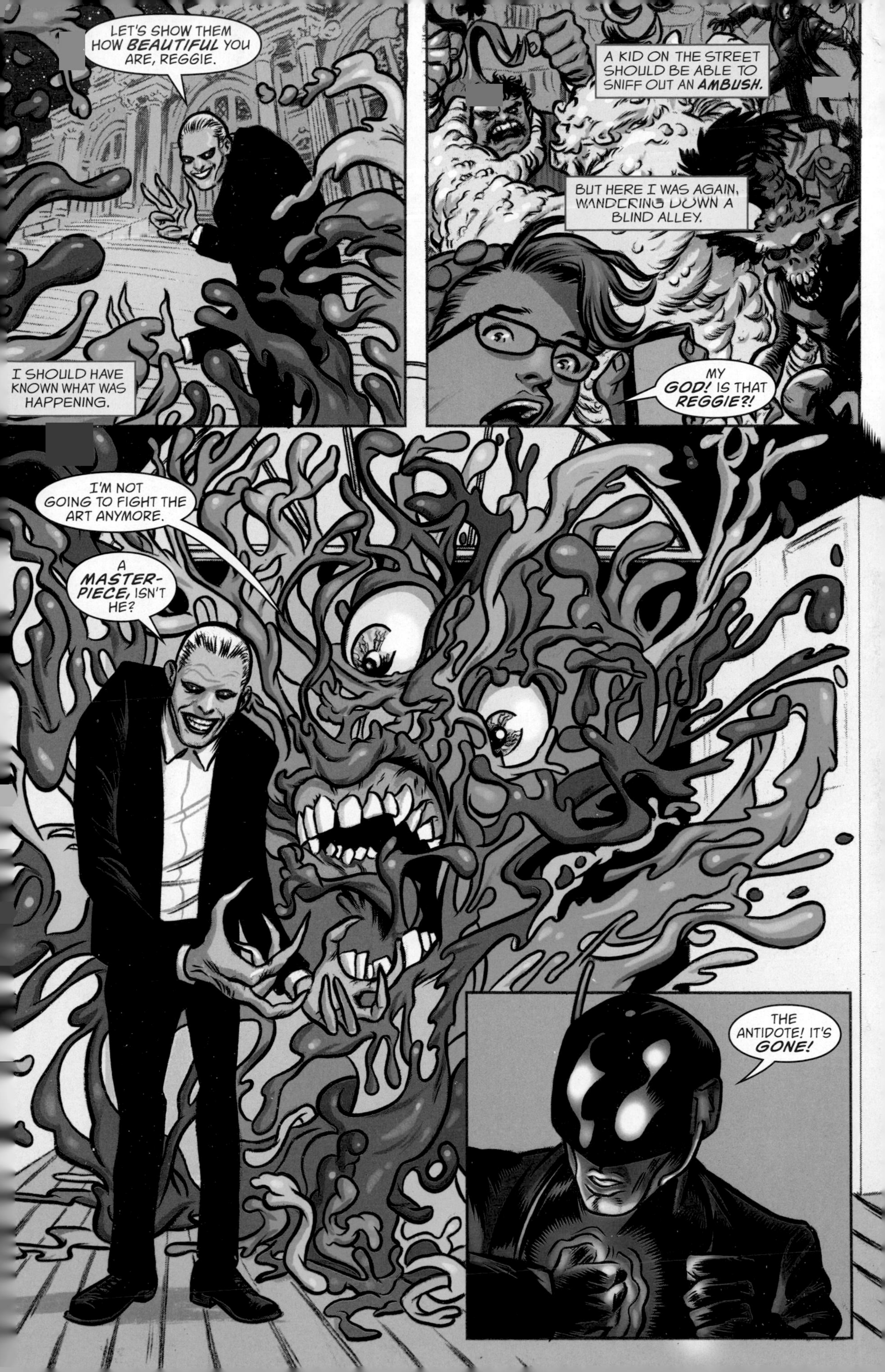
LET'S SHOW THEM HOW **BEAUTIFUL** YOU ARE, REGGIE.
I SHOULD HAVE KNOWN WHAT WAS HAPPENING.
A KID ON THE STREET SHOULD BE ABLE TO SNIFF OUT AN **AMBUSH.**
BUT HERE I WAS AGAIN, WANDERING DOWN A BLIND ALLEY.
MY **GOD!** IS THAT **REGGIE?!**
I'M NOT GOING TO FIGHT THE ART ANYMORE.
A **MASTER-PIECE,** ISN'T HE?
THE ANTIDOTE! IT'S **GONE!**

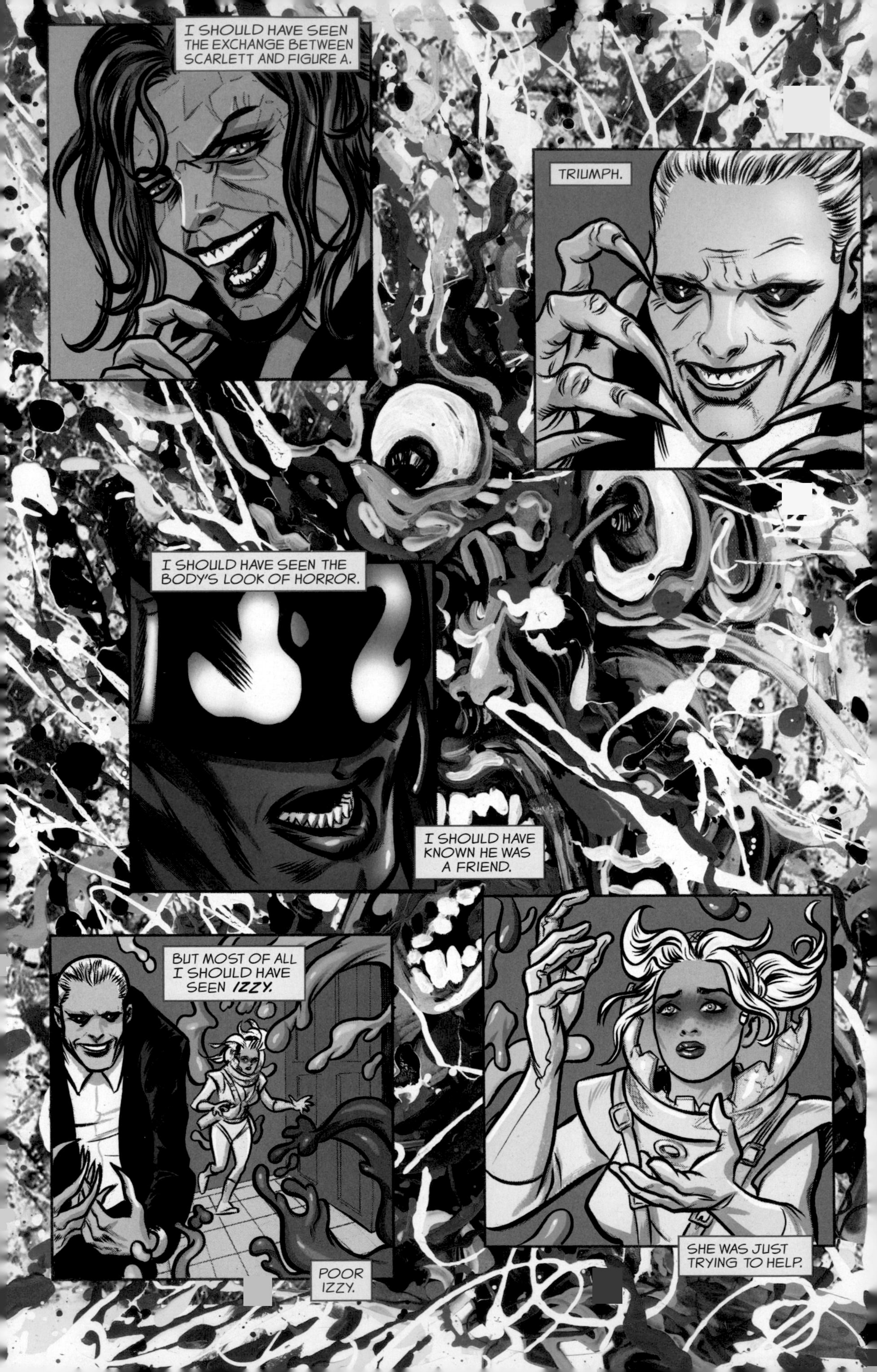
I SHOULD HAVE SEEN THE EXCHANGE BETWEEN SCARLETT AND FIGURE A.
TRIUMPH.
I SHOULD HAVE SEEN THE BODY'S LOOK OF HORROR.
I SHOULD HAVE KNOWN HE WAS A FRIEND.
BUT MOST OF ALL I SHOULD HAVE SEEN *IZZY.*
POOR IZZY.
SHE WAS JUST TRYING TO HELP.

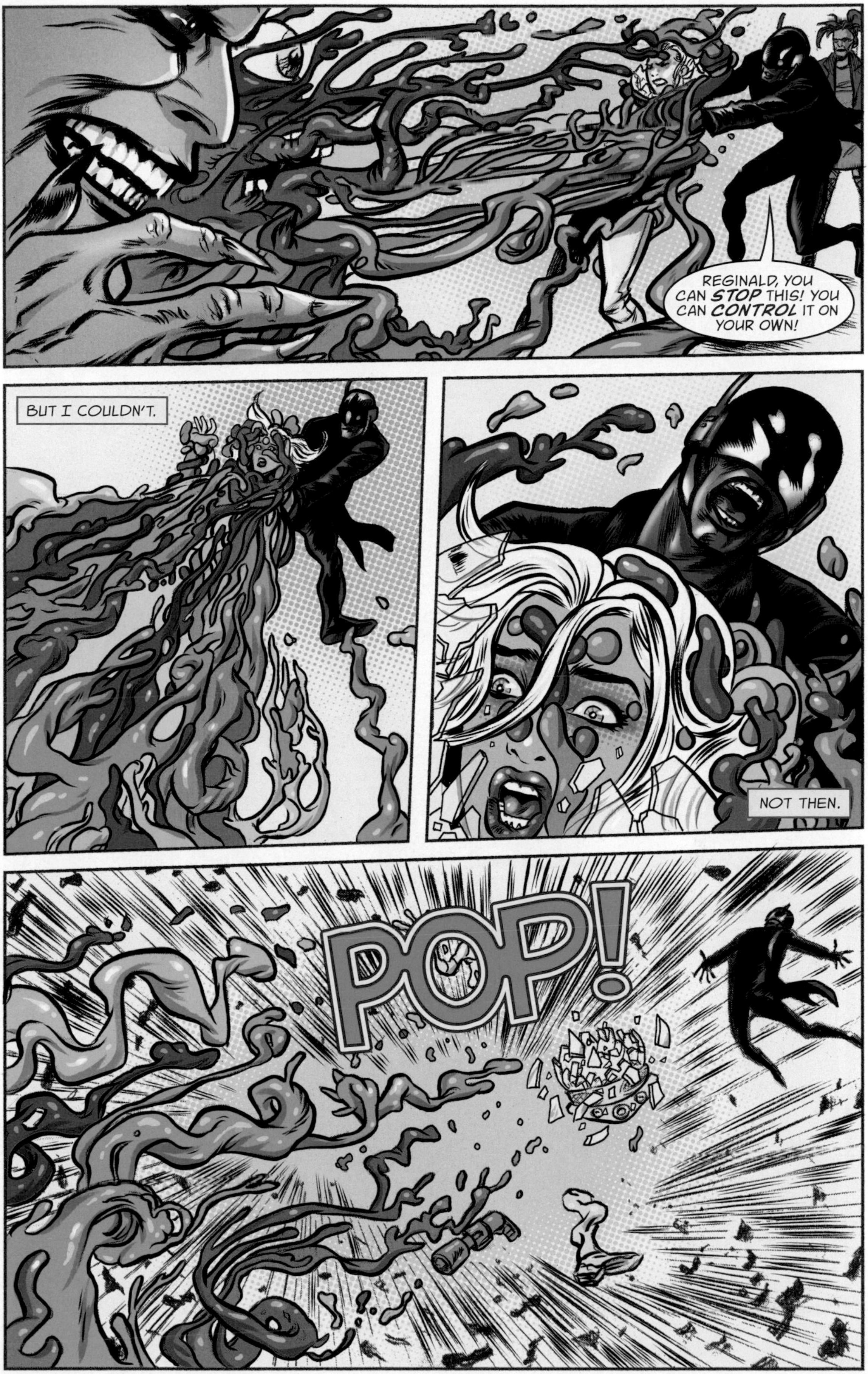
REGINALD, YOU CAN **STOP** THIS! YOU CAN **CONTROL** IT ON YOUR OWN!
BUT I COULDN'T.
NOT THEN.
POP!

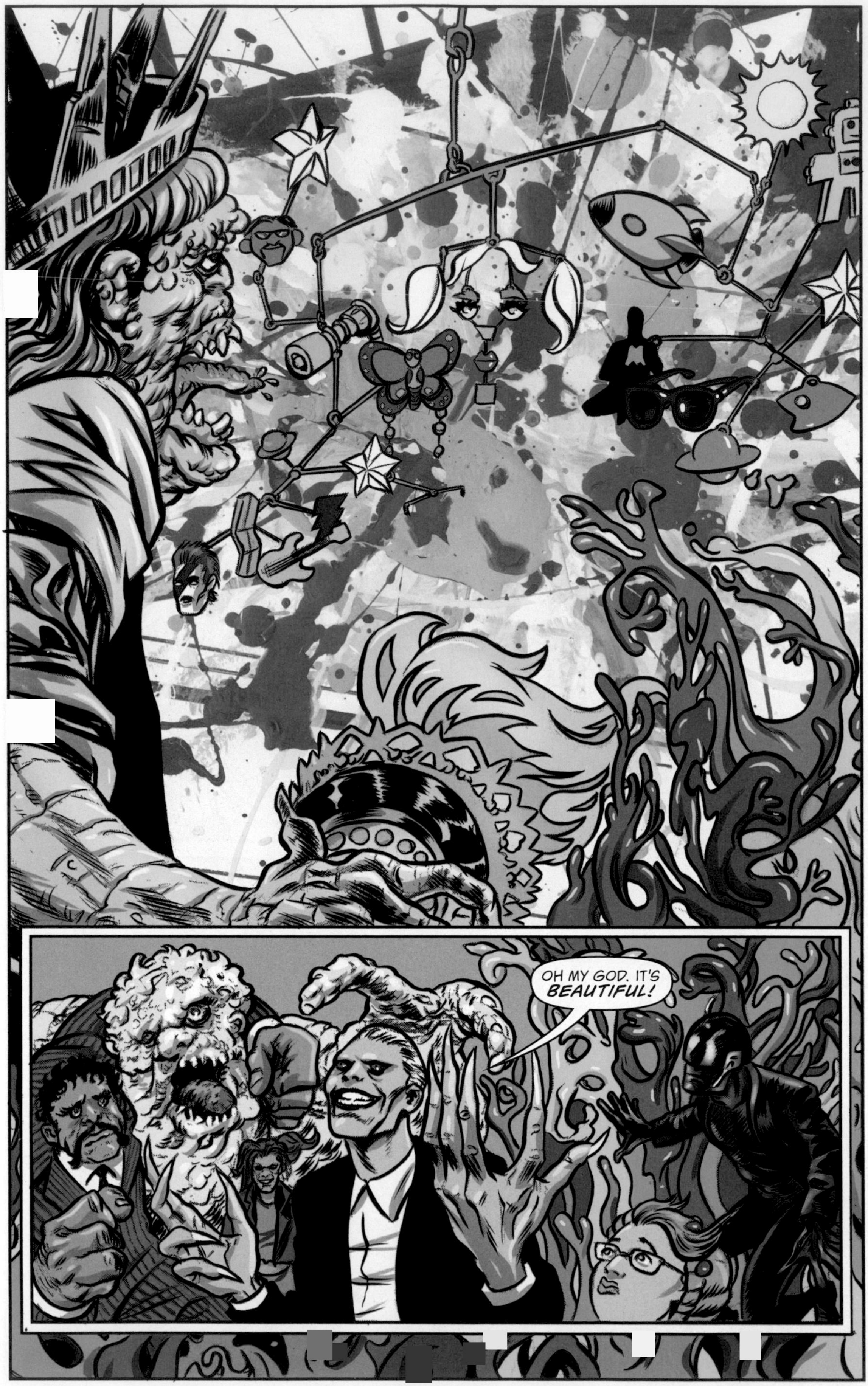
OH MY GOD. IT'S *BEAUTIFUL!*

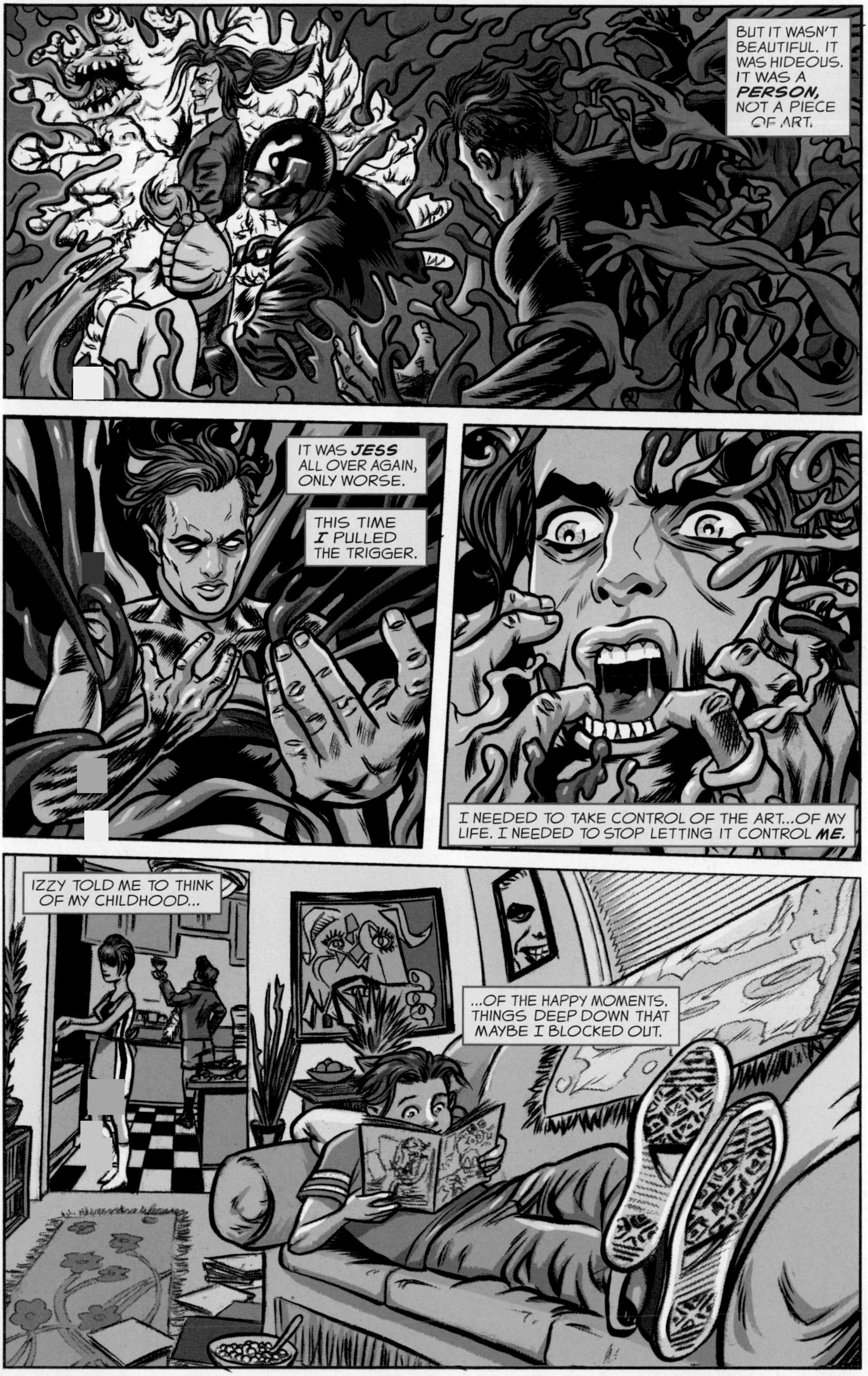
BUT IT WASN'T BEAUTIFUL. IT WAS HIDEOUS. IT WAS A PERSON, NOT A PIECE OF ART.
IT WAS JESS ALL OVER AGAIN, ONLY WORSE.
THIS TIME I PULLED THE TRIGGER.
I NEEDED TO TAKE CONTROL OF THE ART...OF MY LIFE. I NEEDED TO STOP LETTING IT CONTROL ME.
IZZY TOLD ME TO THINK OF MY CHILDHOOD...
...OF THE HAPPY MOMENTS. THINGS DEEP DOWN THAT MAYBE I BLOCKED OUT.

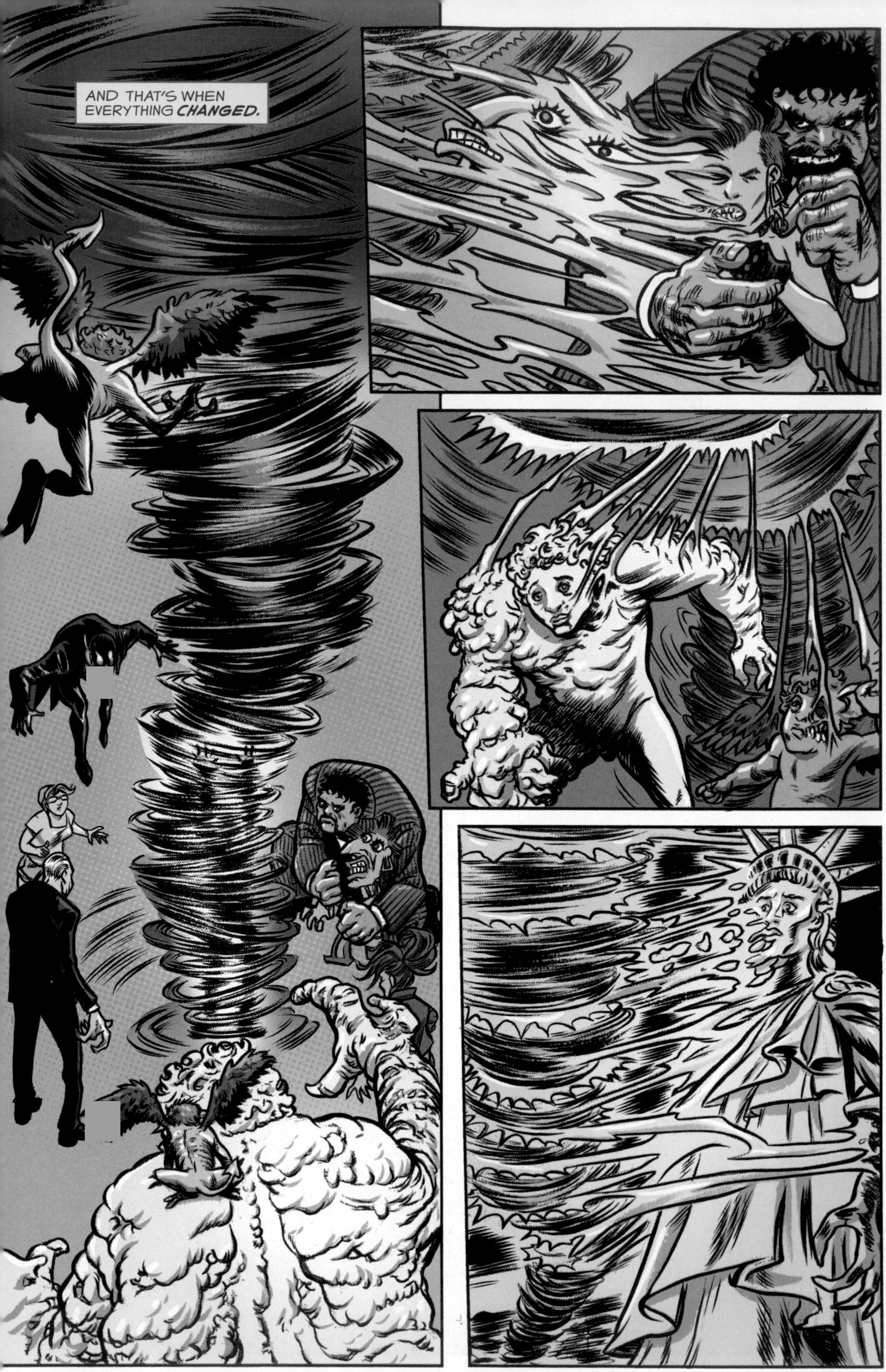
AND THAT'S WHEN EVERYTHING CHANGED.

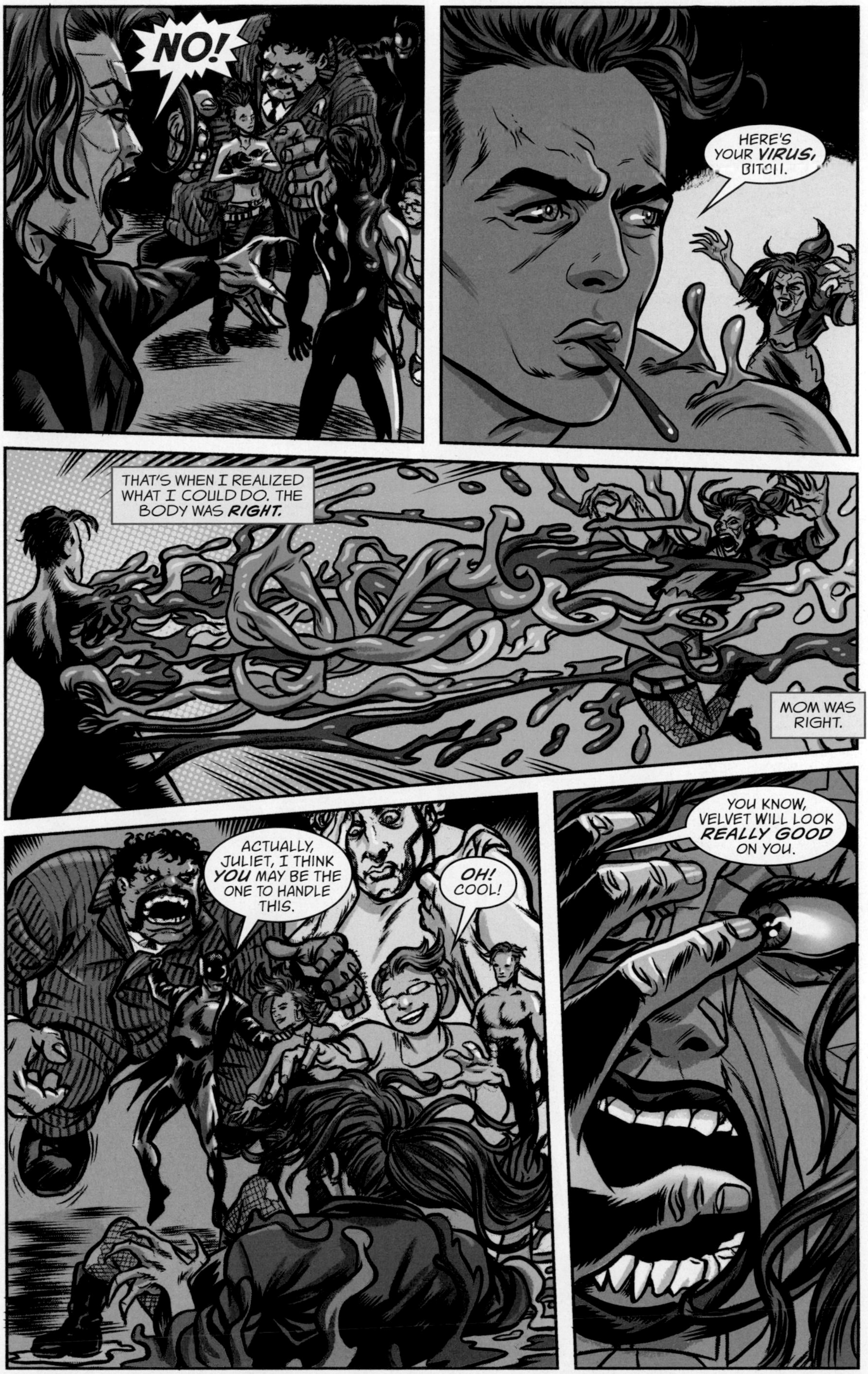
NO!
HERE'S YOUR VIRUS, BITCH.
THAT'S WHEN I REALIZED WHAT I COULD DO. THE BODY WAS RIGHT.
MOM WAS RIGHT.
ACTUALLY, JULIET, I THINK YOU MAY BE THE ONE TO HANDLE THIS.
OH! COOL!
YOU KNOW, VELVET WILL LOOK REALLY GOOD ON YOU.

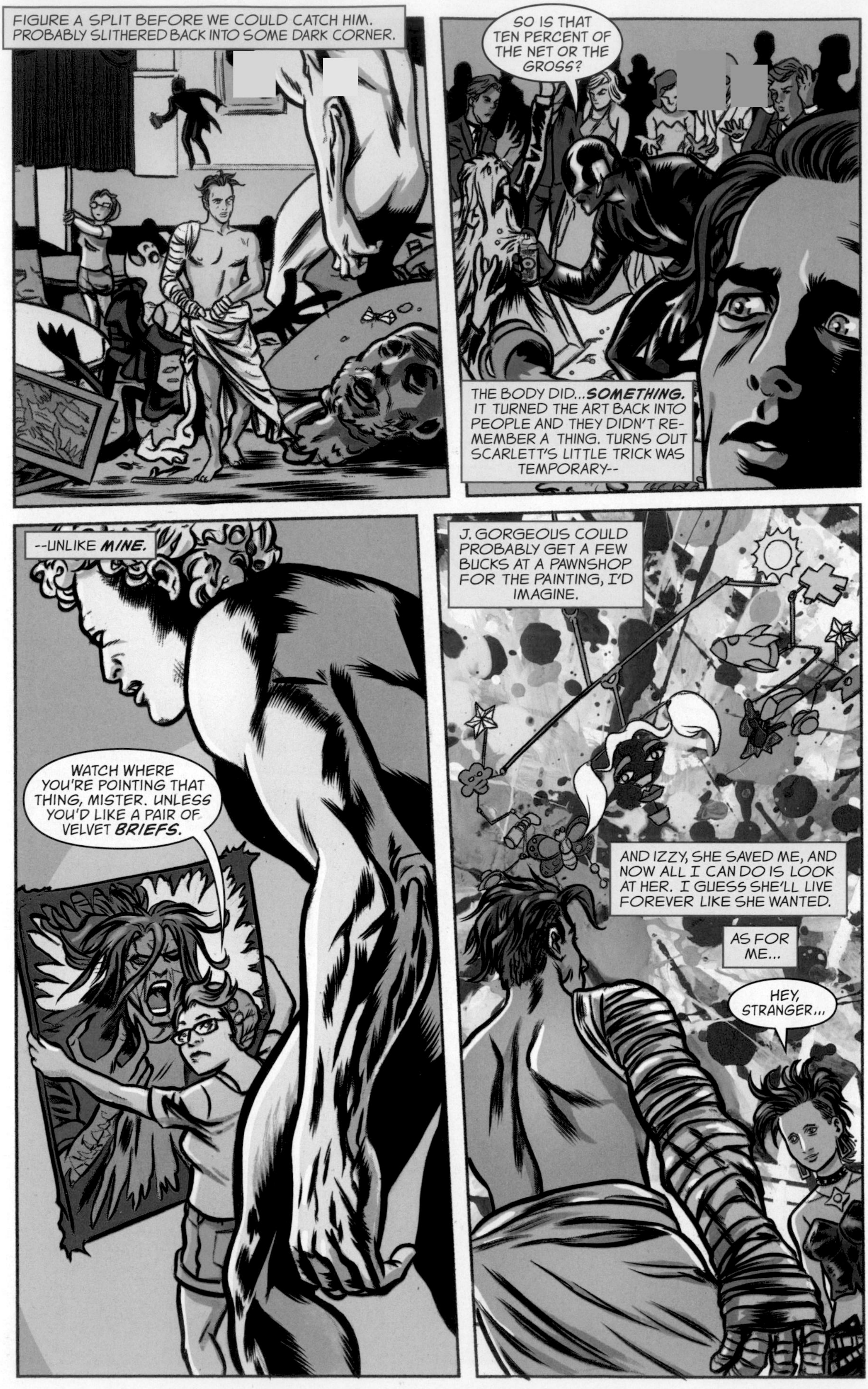
FIGURE A SPLIT BEFORE WE COULD CATCH HIM. PROBABLY SLITHERED BACK INTO SOME DARK CORNER.
SO IS THAT TEN PERCENT OF THE NET OR THE GROSS?
THE BODY DID...SOMETHING. IT TURNED THE ART BACK INTO PEOPLE AND THEY DIDN'T RE-MEMBER A THING. TURNS OUT SCARLETT'S LITTLE TRICK WAS TEMPORARY--
--UNLIKE MINE.
WATCH WHERE YOU'RE POINTING THAT THING, MISTER. UNLESS YOU'D LIKE A PAIR OF VELVET BRIEFS.
J. GORGEOUS COULD PROBABLY GET A FEW BUCKS AT A PAWNSHOP FOR THE PAINTING, I'D IMAGINE.
AND IZZY, SHE SAVED ME, AND NOW ALL I CAN DO IS LOOK AT HER. I GUESS SHE'LL LIVE FOREVER LIKE SHE WANTED.
AS FOR ME...
HEY, STRANGER...

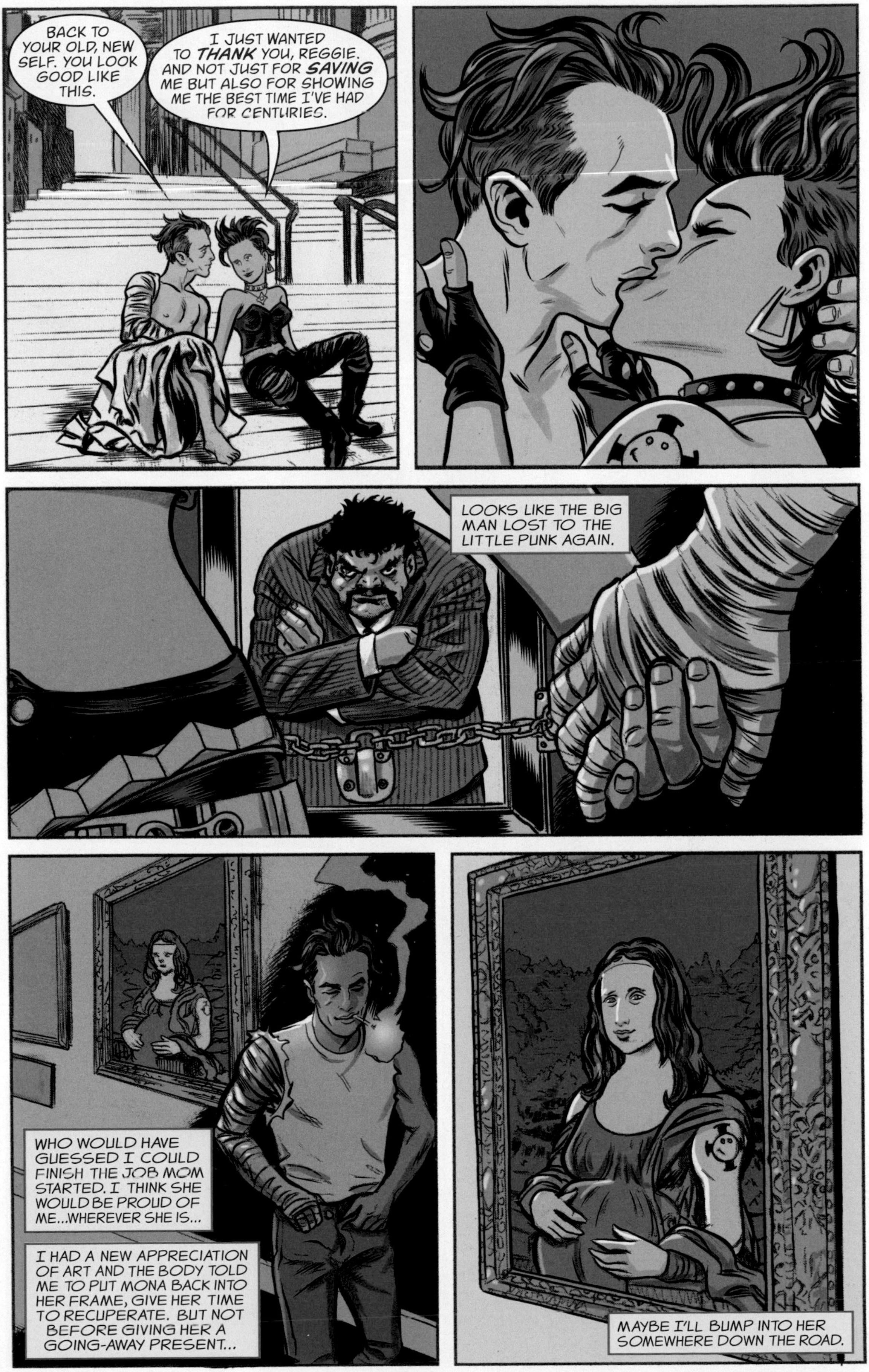
BACK TO YOUR OLD, NEW SELF. YOU LOOK GOOD LIKE THIS.
I JUST WANTED TO THANK YOU, REGGIE. AND NOT JUST FOR SAVING ME BUT ALSO FOR SHOWING ME THE BEST TIME I'VE HAD FOR CENTURIES.
LOOKS LIKE THE BIG MAN LOST TO THE LITTLE PUNK AGAIN.
WHO WOULD HAVE GUESSED I COULD FINISH THE JOB MOM STARTED. I THINK SHE WOULD BE PROUD OF ME...WHEREVER SHE IS...
I HAD A NEW APPRECIATION OF ART AND THE BODY TOLD ME TO PUT MONA BACK INTO HER FRAME, GIVE HER TIME TO RECUPERATE. BUT NOT BEFORE GIVING HER A GOING-AWAY PRESENT...
MAYBE I'LL BUMP INTO HER SOMEWHERE DOWN THE ROAD.

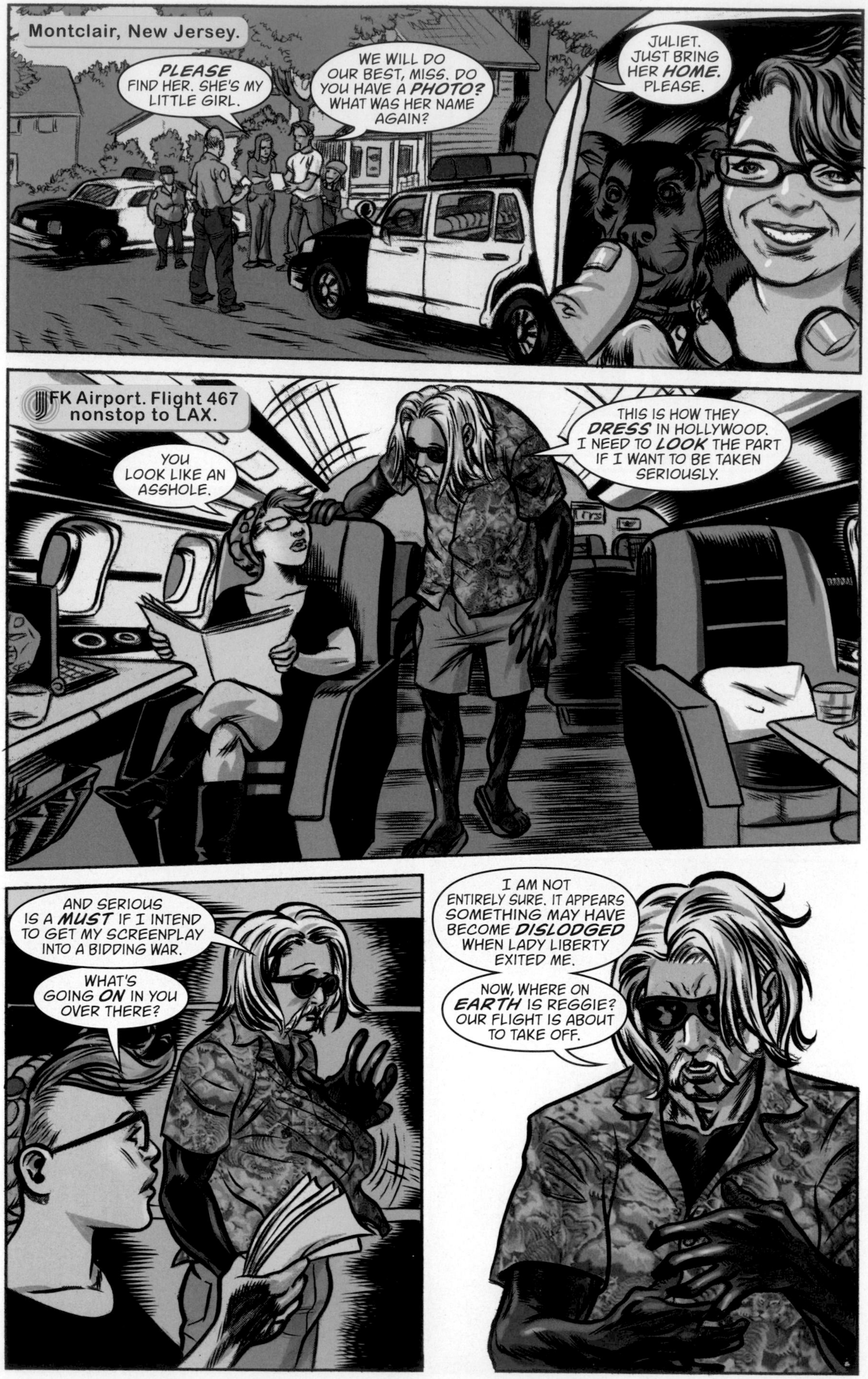
Montclair, New Jersey.
PLEASE FIND HER. SHE'S MY LITTLE GIRL.
WE WILL DO OUR BEST, MISS. DO YOU HAVE A PHOTO? WHAT WAS HER NAME AGAIN?
JULIET. JUST BRING HER HOME. PLEASE.
JFK Airport. Flight 467 nonstop to LAX.
YOU LOOK LIKE AN ASSHOLE.
THIS IS HOW THEY DRESS IN HOLLYWOOD. I NEED TO LOOK THE PART IF I WANT TO BE TAKEN SERIOUSLY.
AND SERIOUS IS A MUST IF I INTEND TO GET MY SCREENPLAY INTO A BIDDING WAR.
WHAT'S GOING ON IN YOU OVER THERE?
I AM NOT ENTIRELY SURE. IT APPEARS SOMETHING MAY HAVE BECOME DISLODGED WHEN LADY LIBERTY EXITED ME.
NOW, WHERE ON EARTH IS REGGIE? OUR FLIGHT IS ABOUT TO TAKE OFF.

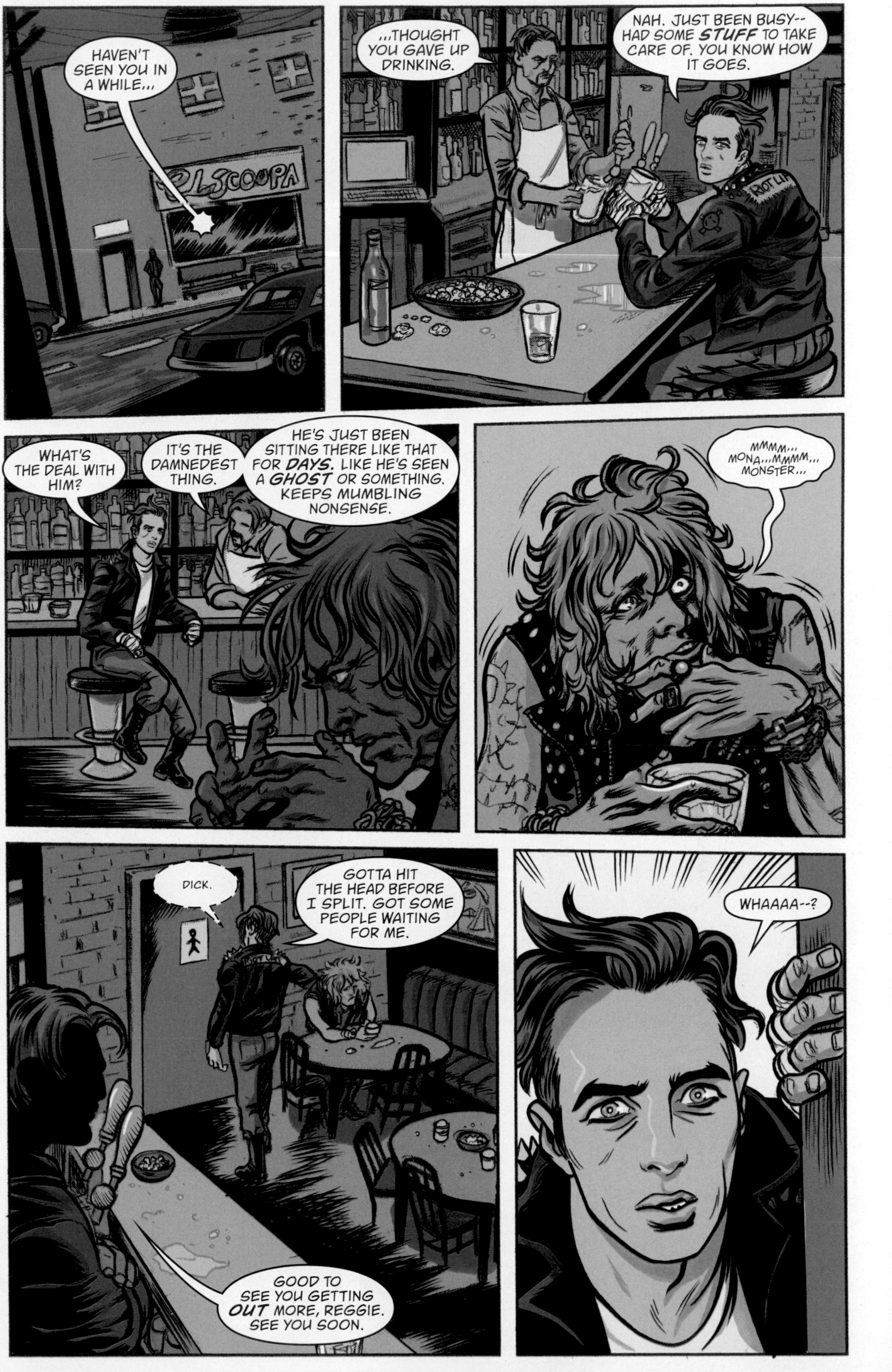
HAVEN'T SEEN YOU IN A WHILE...
...THOUGHT YOU GAVE UP DRINKING.
NAH. JUST BEEN BUSY-- HAD SOME **STUFF** TO TAKE CARE OF. YOU KNOW HOW IT GOES.
WHAT'S THE DEAL WITH HIM?
IT'S THE DAMNEDEST THING.
HE'S JUST BEEN SITTING THERE LIKE THAT FOR **DAYS.** LIKE HE'S SEEN A **GHOST** OR SOMETHING. KEEPS MUMBLING NONSENSE.
MMMM... MONA...MMMM... MONSTER...
DICK.
GOTTA HIT THE HEAD BEFORE I SPLIT. GOT SOME PEOPLE WAITING FOR ME.
GOOD TO SEE YOU GETTING **OUT** MORE, REGGIE. SEE YOU SOON.
WHAAAA--?

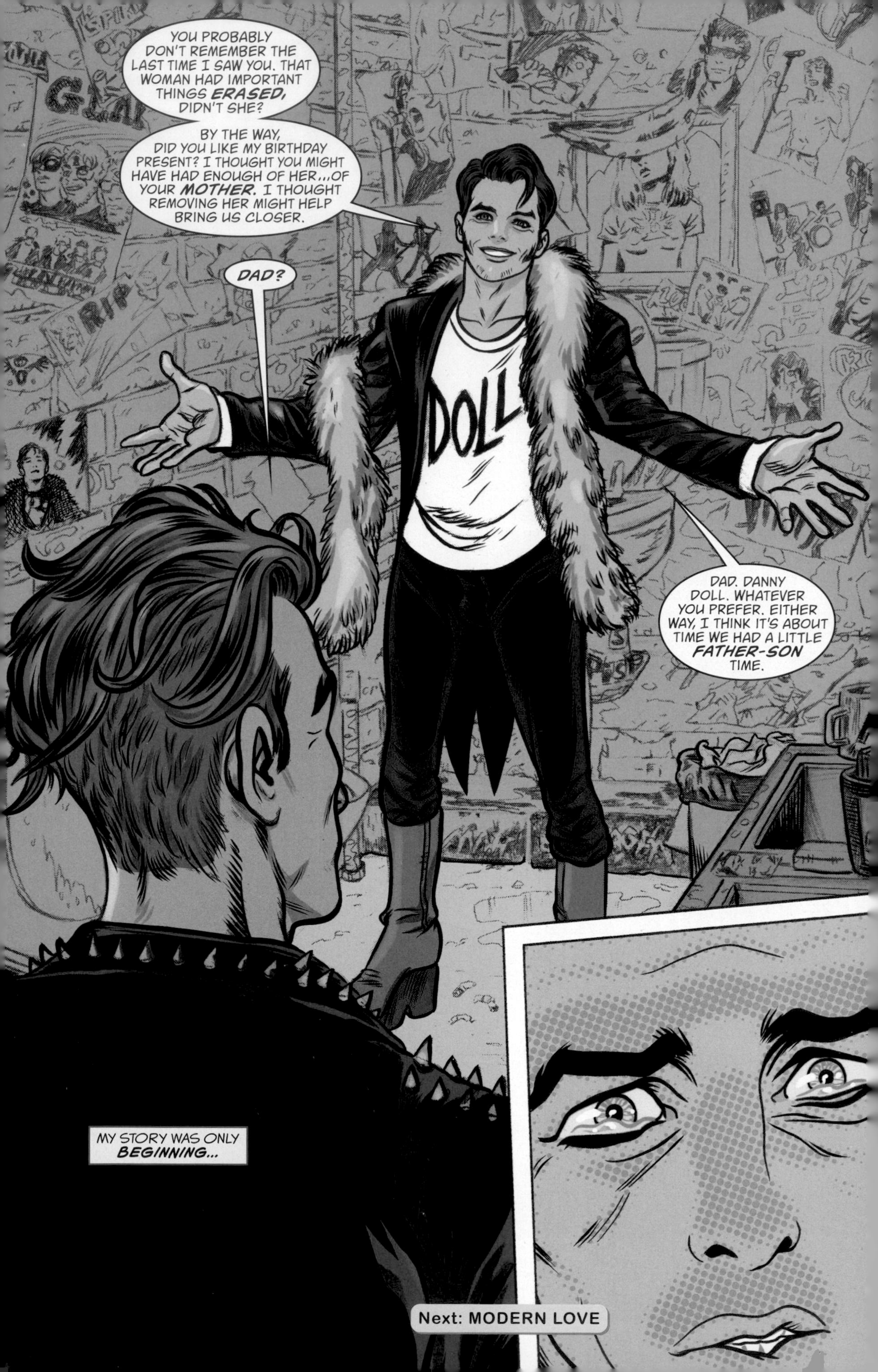
YOU PROBABLY DON'T REMEMBER THE LAST TIME I SAW YOU. THAT WOMAN HAD IMPORTANT THINGS ERASED, DIDN'T SHE?
BY THE WAY, DID YOU LIKE MY BIRTHDAY PRESENT? I THOUGHT YOU MIGHT HAVE HAD ENOUGH OF HER...OF YOUR MOTHER. I THOUGHT REMOVING HER MIGHT HELP BRING US CLOSER.
DAD?
DOLL
DAD. DANNY DOLL. WHATEVER YOU PREFER. EITHER WAY, I THINK IT'S ABOUT TIME WE HAD A LITTLE FATHER-SON TIME.
MY STORY WAS ONLY BEGINNING...
Next: MODERN LOVE

THE OPS FILES

CHARACTER DESIGNS BY **MICHAEL ALLRED** SKETCHES BY **MATT BRUNDAGE**

LOGO DESIGNS BY **STEVE COOK**

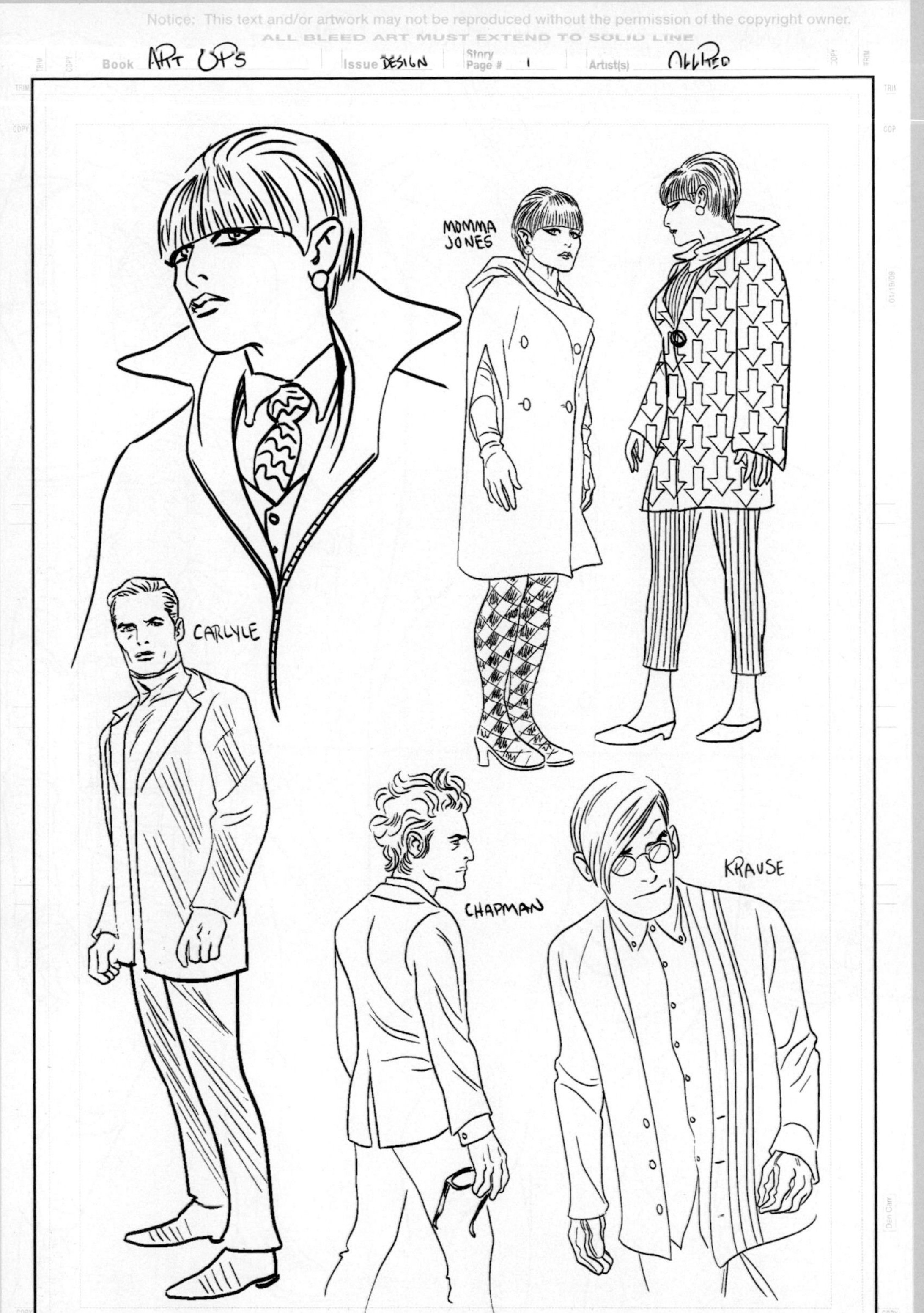
Notice: This text and/or artwork may not be reproduced without the permission of the copyright owner.
ALL BLEED ART MUST EXTEND TO SOLID LINE
Book ART OPS
Issue DESIGN
Story Page # 1
Artist(s) ALLRED
MOMMA JONES
CARLYLE
CHAPMAN
KRAUSE
INSTRUCTIONS FOR DOUBLE PAGE SPREAD: CUT AS SHOWN, ABUT PAGE EDGES, TAPE ON BACK. DO NOT OVERLAP.

Book ART OPS | Issue DESIGN | Story Page # 3 | Artist(s) ALLRED

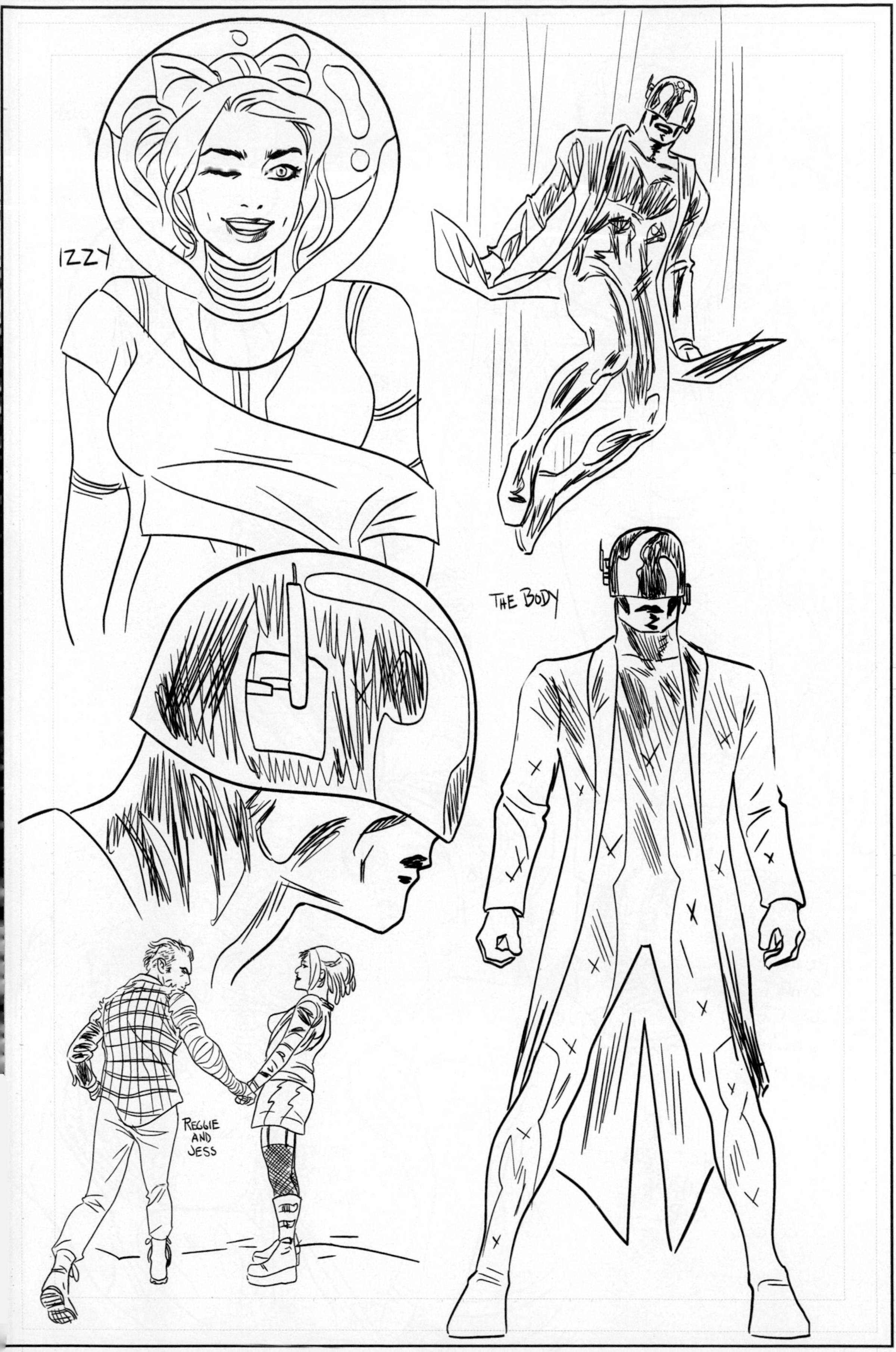
IZZY
THE BODY
REGGIE AND JESS

Book ART OPS | Issue DESIGN | Story Page # 4 | Artist(s) ALLRED

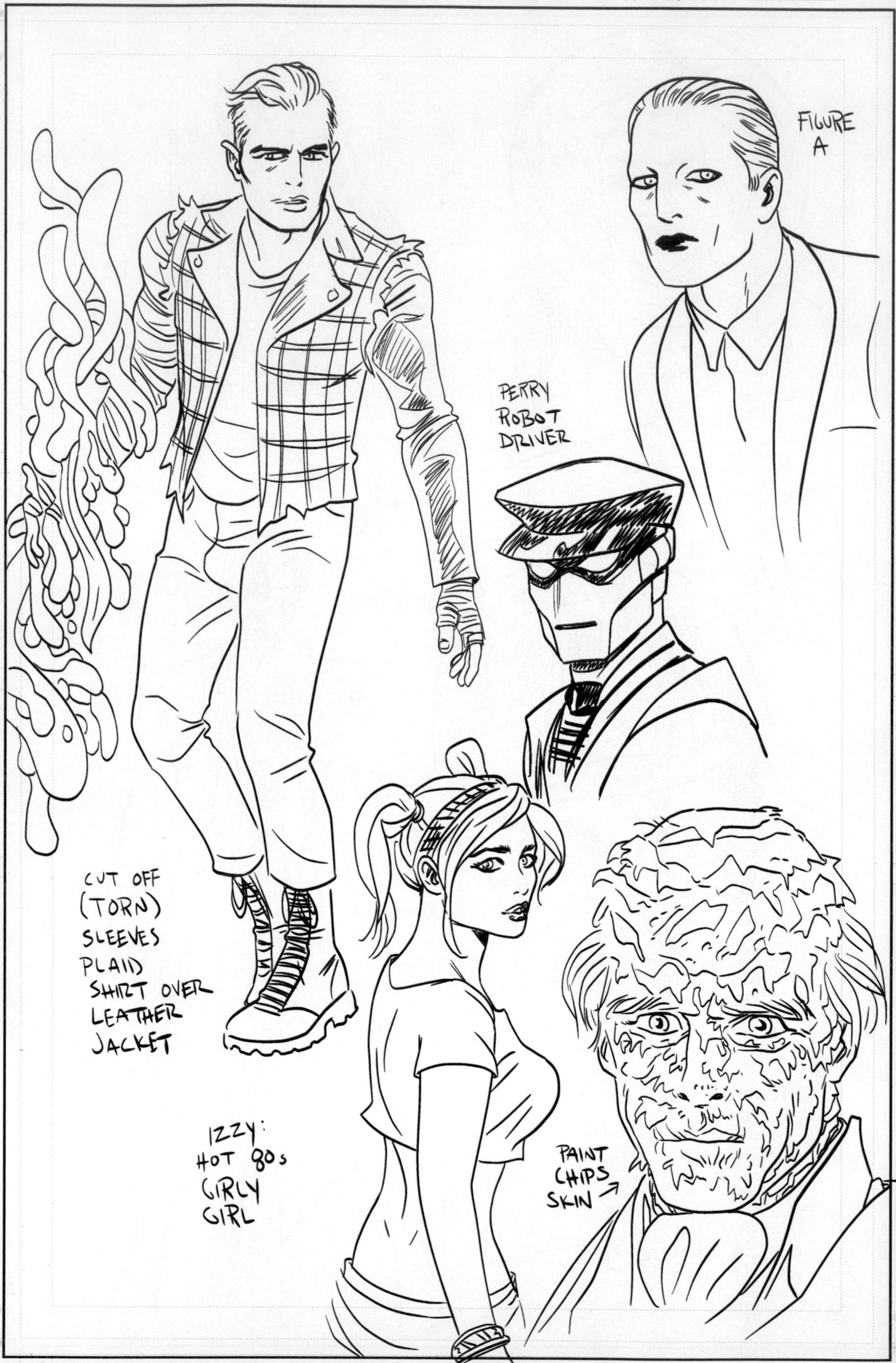
FIGURE A
PERRY ROBOT DRIVER
CUT OFF (TORN) SLEEVES PLAID SHIRT OVER LEATHER JACKET
IZZY: HOT 80s GIRLY GIRL
PAINT CHIPS SKIN →

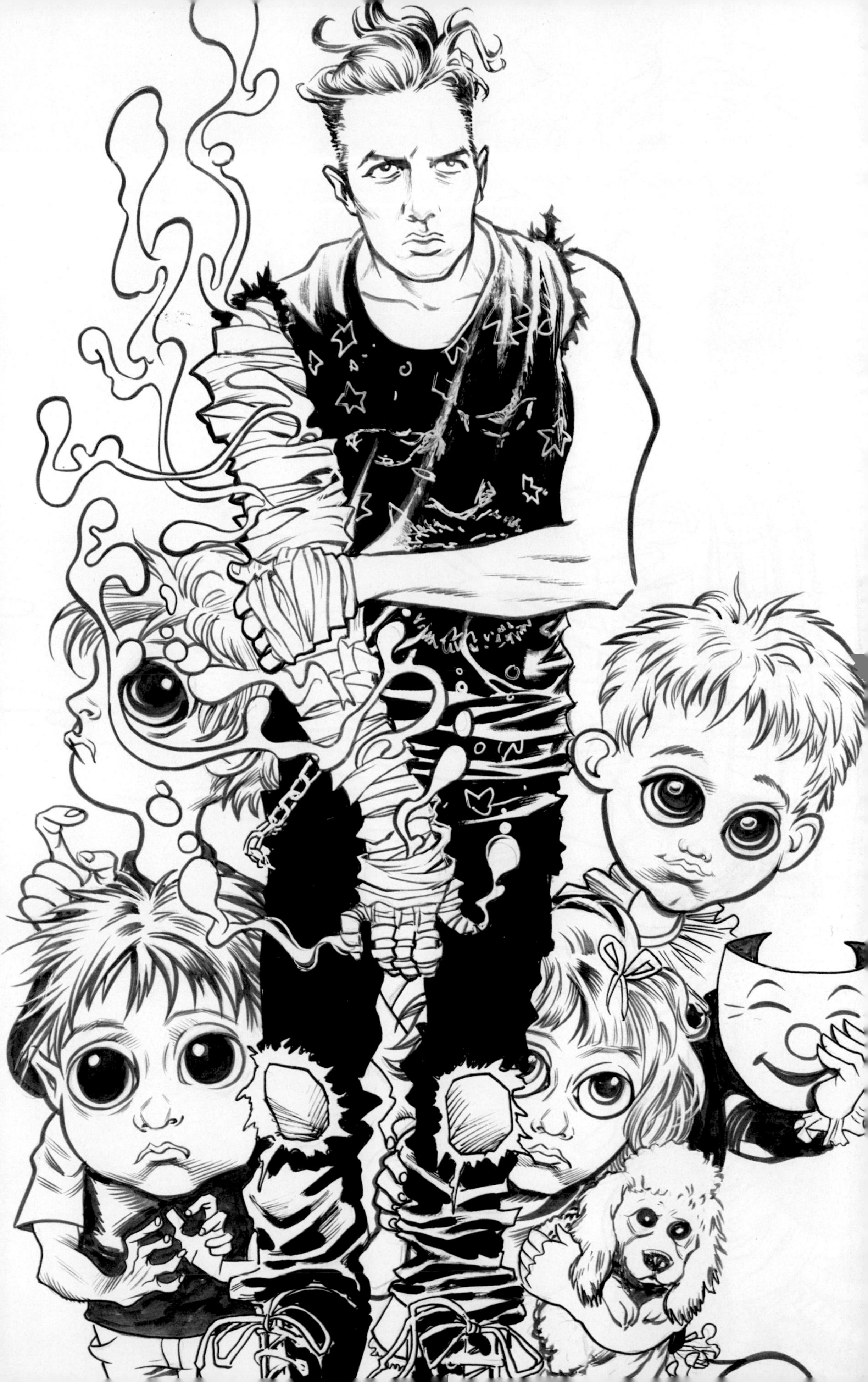

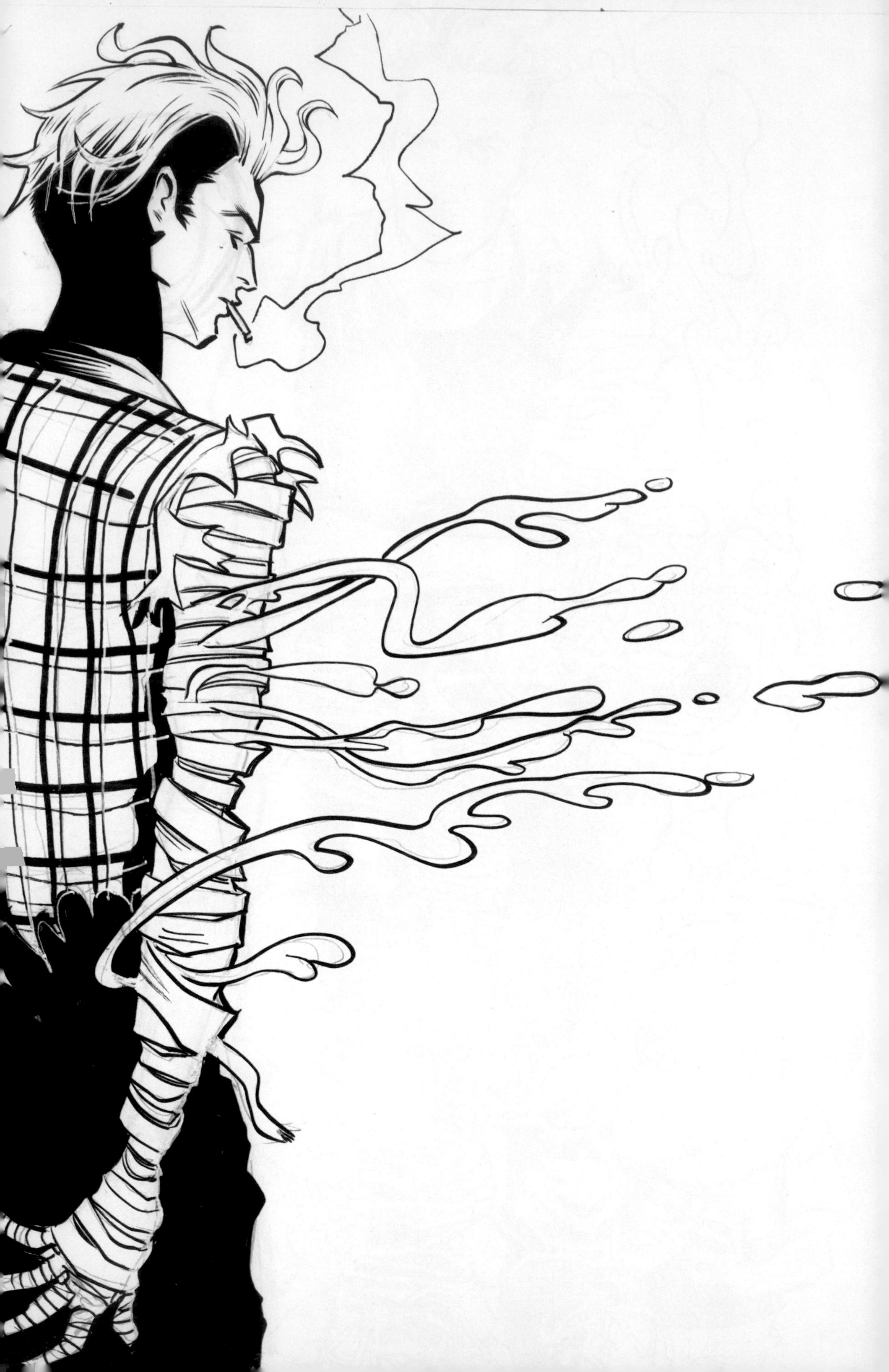

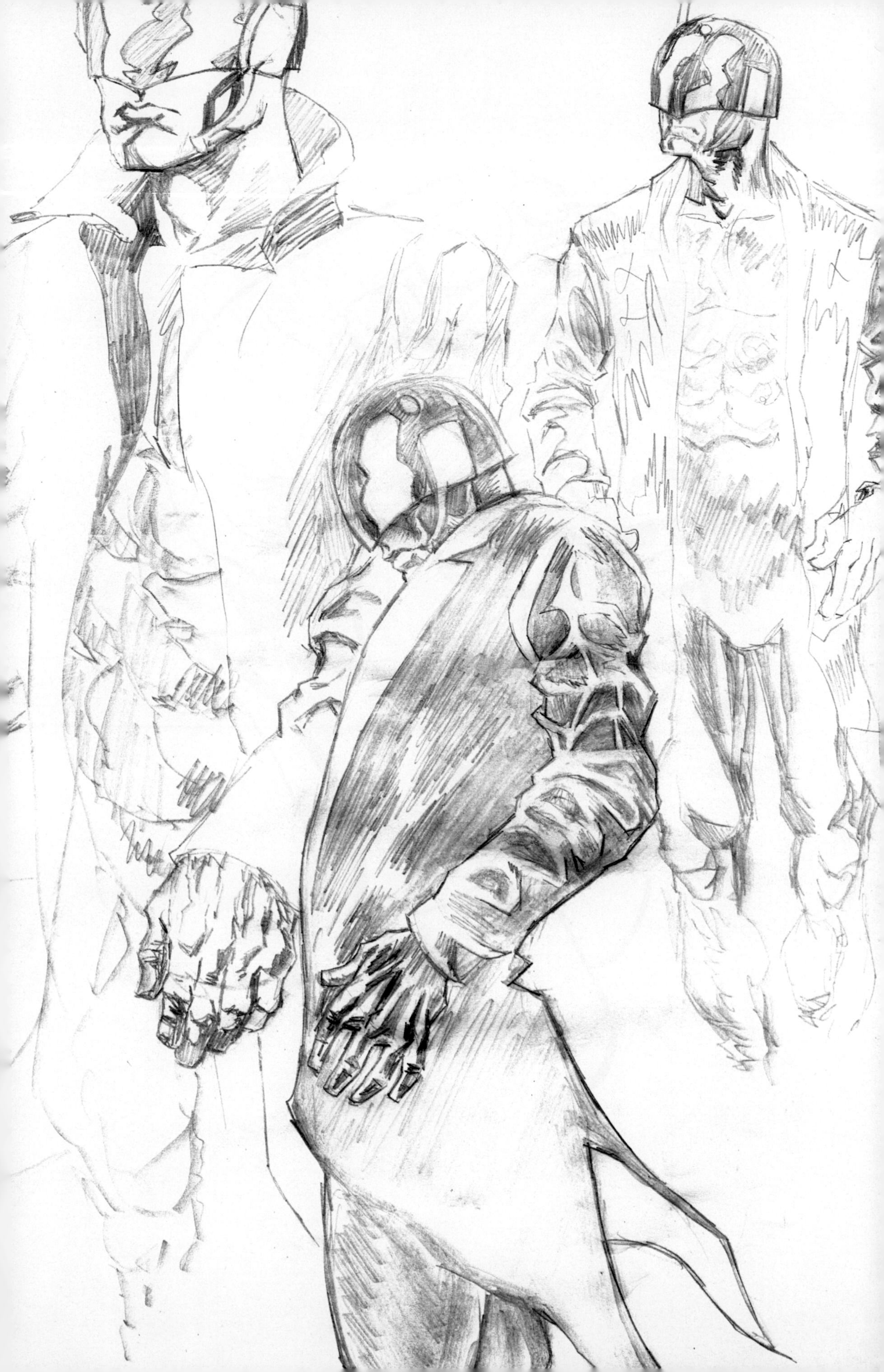

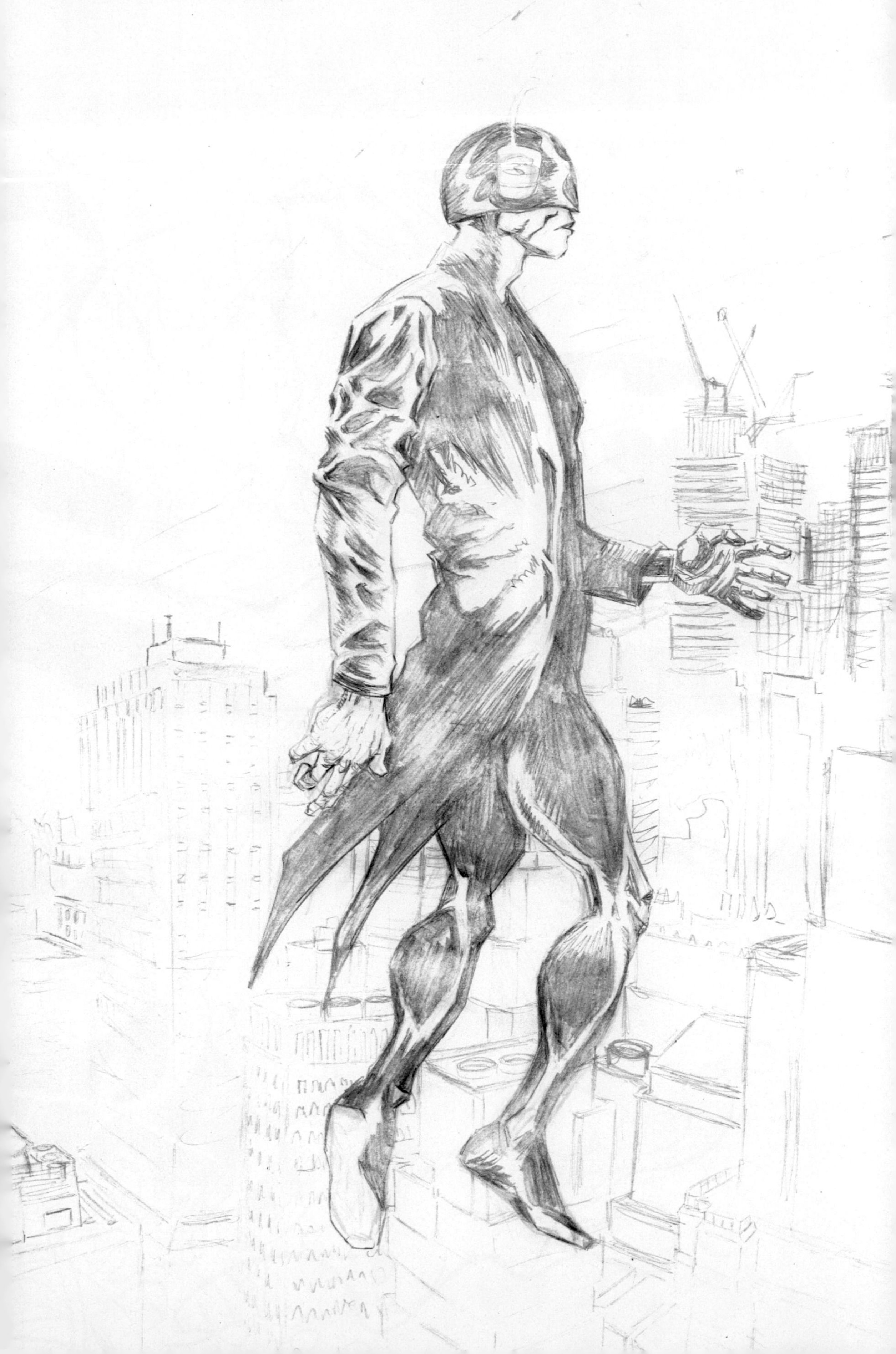

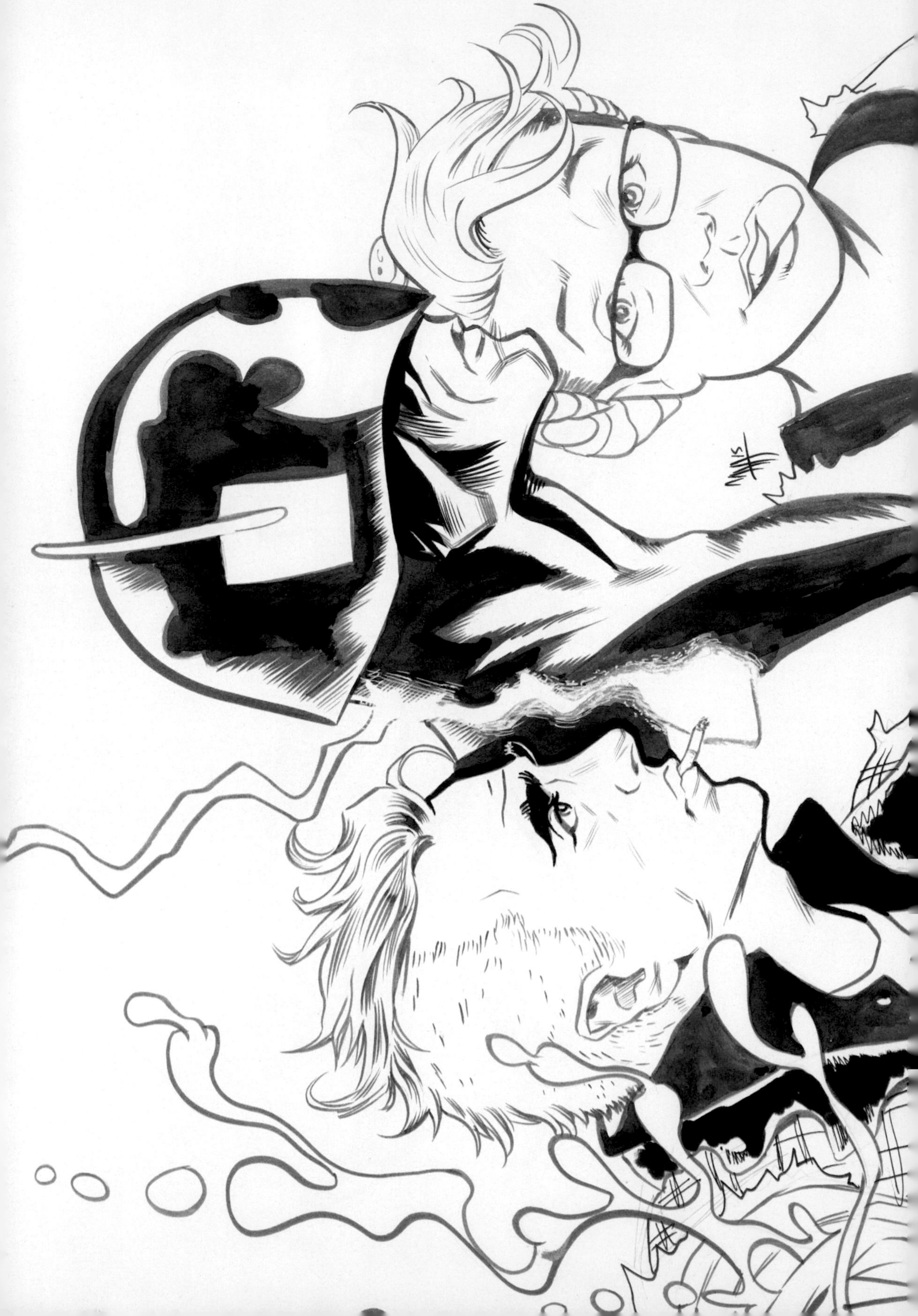

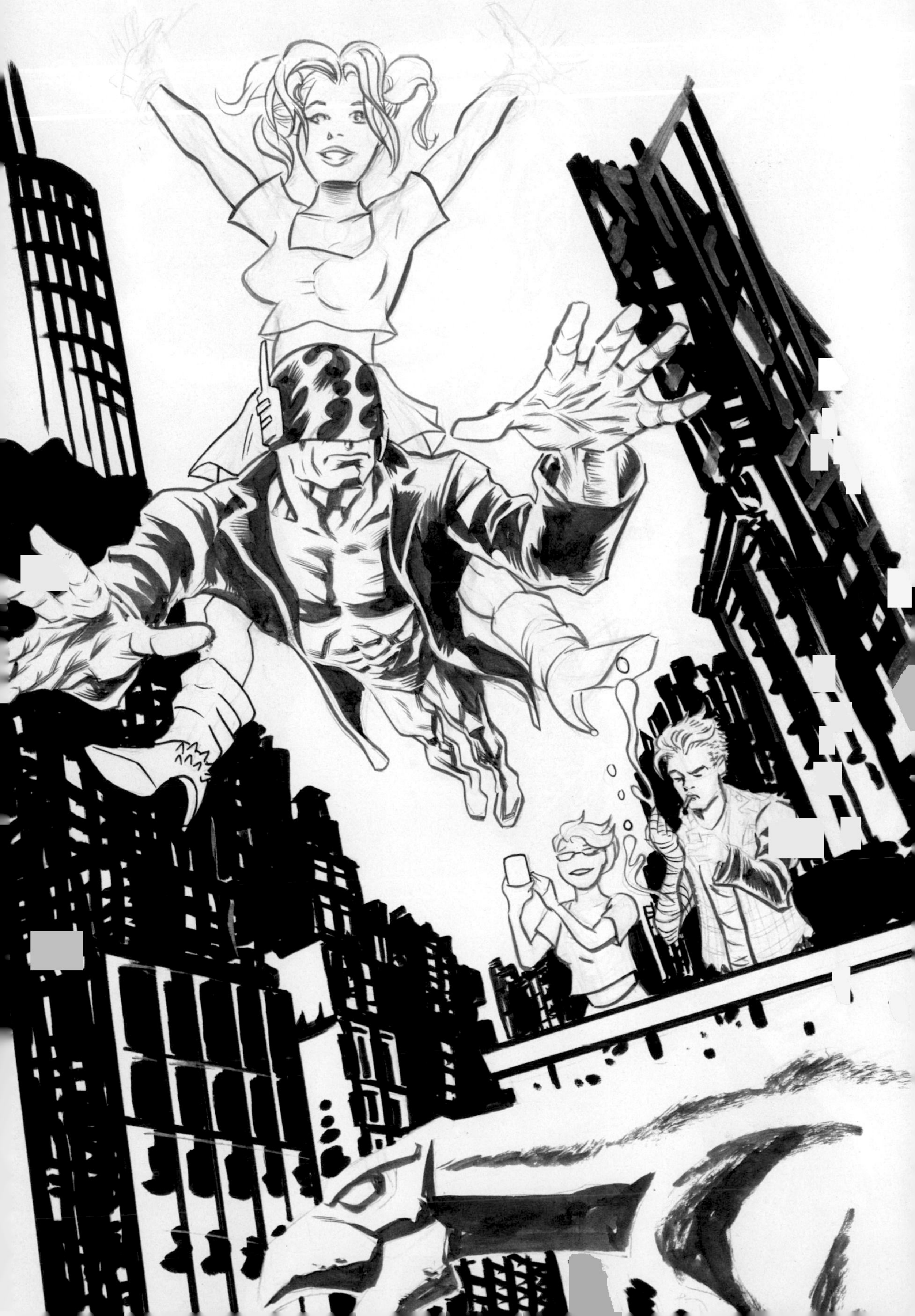

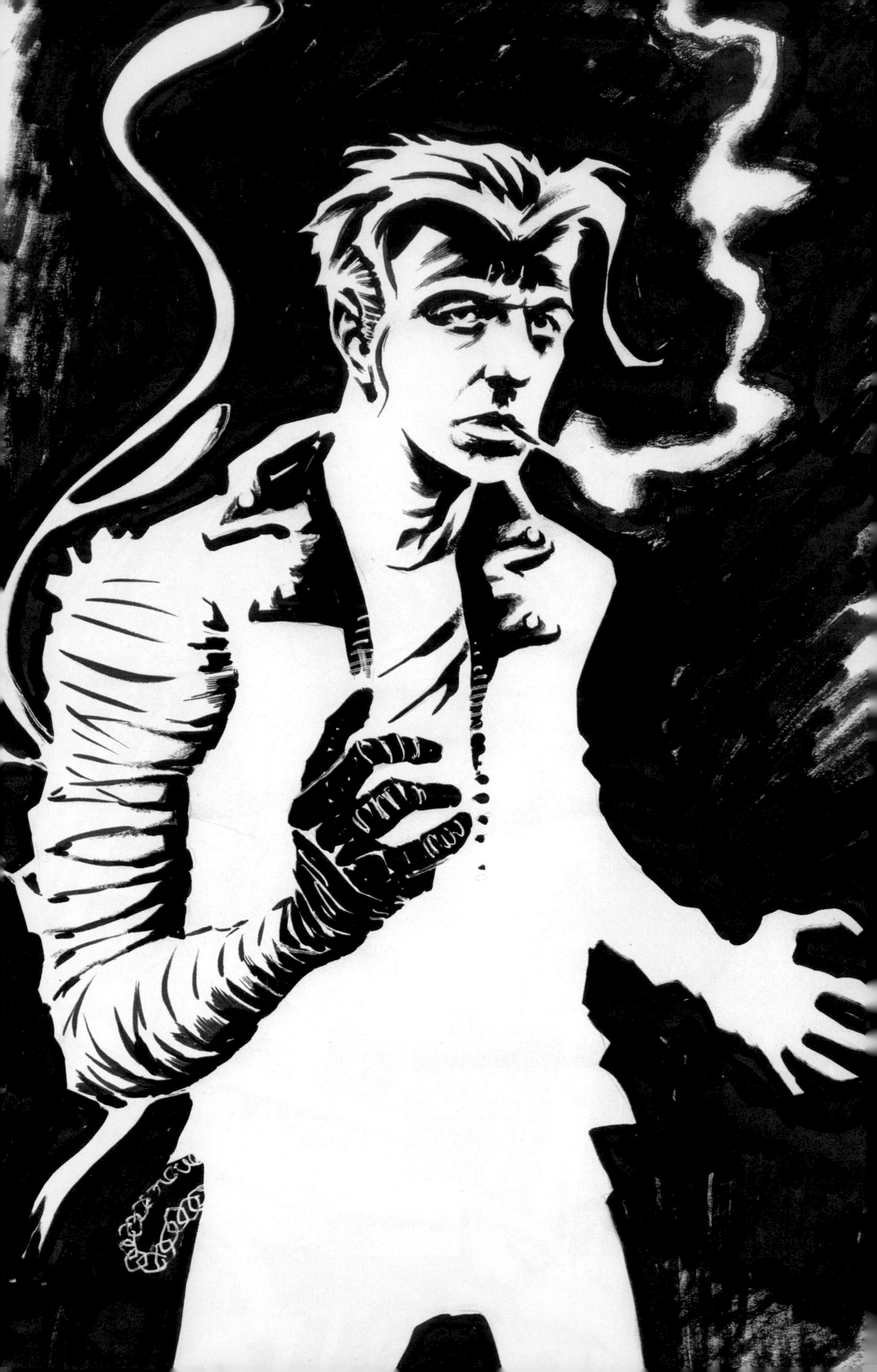

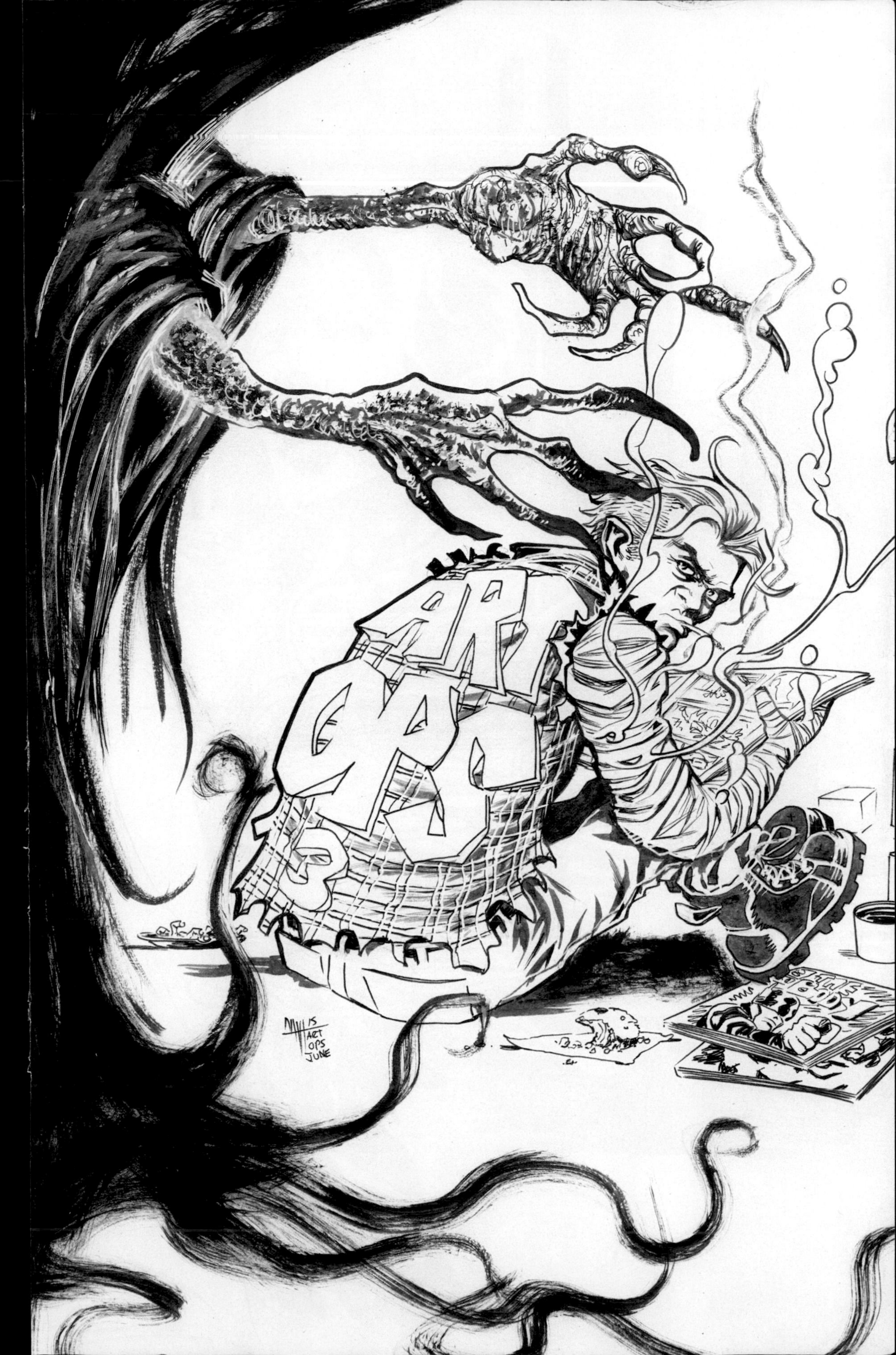
'15
ART
OPS
JUNE

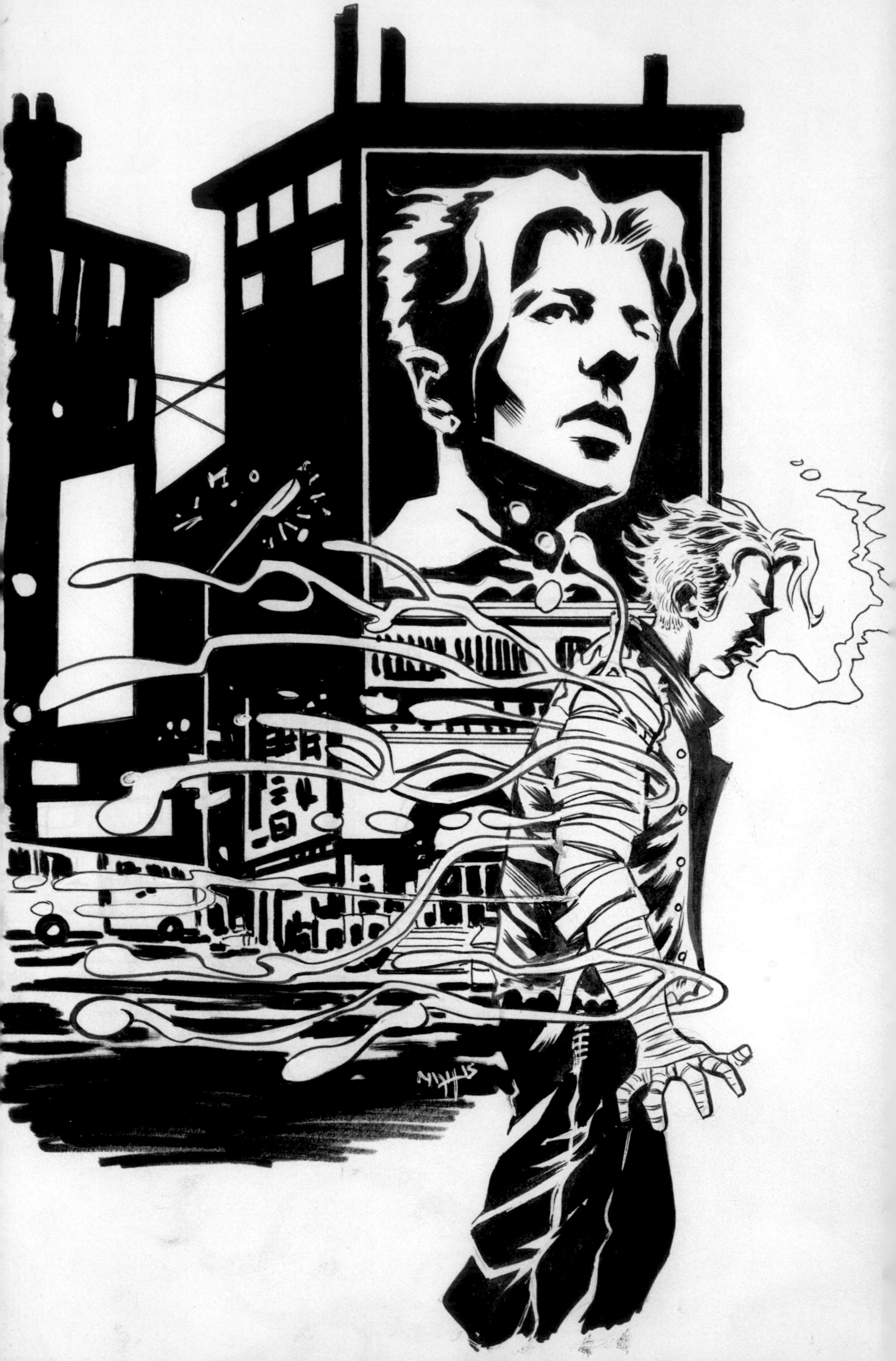

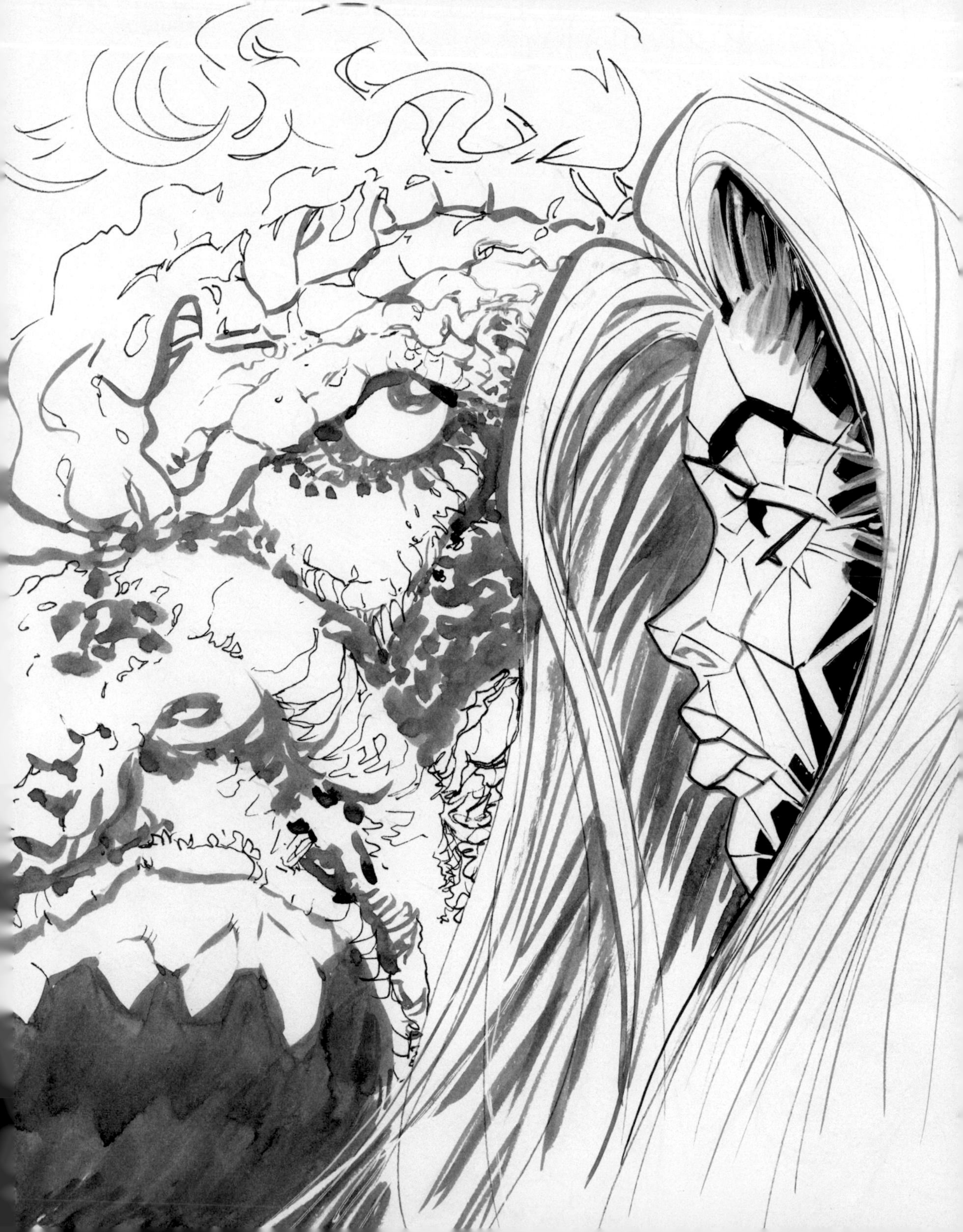

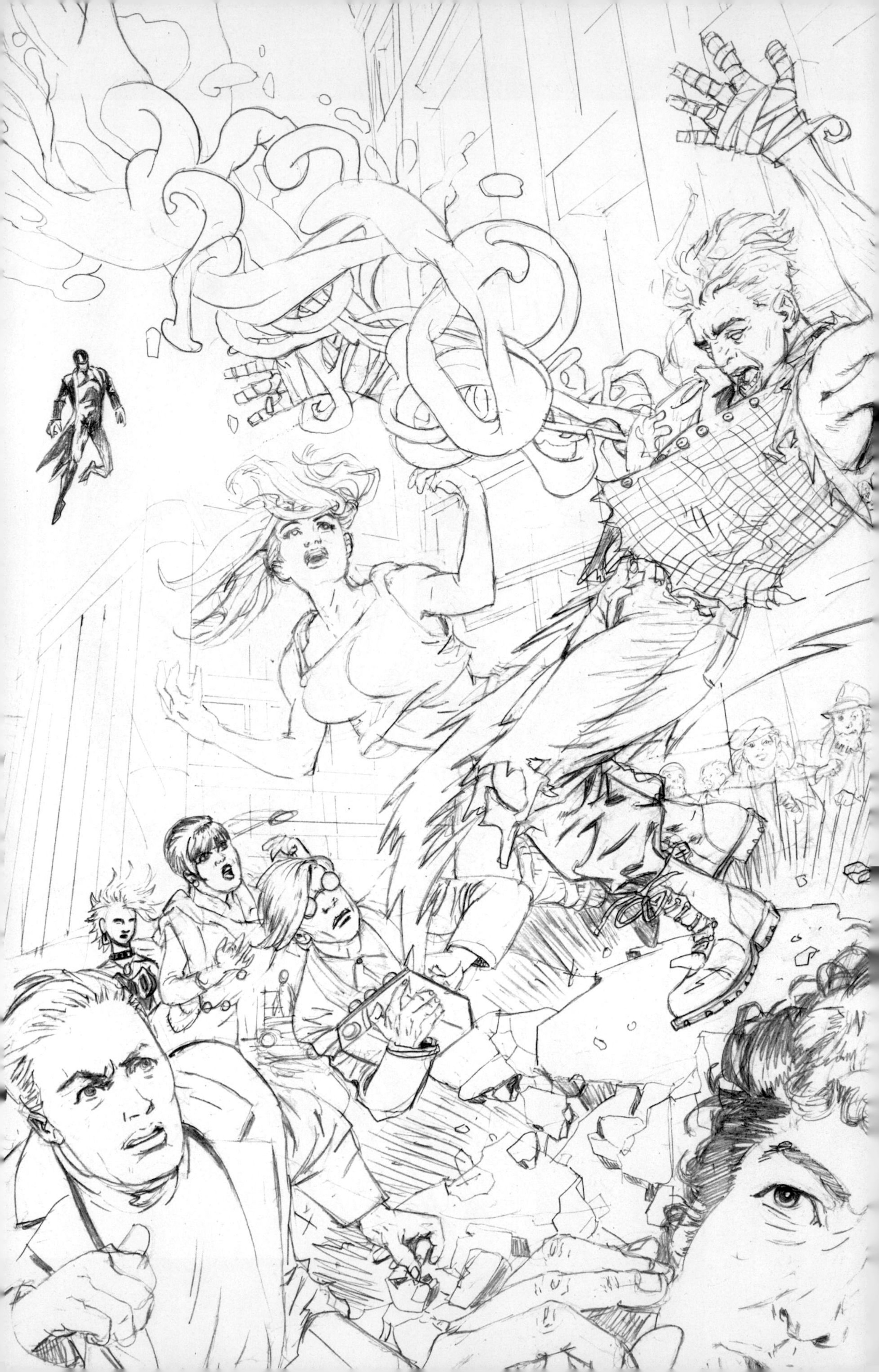

LOGO PROPOSALS BY STEVE COOK

Here are a few working roughs of draft logos for ART OPS, which were ultimately not used.

art ops
$3.99
May '13
VERTIGO
#1
On Tour!

ART OPS
$3.99
Jan '15

ART OPS
On Tour!

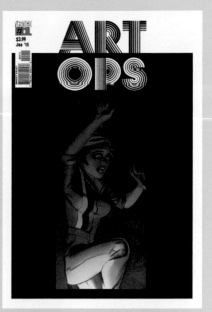

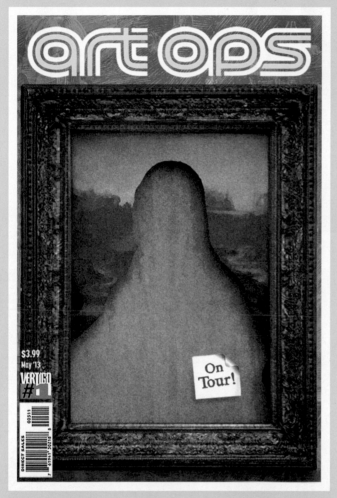

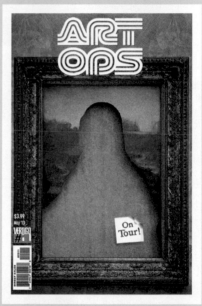

THE HISTORY OF LOGO DESIGN

The logo designer is often a silent contributor to the creation of a comic book, which is an absolute travesty. The title of a comic must be clearly displayed in a bold composition that makes it instantly readable, near or far. It must also communicate the tone of a series and complement the arresting cover imagery. Without a strong logo you have absolutely nothing. This is one of the many reasons why you see a logo design credit in the Vertigo titles. We value the importance of the logo designer, and we work with the best in the business. Steve Cook, a provocative photographer and artist in his own right, has been crafting logos for my titles since Vertigo's inception. He has an innate understanding of the stories that I edit and brings his own audacious, pop art sensibility to each project. The creative team on ART OPS was so excited when the series was approved that even though Mike Allred needed a few months to wrap up other projects before he could illustrate the cover and first issue, we wanted Steve to get on board fast. I sent him the proposal and samples of Mike's iZOMBIE covers to use for positioning when he was working on concept designs. And in typical Cook fashion, he not only came up with many a great logo to choose from but also a clever placeholder image that clearly conveyed the high concept of the series. The creators loved it so much that the idea evolved into the first issue's cover. And the rest, as they say, is design history.

– **SHELLY BOND**, Editor

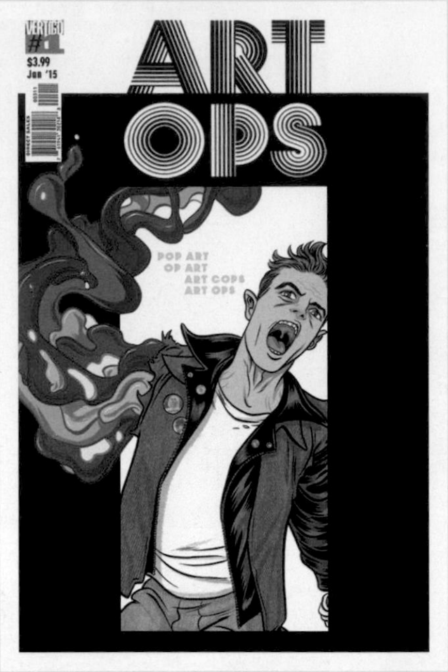
VERTIGO #1
$3.99
Jan '15
ART OPS
POP ART
OP ART
ART COPS
ART OPS
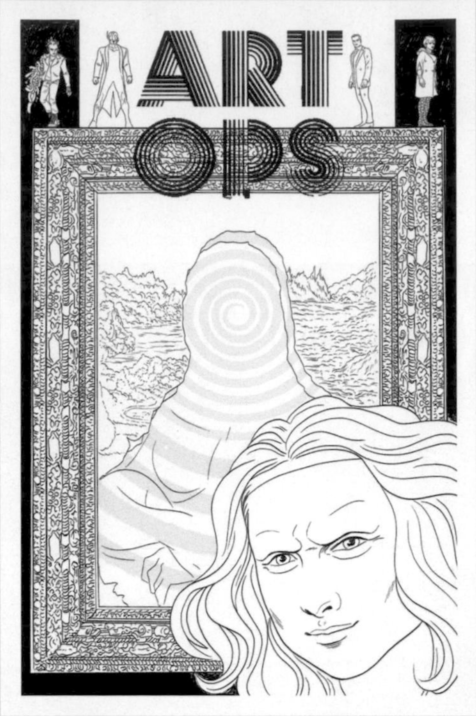
ART OPS
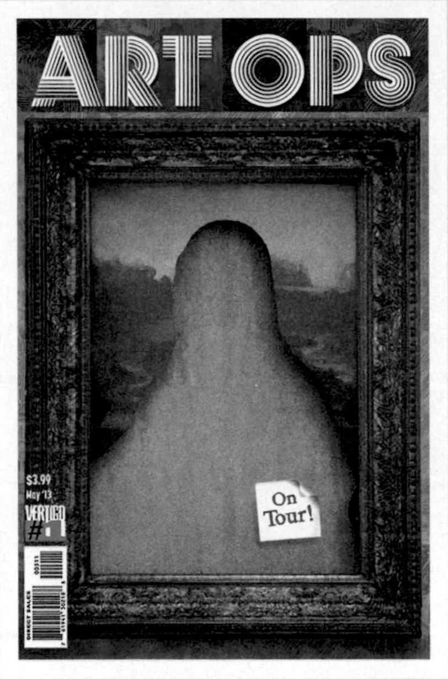
ART OPS
$3.99
May '13
VERTIGO #1
DIRECT SALES
On Tour!
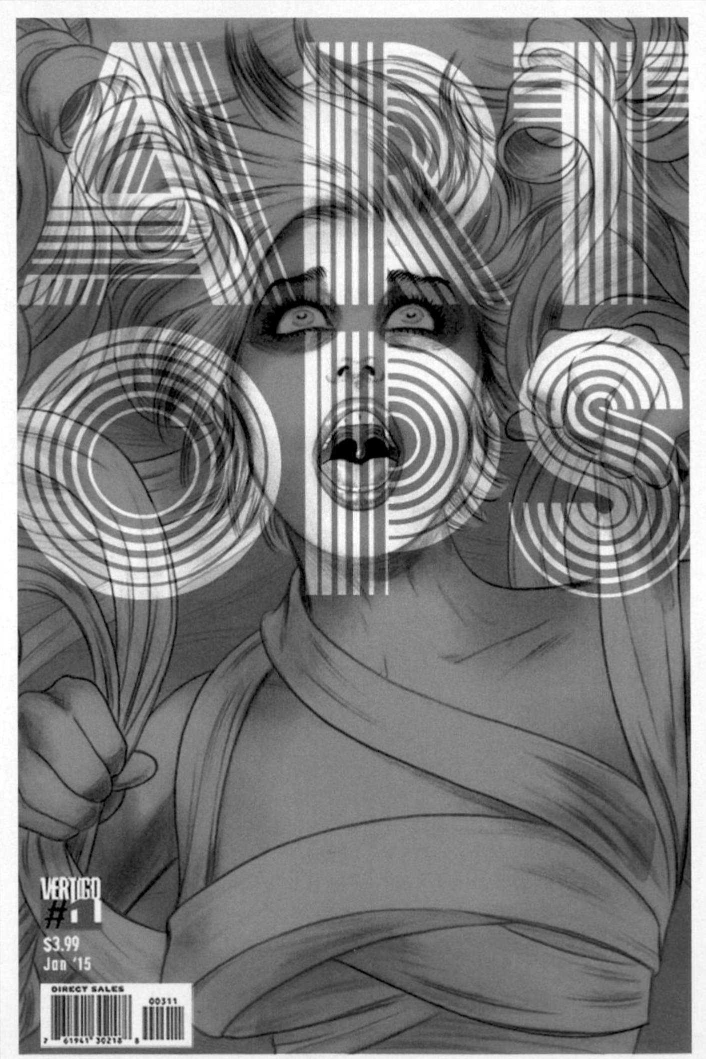
ART OPS
VERTIGO #1
$3.99
Jan '15
DIRECT SALES

FROM THE WRITER OF *HELLBLAZER*

MIKE CAREY
with PETER GROSS

LUCIFER BOOK TWO

LUCIFER BOOK THREE

LUCIFER BOOK FOUR